PEACE BY DESIGN

PEACE BY DESIGN

Managing Intrastate Conflict through Decentralization

Dawn Brancati

OXFORD
UNIVERSITY PRESS

OXFORD

UNIVERSITY PRESS

Great Clarendon Street, Oxford OX2 6DP

Oxford University Press is a department of the University of Oxford.
It furthers the University's objective of excellence in research, scholarship,
and education by publishing worldwide in

Oxford New York

Auckland Cape Town Dar es Salaam Hong Kong Karachi
Kuala Lumpur Madrid Melbourne Mexico City Nairobi
New Delhi Shanghai Taipei Toronto

With offices in

Argentina Austria Brazil Chile Czech Republic France Greece
Guatemala Hungary Italy Japan Poland Portugal Singapore
South Korea Switzerland Thailand Turkey Ukraine Vietnam

Oxford is a registered trade mark of Oxford University Press
in the UK and in certain other countries

Published in the United States
by Oxford University Press Inc., New York

British Library Cataloguing in Publication Data
Data available

Library of Congress Cataloging in Publication Data
Data available

Typeset by SPI Publisher Services, Pondicherry, India
Printed in the UK on acid-free paper by
the MPG Books Group

ISBN 978-0-19-954900-9

1 3 5 7 9 10 8 6 4 2

To my parents

Acknowledgements

I owe a profound debt to many people who helped make this book possible. At Columbia University, where I received my PhD, John Huber, Bob Shapiro, Jack Snyder, and Steven Solnick offered me excellent advice and inspiration at every stage of the project. The *Department of Political Science* at Columbia supported my training with various fellowships, as did the *Saltzman Institute for War and Peace* and the *Center for International Conflict Resolution*.

Beyond the gates of 116th Street, the *Leopold Schepp Foundation* provided with support to complete my training, as did the *German Marshall Fund*, whose two fellowships allowed me to do field research in the Czech Republic, Slovakia, and Spain. In the Czech Republic, I am grateful to the *Národní Knihovna České Republiky* for use of the library's abundant resources. In Spain, I owe the same to the *Fundación Juan March*, directed by José María Maravall. In both of these countries, I acknowledge the generosity of the many politicians who had lengthy discussions with me at their parliamentary offices, party headquarters, and even local cafés.

At Princeton University, I am very grateful to the *Center for the Study of Democratic Politics* (CSDP) for postdoctoral support, and especially the center's director, Larry Bartels. Not only did CSDP afford me the luxury of time to expand my elections dataset exponentially and publish my first articles, but it also offered a stimulating intellectual environment with great espresso. I am likewise grateful to the *Harvard-MIT Data Center* and the *Institute for Quantitative Social Science*, where the coffee was not nearly as good, but the environment was equally percolating. I owe special thanks to Gary King, director of both institutions, who fielded many questions from me and offered helpful professional advice from all corners of the globe at all hours of the day.

Also, at Harvard, I owe much thanks to Yoi Herrera, who integrated me into the university's intellectual community and offered me very detailed and insightful comments on every chapter of the book. Elise Giuliano also read the entire manuscript while at the Davis Center and offered especially helpful comments on the theory chapter and case studies. For comments on various chapters and papers related to this book, I also thank participants of the *Comparative Politics Workshop* and *Political Economy Workshop* at Harvard, as well as Jim Alt, Micah Altman, Nancy Bermeo, Hanna Birnir, Bear Braumoeller, Kanchan Chandra, Barry Friedman, Tulia Falleti, Shigeo Hirano, Simon Hug, Sandra León Alfonso, Andy Kydd, Evan Lieberman, and Olga Shvetsova. At Oxford University, I would also like to thank the editor Dominic Byatt and the anonymous reviewers of this book.

To my friends, many of whom are also colleagues, I am very grateful for their advice on different aspects of the book, their exuberant cheerleading, and the much-needed distractions they offered from the book, especially Ruth Ben-Artzi, Christine Chua, Rebecca Green, Shareen Hertel, Ruta Kellogg, Andrew Lund, Natalie Mindrum, Adam Pollet, Rose Razaghian, and Donald Swinton. Finally, and most importantly, I thank my parents, Dolores and Rudy, to whom this book is dedicated. Were it not for the way they revered education, the determination, if not stubbornness, they instilled in their children, and their parenting ethic of always putting their children first, undoubtedly neither the career nor the book would have been possible.

Contents

List of Figures   xi
List of Tables   xiii

1. Introduction   1

Part I Theory Development

2. Decentralization: Fueling the Fire or
   Dampening the Flames of Intrastate Conflict?   29

Part II Case Study Analysis

3. Czechoslovakia   65

4. Spain   90

5. India   122

Part III Quantitative Analysis

6. Ethnic Conflict and Secessionism   157

7. Regional Parties   195

8. Conclusion   225

References   232
Endnotes   257
Index   279

List of Figures

3.1 The electoral strength of regional parties in Czechoslovakia's
two national legislatures, 1990–92   75

3.2 The electoral strength of regional parties in Czechoslovakia's
National Councils, 1990–92   76

3.3 The electoral strength of regional parties in interwar
Czechoslovakia, 1920–35   79

4.1 Public support for the right to be independent in Spain,
2003   94

4.2 Subnational expenditure in Spain, 1976–97   97

4.3 FCI transfers to Spain's autonomous communities,
1997–2008   99

4.4 Regional party vote in Spain's national legislatures,
1977–2000   101

4.5 Regional party vote in Spain's autonomous community
elections, 1980–99   103

4.6 Regional identities in Spain's autonomous communities,
1996 and 2003   106

4.7 The percentage of seats held by regional parties in Spain's
Senate by aspect, 1980–2004   118

5.1 Subnational expenditure in India, 1974–2000   130

5.2 Subnational revenue in India, 1950–2004   130

5.3 The electoral strength of regional parties in elections to
India's House of People, 1952–99   133

5.4 Regional party vote in elections to India's House of People
by region, 1952–99   134

5.5 Regional parties elected to India's Council of States by the state assemblies, 1952–99   136

5.6 Regional party vote in elections to India's state assemblies by region, 1977–98   137

6.1 Predicted probability of no anti-regime rebellion (ordered logit)   178

6.2 Predicted probability of no intercommunal conflict (ordered logit)   185

7.1 Electoral strength of regional parties in centralized versus decentralized systems of government (national lower and upper house elections, 1944–2002)   197

List of Tables

3.1 Public opinion on the optimal political system in Czechoslovakia, July 1992   68

6.1 Anti-regime rebellion: base models   174

6.2 Anti-regime rebellion: alternative measures of decentralization   175

6.3 Anti-regime rebellion: interaction models   177

6.4 Intercommunal conflict: base models   180

6.5 Intercommunal conflict: alternative measures of decentralization   181

6.6 Intercommunal conflict: interaction models   183

6.7 Instrumental variable regression   191

7.1 National elections: base models (national level results)   207

7.2 National elections: full models (national level results)   208

7.3 National elections: alternative measures of decentralization (national level results)   211

7.4 National elections: full models (regional level results)   215

7.5 Regional elections   218

7.6 Instrumental variable regression   222

1
Introduction

Ethnic conflict and secessionism pose a major threat to peace and stability in the twenty-first century. Together they are responsible for the deaths of millions of people around the world as well as the rape, torture, and disfigurement of many more. In the early 1990s, an estimated 200,000 people died in Yugoslavia alone, while almost 1 million died in Rwanda during a single year of fighting in 1994. No corner of the world is immune to these phenomena. Both ethnic conflict and secessionism have afflicted large countries as well as small ones, advanced economies as well as developing ones, and robust democracies as well as clear dictatorships. Regrettably, many existing conflicts continue unabated today while many other seemingly resolved ones have reignited (Fearon and Laitin 2003; Hewitt et al. 2008).

The consequences of these conflicts extend far beyond a loss to human life and endure long after the fighting ends. Invariably, ethnic conflict and secessionism destroy national economies, spread infectious disease, and damage the environment (Murdoch and Sandler 2002; Ghobarah et al. 2003). Violence resulting from each euphemistically depletes labor markets, damages physical infrastructures, and diverts resources away from more economically valuable pursuits. Recovering from these hardships is challenging for post-conflict countries since foreign companies are often reluctant to invest in countries where conflict might unexpectedly reignite (Abadie and Gardeazabal 2003; Jensen and Young 2008).

Infectious diseases, such as cholera and dysentery, are likewise endemic in many post-conflict countries because of poor nutrition, inadequate sanitation, and deficient water treatment facilities. Combatants often transmit AIDS and other sexually transmitted diseases while using rape as a military weapon to intimidate and humiliate women, extract information from civilians, and obliterate entire ethnic groups through miscegenation (Wood 2006). Lacking the funds to rebuild hospitals, pay medical staff, and purchase drugs and supplies, post-conflict countries confront significant challenges treating diseases and revitalizing their healthcare systems.

Given the devastating consequences of intrastate conflict both in the long and short terms, politicians, as well as scholars, have sought tools with which to reduce its occurrence, if not eradicate it entirely. One such tool is political decentralization (Lijphart et al. 1993; Bermeo 2002; Hartzell and Hoddie 2003). In democracies, political decentralization is thought to reduce conflict by extending threatened or embattled minority groups control over their own political, social, and economic affairs. For this reason, stable democracies with well-developed economies (e.g. Belgium, Canada, Italy, and Spain), as well as fledgling democracies with developing economies (e.g. Bosnia-Herzegovina and postcommunist Czechoslovakia), have all used political decentralization to manage tensions within their borders. Interest in decentralization as a tool to reduce ethnic conflict and secessionism is still intense today, with recent attempts at decentralization including the beleaguered states of Afghanistan and Iraq.

1.1. The puzzle of political decentralization

In practice, however, decentralization's ability to reduce ethnic conflict and secessionism has been rather mixed.[1] Decentralization, in other words, has been much more successful in mitigating ethnic conflict and secessionism in some democracies than in others. While decentralization seems to have helped prevent the secession of Quebec from Canada and the Basque Country from Spain, decentralization seems to be much less successful in mitigating ethnic conflict and secessionism in other countries, including Czechoslovakia, Yugoslavia, and Nigeria. Czechoslovakia dissolved into two separate states in 1993 despite widespread support for state unity and amicable relations among Czechs and Slovaks, while Yugoslavia, despite a long tradition of decentralized governance, fragmented into several independent countries through a bloody civil war in the 1990s. While Nigeria has not dissolved into separate states, violence has marred the country's brief experiment with democracy following elections in 1999.

From a normative point of view, secessionism may not seem intrinsically undesirable. After all, secessionism may be an expression of the public's will and some regions might fare better politically, as well as economically, as independent states. From a practical point of view, however, secessionism is problematic. While regions may express secessionist sentiment peacefully through political demands for independence, national governments usually oppose secession, even if separatist regions are not economically valuable, since one region's independence may prompt another region to secede as well (Walter 2006). Attempts at independence, as a result, tend to be violent. Moreover, as the case of Czechoslovakia (a rare example of peaceful secession) illustrates, secession does not always represent the expression of the public's will, nor does it necessarily leave regions better off economically or politically. The legitimation of secession as an appropriate means of resolving differences within countries also creates a dangerous norm, suggesting that people of different ethnicities, languages, and religions cannot live together peacefully.

The fact, however, that at least under the right circumstances decentralization can bring frustrated populations closer to the government and provide them with an outlet in which to address their grievances has led many politicians, especially those representing minority groups, to tout decentralized governance as the key to reducing, if not preventing, ethnic conflict and secessionism. Despite a tortured history of political and civil rights abuse, the Kurds in Iraq ardently support decentralization as a means of protecting their rights and maintaining Iraq's unity, a position with which US Senator Joseph Biden agrees. According to Biden, Chairman of the Senate Foreign Relations Committee, "Federalism is Iraq's best possible future."[2] Political leaders in other countries, including Indonesia and Uganda, have also advocated decentralization as a solution to protracted civil war. John Ken Lukyamuzi, an outspoken advocate of federalism in Uganda and a Conservative Party leader, claims, for example, that "[f]ree and fair elections are not a panacea for political instability" – only "[f]ederalism ensures freedom."[3]

Support for decentralization extends well beyond fragile democracies and members of minority groups to include politicians representing major ethnolinguistic groups in well-established democracies. Former Canadian Prime Minister Pierre Trudeau has heralded decentralization as the best way to integrate diverse groups within a large country. Trudeau, known for his staunch opposition to Quebecois separatism, considers the ideal state to be "one with different sizes for different purposes" and believes that "the federal state comes closest" to this ideal (1968: 35). Former US President Bill Clinton has similarly extolled the virtues of decentralization. Clinton has even gone so far as to identify decentralization as the force "most likely to advance our common humanity in a small world" and the "arrangement of government most likely to give us the best of both worlds, the integrity...self-government...and self-advancement we need."[4]

However, the failure of decentralization to reduce ethnic conflict and secessionism in some countries has led many politicians and scholars to question the effectiveness of decentralization (Nordlinger 1972; Dikshit 1975; Gleason 1990; Horowitz 1991; Roeder 1991; Hardgrave 1994; Suberu 1994; Brubaker 1996; Snyder and Ballentine 1996; Kymlicka 1998; Bunce 1999; Leff 1999; Snyder 2000). Shortly after leaving office, UK Prime Minister John Major called decentralization "the Trojan horse that will lead to friction, frustration and the demand for full independence."[5] Impassioned opposition to decentralization like this persists in faltering democracies as well, including Sri Lanka, a former British colony, where demands for Tamil independence have embroiled the country in war since the mid-1980s. Past promises to implement decentralization in Sri Lanka have been largely unfulfilled because of fears that decentralized governance could trigger the country's dissolution. Epitomizing this fear, H. L. de Silva, once Sri Lanka's Permanent Representative to the United Nations, has likened decentralization to "[a] beguiling serpent, which by its fatal sting will bring about the death of the Republic."[6]

So why is political decentralization a *Trojan horse* and *beguiling snake* in some countries and a panacea in others? In other words, why is decentralization more successful in reducing ethnic conflict and secessionism in some democracies than in others? This question constitutes the central focus of this book. In brief, I argue that the impact of decentralization depends on the electoral strength of regional parties, which tend to promote ethnic conflict and secessionism by creating regional identities, advocating legislation that threatens other regions in a country and/or regional minorities, and by mobilizing groups to engage in ethnic conflict and secessionism or supporting extremist groups that do. The extent to which regional parties behave in these ways, however, is influenced by a number of other factors. Ironically, decentralization also increases the electoral strength of regional parties, but the extent to which it does depends on the institutional structure of decentralization. The features of decentralization, which I argue significantly influence the strength of regional parties, include, but are not necessarily limited to, the following: the proportion of seats individual regions have in a national legislature, the number of regional legislatures in a country, the method used to elect upper houses, and the timing of national and regional elections. In the remainder of this book, I develop these ideas further, and provide evidence of decentralization's effect on ethnic conflict and secessionism through case studies and statistical analysis, in order to explain why decentralization is not always successful in reducing intrastate conflict in *all* countries.

1.2. Political decentralization defined

In order to understand the role that political decentralization plays in reducing conflict and secessionism, it is first necessary to define decentralization and elaborate on its features. Political decentralization is a system of government in which there is a hierarchical division of power among multiple levels of government, where each level has independent decision-making power over at least one issue area. Independent decision-making means that different levels of government (i.e. national, regional, and local levels) legislate on certain matters. Countries in which governments only administer or carry out decisions made at a higher level are not politically decentralized.[7,8] As I employ the term here, political decentralization is synonymous with federalism (Riker 1964). I deliberately use the term political decentralization, however, because federalism connotes a dichotomy between federal and nonfederal countries whereas decentralization suggests a spectrum of degrees of decentralization. Throughout this book, I frequently drop the modifier *political* in referring to decentralization. Unless otherwise noted, decentralization refers to political decentralization.

Typically, in decentralized systems of government, national governments have legislative authority over issues that benefit from a uniform policy throughout a country and that are too costly for subunits of states to provide for individually (e.g. currency, defense, foreign affairs, and immigration). Subnational governments, in contrast, tend to legislate on issues which are addressed more effectively when tailored to the specific needs of different locales, such as health, education, and transportation. Beyond these more general trends, the legislative authority of national and subnational levels of government varies widely within and across countries.

The number of issues over which subnational legislatures have control, as well as the saliency of these issues, determines in large part how extensive decentralization is within countries. The more salient are the issues over which subnational legislatures have control, the more decentralized systems tend to be. Also important in this regard is whether subnational authority is singular or shared, and whether it is explicit and codified in law, or implicit and easily rescinded. Obviously, having independent authority codified in law is indicative of greater decentralization than the latter.

Often, decentralized countries also have constitutional courts that help to maintain a division of authority between levels of government, although this is not a necessary feature of decentralization. Neither is bicameralism. Nonetheless, most decentralized systems of government have upper houses of government, and many of these legislatures differ significantly in structure from those that exist in centralized systems. Often, in decentralized systems of government, upper houses have special jurisdiction over regional issues or committees authorized to address these issues in particular. Frequently, they also extend special representation to regions by giving disproportionate weight to smaller regions and they are also often elected, either in part or in full, by regional legislatures.

Nevertheless, national governments can erode the authority of subnational governments even where there is an extensive division of authority codified in law and constitutional courts charged with protecting it. Not only can national governments infringe on the jurisdiction of subnational legislatures, but they can also flout the laws subnational legislatures produce and even overturn them entirely. National governments can also exert control over subnational legislatures by appointing politicians "friendly" to national governments or disbanding subnational legislatures indiscriminately. While these actions, which undermine decentralization, can and do occur in democracies, decentralization is shallowest in nondemocracies, where one-party states and absolute leaders invariably erode the decision-making authority of subnational legislatures. It is, therefore, not very surprising that decentralization does not reduce conflict and secessionism in these countries. The eruption and persistence of conflict in democracies is far more puzzling because democracies tend to have a more genuine division of power and people expected to resolve their grievances through the legislative process. The book, thus, focuses on the paradox of decentralization in these cases.

1.3. Decentralization as a conflict deterrent

Decentralization is widely assumed to reduce ethnic conflict and secession in democracies although the specific reasons for this are quite varied (Lijphart 1977, 1996; Tsebelis 1990; Horowitz 1991; Ornstein and Coursen 1992; Narang 1995; Kaufman 1996; Stepan 1999; Gurr 2000; Bermeo 2002; Lustik et al. 2004). For one, decentralization is supposed to reduce conflict by increasing the number of opportunities for citizens to influence policy and bring the government closer to the people. It does so through the presence of many small governments with independent decision-making powers dispersed throughout a country (Duchacek 1987). This not only reduces the physical distance people must travel to bring issues of concern to the government, but it is also supposed to raise people's awareness of government activities, and give them a greater stake in the maintenance of that political system. Citizens, in turn, with a greater stake in the political system are supposed to be less likely to secede from a country and more likely to work from within the government to achieve their goals.

In principle, decentralization is also thought to reduce conflict by habituating politicians, who represent different ethnic groups, into dealing with each other at the subnational level before they need to work together at the national level (Horowitz 1991). Others suggest, meanwhile, that decentralization obviates the need for multiethnic accommodation by moving the locus of politics to the subnational level, where groups can legislate on areas of greatest interest to them without the involvement of others (Tsebelis 1990). By moving the locus of politics to the subnational level, other scholars suggest that decentralization quarantines conflicts to particular regions and prevents them from spreading throughout an entire country (Manor 1998).

However, the most commonly suggested, and in this sense, perhaps the most important, way in which decentralization is supposed to reduce ethnic conflict and secession is by giving territorially concentrated minority groups control over their own political, social, and economic affairs (Lijphart 1977, 1996; Tsebelis 1990; Horowitz

1991; Ornstein and Coursen 1992; Narang 1995; Kaufman 1996; Stepan 1999; Gurr 2000; Bermeo 2002; Lustik et al. 2004). Minority groups have little impact on policy at the national level because they constitute a small proportion of a country's total population. Under decentralization, however, minorities can exert significant influence at the subnational level if they are concentrated in particular regions or geographic locales. Decentralization has no effect on conflict, though, where groups are not territorially concentrated. For this reason, ethnic conflict that is not regionally based is outside the scope of this study.

For groups that are geographically concentrated, having access to and influence on politics enables minorities to redress the concerns that drive them to fight others and seek independence in the first place. If, for example, physical insecurity provokes conflict, decentralization can prevent conflict by granting minorities control over their own police forces. On the other hand, if fears of social extinction are the cause, decentralization can extend groups control over issues, such as education and justice, to help protect their languages and religious practices. Finally, if feelings of economic disadvantage prompt secessionism, then decentralization can lessen demands for independence by allowing groups to decide on how money is allocated within their regions. Interestingly, even when decentralization extends real powers to territorially concentrated groups, it has failed to reduce ethnic conflict and secessionism in many countries. The compelling question remains why.

1.4. Decentralization as a conflict agent

Extant scholarship offers several potential explanations for decentralization's failure to reduce, and even intensify, ethnic conflict and secessionism in particular countries. One argument suggests that decentralization fails to hold countries together because its citizens lack a sense of unity and commitment to decentralized governance (Dikshit 1975; Lijphart 1977; Duchacek 1987, 1988; Elazar 1987;

Burgess 1993; Narang 1995). Elazar identifies this as a "federal culture," while Burgess refers to it as a "federal ideology" and Narang calls it a "federal spirit." A sense of unity is undoubtedly an important factor in explaining national cohesion. One must ask, however, as these authors would likely agree, why some countries possess these unifying characteristics while others do not, and what role institutions and political leaders play in fostering these identities, if any at all (Penn 2007*a,b*).

A second argument suggests that decentralization intensifies conflict and secessionism by reinforcing regional identities, as well as ethnic identities that are regionally based. Some scholars suggest that decentralization accomplishes this by merely recognizing and legitimizing certain groups within a country (Hardgrave 1994; Kymlicka 1998). Others claim that it does so by allowing groups to pass legislation at the subnational level that actively promotes their languages, customs, histories, etc. (Roeder 1991; Brubaker 1996; Bunce 1999). This argument only offers a partial explanation for why decentralization reduces conflict more in some countries than in others. All decentralized systems of government recognize and legitimize subnational groups and most, if not all, give regions legislative authority through which they can promote regional identities. However, not all regions exploit these authorities to the same degree and not all result in conflict or state dissolution. The question then remains why certain subnational actors promote regional identities more than others. Equally important are the factors that give rise to these actors in the first place.

A third argument claims that decentralization fosters secessionism by encouraging groups to desire more and more autonomy until they finally demand complete independence from the state (Nordlinger 1972; Gleason 1990; Kymlicka 1998; Hechter 2000). According to this argument, groups seek further autonomy because they realize that after gaining a certain amount of autonomy, regardless of the actual amount, that they are able to manage their affairs better than the state (Nordlinger 1972; Gleason 1990; Kymlicka 1998). Supposedly, autonomy also triggers demands for more authority because it gives rise to regional elites who want to aggrandize their personal power through increased autonomy (Meadwell 1993). However, as with the previous argument, more attention needs to be paid to the role of subnational actors. Who are these actors? Why do some seek more autonomy than others, even though increasing autonomy enhances the personal power of all subnational actors? Furthermore, why do some subnational actors demand complete independence, while others are satiated with more limited forms of autonomy?

Still a fourth argument emphasizes decentralization's tendency to allow groups to produce subnational legislation that discriminates against regional minorities (Nordlinger 1972; Horowitz 1991; Lijphart et al. 1993; Suberu 1994). Discriminatory legislation, in turn, can incite conflict between minority and majority groups and prompt demands by the former for autonomy or independence. For example, adoption of the Shari'ah in northern Nigeria has fueled conflict among Christians and Muslims. Although the Shari'ah is supposed to apply only to Muslims, many Christians claim that they are also forced to comply with its dictates. Russians have similarly sparked tensions with Romanians in Transnistria by adopting a law in 2004 closing all schools in the region that do not use the Cyrillic alphabet. Although such legislation may be the immediate cause of conflict in some countries, one must still look deeper, though, to understand why particular subnational actors and not others choose to adopt this legislation in the first place.

A fifth and final argument suggests that decentralization encourages ethnic conflict and secessionism by providing groups with certain resources at the subnational level (e.g. legislatures, media, and militia/police forces), which make engaging in these activities easier to achieve (Riker 1964; O'Leary and McGarry 1995; Snyder and Ballentine 1996; Kymlicka 1998; Bunce 1999; Leff 1999; Snyder 2000). Subnational governments and forms of media (e.g. television, radio, and newspapers) provide regional leaders with platforms through which they may effectively elevate tensions among groups and demand independence. Subnational legislatures also give regional leaders experience governing, while subnational security forces provide regions with the machinery necessary to engage in ethnic conflict or fight for independence. Although decentralization provides all regions with at least some of these resources, only some regions utilize these resources to engage in ethnic conflict and secessionism. To understand why, we must look at the types of actors that are in power at this level of government.

With few notable exceptions (Riker 1964; Brancati 2003, 2006; Filippov et al. 2004; Hale 2004; Bakke and Wibbels 2006), the literature on decentralization has not addressed the question of why decentralization is more successful in reducing ethnic conflict and secessionism in some countries than in others. In this book I attempt to explain this puzzle. Building on the work of others who have also stressed the importance of political parties (Riker 1964; Filippov et al. 2004), I argue that a key factor in explaining decentralization's failure to reduce ethnic conflict and secessionism are regional parties. In contrast to previous work on this issue, I stress the importance of regional parties over incohesive statewide parties. I also attempt to explain the origins of these parties in terms of decentralization, and independent of the underlying social and economic differences within countries. I further try to identify different aspects of decentralization that favor these parties over others. Finally, in contrast to previous studies on decentralization, I test my argument through statistical and case study analysis, whereas previous studies have been based almost entirely on case studies.

1.5. Regional parties: The linchpins of decentralization

At their most basic level, regional parties are parties that compete and win votes in only one region of a country. The geographic basis of their support distinguishes them from all other types of political parties. Regional parties also share much in common in terms of their political goals. Their primary focus is on issues that relate to and/or impinge on the well-being of their regions. These issues may be specific to a particular region (e.g. dam project within a region), or have effects that traverse more than one region (e.g. interregional highway system). Regional parties may also have positions on national policies (e.g. minimum wage and state pensions), but when they do, they tend to focus on these policies in terms of the needs and interests of their particular regions.

Often, regional parties demand political, fiscal, and administrative autonomy over decision-making within their regions and, in many cases, outright independence. Not all regional parties seek autonomy, at least not in each of these areas. Regional parties from poor regions often do not demand fiscal autonomy from the national government but rather financial subsidies, which fiscal decentralization necessarily curtails. At the same time, they often demand political and administrative authority over how these subsidies are allocated within regions. Where regional and ethnic boundaries coincide, regional parties may also couch their goals in terms of particular ethnic groups. Often, parties that do so are dubbed ethnoregional parties.

These goals are not unique to regional parties. Many statewide parties advocate the interests of particular regions, especially at the subnational level. Many also support decentralization and even agitate for more extensive forms of subnational autonomy. Generally, however, these issues constitute a much smaller aspect of a statewide party's political agenda. Statewide parties also tend to make demands regarding regional issues that are more moderate than those of regional parties, especially as they relate to autonomy, since statewide parties need to balance the interests of competing regions against each other. Above all, unlike regional parties, statewide parties never appear to demand independence or state dissolution.

In order to achieve their goals, regional parties utilize a range of tactics. The strategies some parties employ are purely electoral. That is, they compete for the public's support during elections and try to influence outcomes through the political system. Incidentally, regional parties may compete in either national elections, subnational elections, or both, as long as they compete in only one region of a country. Other parties compete in elections but refuse to assume the offices to which they are elected in order to register their opposition to the political system itself. Still others work even further outside the system using violence to achieve their goals and supporting groups that employ these tactics. Many regional parties use a combination of all three strategies, either simultaneously, or at different points in history.

Importantly, my argument about the ways in which regional parties affect conflict and secessionism is premised upon constructivist assumptions about identity and interest formation, a position that is widely shared by many scholars (Laitin 1985; Gagnon 1994, 1995; Malcolm 1996; Brass 1997; Bunce 1999; Giuliano 2000; Mueller 2000; Snyder 2000; Chandra 2004; Herrera 2005). Accordingly, I assume that identities, beliefs, and grievances are not derived from ascriptive characteristics (e.g. biological, ethnic, and racial), but instead are created by the environment in which people live, the interactions they have with others, and the influence of political leaders; in this case, regional parties. Identities, beliefs, and grievances do not necessarily follow from each other. Grievances are not necessarily derived from beliefs, while neither is necessarily derived from identities. They are instead constructed individually albeit from similar or even identical processes.

Given these assumptions, I further suggest that regional parties are not a function of regional differences, but instead create political identities along regional lines. They create these identities by presenting and/or framing particular issues as regional issues (and as ethnic issues where the two coincide). Regional parties also do so by emphasizing certain issues and ignoring others. Regional party leaders may use regional differences to craft these identities, but regional differences do not preordain regional identities or the appeals that regional parties make based on them. In some cases, regional parties contrive regional differences. Whether or not politicians choose to form regional parties and foster regional identities is largely a function of the incentives institutions provide them in terms of whether or not regional parties may be electorally successful and politically influential.

With this in mind, I argue that regional parties can intensify ethnic conflict and secessionism in at least three different ways. First, as already discussed, regional parties create regional cleavages that may be rooted in, but are not preordained by, political, social, and economic differences across regions, and may even be fabricated entirely (de Winter and Türsan 1998; Keating 1998). Statewide parties do not generally promote regional identities because the former strives to make people living in a country feel united in a common fate. Strong regional identities do not necessarily lead to conflict and secessionism but they do form a basis around which groups are mobilized toward these ends. Second, regional parties often advocate legislation that harms other regions of a country, including legislation curtailing the autonomy or funding of those regions, and that harms minorities within their own regions. Because statewide parties must accommodate the interests of many regions in order to win elections, they are less likely to support this type of legislation.

Finally, regional parties often increase ethnic conflict and secessionism directly by mobilizing groups toward these ends, encouraging them to demonstrate their will through rallies, demonstrations, and boycotts, and to pick up arms in pursuit of these goals. To this end, regional parties may exploit the subnational resources decentralization affords them (e.g. legislatures, media, and militia/police forces). They may also support terrorist organizations, such as the Irish Republican Army (IRA) or Euskadi Ta Azkatasuna (ETA), which employ both violent tactics and intimidation to achieve their goals. Often, this support is mutual. Statewide parties have these resources at their disposal as well, but are much less likely to use them for this purpose.

Of course, regional parties do not always intensify intrastate conflict in these ways, nor do statewide parties invariably reduce conflict. Particular conditions may make these outcomes more or less likely to occur. These conditions can affect the incentives of parties to compete in certain regions of countries or to incorporate particular groups into their agendas. Conditions that influence parties in this respect include, but are not limited to, the heterogeneity of regions, the dispersion of regional minorities throughout a country, the pivotalness of certain voters to electoral outcomes, and leadership style. These conditions may also influence the effectiveness of regional party appeals (e.g. democratic transitions) or the ability of statewide parties to successfully attract votes in regions (e.g. the ideological proclivities of regions). Finally, they may also affect the opportunity regional parties have to implement their policies (e.g. the political authority of legislatures in which parties have strong positions and the rules governing these legislatures).

Political decentralization, in turn, I argue, encourages the growth of regional parties and is not simply a product of them. Decentralization promotes regional parties because they have a much greater chance of governing in subnational legislatures than in national legislatures. At the national level, seats are apportioned among multiple regions largely according to size. Parties that represent individual regions are limited, therefore, in their ability to govern at this level. At the regional level, in contrast, regions usually have their own legislatures, making parties that compete in only one region more likely to govern. The strong presence, moreover, of regional parties at this level tends to increase their presence at the national level in decentralized systems of government for at least two reasons. First, the fact that regional parties already exist for the purpose of competing in regional elections lessens their costs of participating in national elections. Second, the strong standing of regional parties at the subnational level makes it likely that regional legislatures will elect regional parties to national legislatures when given the opportunity (Patterson and Mughan 1999).

Yet, the extent to which decentralization increases the electoral strength of regional parties, I maintain, depends on the specific characteristics of decentralization. This is precisely the reason why decentralization does not reduce ethnic conflict and secessionism equally in all countries. In addition to the size of regions (as previously described), I identify three other features of decentralization that affect the electoral strength of regional parties. These characteristics include the number of regional legislatures in a country, the method used to elect upper houses of government, and the sequencing of national and subnational elections.

A large number of regional legislatures may increase the electoral strength of regional parties at the subnational level by giving regional parties more chances to participate in government. Put simply, the more regional legislatures there are in a country, the more regional parties will arise in order to compete within them. Having more regional legislatures at the subnational level may also strengthen the presence of regional parties at the national level since many regional parties that compete at the regional level may participate at the national level for reasons already described.

The method used to elect upper houses of government at the national level may also influence the electoral strength of regional parties at this level. In some countries regional legislatures elect national upper houses either in part or in full. This may strengthen regional parties at the national level because regional parties tend to have sizeable positions in regional legislatures, and these legislatures are likely to elect regional parties to upper houses if given the opportunity.

Finally, the timing of national and regional elections may also influence the electoral strength of regional parties at the subnational level. Typically, national elections influence regional elections whereby parties that perform well in the former tend to perform well in the latter, if elections occur at the same time. Consequently, statewide parties, which typically perform better than regional parties in national elections, should have stronger positions in regional elections when the two occur at the same time. However, nonconcurrent elections disrupt this coat tails effect. Therefore, when national and regional elections are nonconcurrent, regional parties are likely to have stronger positions in regional elections than otherwise. Only in understanding both the influence of regional parties on intrastate conflict, and the effect of decentralization on regional parties, is the overall impact of decentralization on conflict apparent.

1.6. Methodology

In order to understand the effect of decentralization and regional parties on ethnic conflict and secessionism, I use case studies as well as statistical analysis (King et al. 1994; Brady and Collier 2004; Lieberman 2005). This approach is different from previous studies of decentralization, which have relied almost exclusively on case studies to build and support their arguments – most of which have been on Eastern Europe (Riker 1964; Nordlinger 1972; Horowitz 1991; Roeder 1991; Ornstein and Coursen 1992; Brubaker 1996; Kymlicka 1998; Bunce 1999; Leff 1999; Snyder 2000; Filippov et al. 2004). Prior analyses of regional parties have likewise relied on case studies either of specific regional parties, such as the Scottish National Party and the Northern League, or specific regions of countries, such as the Basque Country and Catalonia in Spain and the North East of India (Banerjee 1984; Kumar 1988; Gassah 1992; Llera 1993; Newell 1998; Bhatnagar 1988; Christiansen 1998; Holzer and Schwegler 1998; Marcet and Argelaguet 1998; Tarchi 1998; Ugarte and Pérez-Nievas 1998). Some studies have focused even more narrowly on particular regional party leaders, such as Umberto Bossi of the Northern League (Rocca 1999) or Slobodan Milošević of the Socialist Party of Serbia (Malcolm 1996; Blumi 2001).

In this study, I also use case studies to develop a theory about the effects of decentralization and regional parties on ethnic conflict and secessionism, while I employ the statistical analysis to test the generalizability of this argument and to address potential alternative explanations. I also rely on the case studies to examine the mechanisms through which regional parties increase conflict and secessionism. The case studies complement the statistical analysis by providing more nuanced measures of particular variables included in the analysis (e.g. the intensity of social grievances and the depth of nonviolent secessionist sentiment) and by offering more freedom to explore earlier periods of history not covered by the statistical analysis.

Finally, I use both the case studies and statistical analysis to help disentangle the causal relationships among my key variables and to demonstrate how decentralization influences regional parties, which in turn may affect ethnic conflict and secessionism. In the case studies, I trace out the processes through which countries decentralize and regional parties arise to show how decentralization is not simply a function of regional parties and/or ethnic conflict and secessionism. In each case I demonstrate how statewide parties made the decision to decentralize and how regional parties have grown in regions that did not demand decentralization prior to its adoption. I also highlight how regional parties are weaker in different regions of countries and in different periods of history despite similar ethnolinguistic and economic differences. I further call attention to how patterns in regional party strength are consistent with the presence or absence of decentralization, as well as specific features of this system.

In the statistical analysis I explore the question of causality using instrumental variable regression, which disentangles the relationship between two potentially endogenous variables by using instruments for one variable to proxy for its effects on the other (Hug 2007). To proxy for the effect of decentralization, I use instruments that affect the decision to decentralize and not the intensity of ethnic conflict and secessionism. In a similar fashion, I use factors that affect regional parties, but not the decision to decentralize or the intensity of conflict and secessionism, to proxy for their effect on both. The results of this analysis dovetail nicely with the three case studies to show the independent effect of decentralization on regional parties, and regional parties, in turn, on ethnic conflict and secessionism.

1.6.1. *Case studies*

The case study analysis focuses on three countries: postcommunist Czechoslovakia, Spain, and India. The first two case studies are based on extensive field research in Europe and draw on interviews with regional and statewide party leaders at the national and subnational levels of government. All of the case studies are rooted in a very close examination of newspaper coverage on issues related to conflict and independence. They also draw extensively on primary data on elections, censuses, budgets, legislation, and court cases, among other things.

I selected these case studies based on variation in my two independent variables, decentralization and regional parties (Geddes 1990). All three countries have decentralized systems of government filled through democratic elections. However, their systems of government vary in ways that affect the electoral strength of regional parties. While Czechoslovakia, for example, had only two large regions, Spain has nineteen, and India has thirty-five today. Czechoslovakia directly elected its upper house and held national and regional elections concurrently, while Spain directly elects only part of its upper house and holds most national and regional elections nonconcurrently. India indirectly elects its entire upper house and has staggered elections in certain regions of the country. The extent to which countries divide authority between the national and subnational levels of government, the issues over which each level has jurisdiction (particularly in terms of constitutional decision-making), and the extent to which the national level of government can interfere with the subnational level are also different across these three countries.

The electoral strength of regional parties also varies considerably in these three countries. In Czechoslovakia, regional parties were very strong at the national and subnational levels of government and controlled the legislative agenda in both. In Spain they have had a much more moderate position, never participating in the national government and controlling subnational legislatures in only a few regions. In India, in contrast, regional parties have controlled many regional legislatures and have participated in the national government since the early 1990s.

I also selected these cases because they are similar in terms of a number of alternative explanations for the rise of regional parties and the occurrence of ethnic conflict and secessionism. This helps eliminate these factors as alternative explanations for my three cases. All three countries are ethnically diverse and have ethnic groups that are regionally concentrated. Not only do they have regions that differ in terms of ethnolinguistic or religious identity, but they also have regions that vary in terms of economic wealth. The two most secessionist regions in Spain, the Basque Country and Catalonia, are wealthier than the rest of the country (although the relative wealth of the Basque Country has declined considerably over time), while Slovakia was poorer than the Czech Lands. The conflict-prone areas of India are more of a mixed bag in terms of economic wealth.

Further, Czechoslovakia, Spain, and India all underwent democratic transitions after World War II, and are considered "free" or "partly free" by Freedom House.[9] All three countries have parliamentary systems and two – Czechoslovakia and Spain – have proportional representation systems. None, meanwhile, have cross-regional voting laws, which could artificially manipulate the strength of regional parties.

More than three countries in the world meet these requirements. Of these, I selected Czechoslovakia, Spain, and India in particular for the following additional reasons. I selected Czechoslovakia because studying the breakup of Czechoslovakia initially gave me the idea to look at regional parties as an explanation for decentralization's varied success. The role that regional parties played in Czechoslovakia's dissolution was quite dramatic, with regional parties breaking up the country in 1993 against the tide of public opinion in both the Czech and Slovak Lands. The overwhelming presence of regional parties in the country is quite remarkable since ethnic, religious, and economic differences between the Czech Lands and Slovakia were not very large at the time, and definitely not larger than many countries that have remained united. If decentralization were to keep a country united anywhere, it should have been in Czechoslovakia. I also sought to include a country from Eastern Europe in this study because most of the theories about why decentralization fails to reduce ethnic conflict and secessionism are based on the three failed cases of decentralization in Eastern Europe – Czechoslovakia, Yugoslavia, and the Soviet Union. The latter two cases are very well studied with many books written on each, while the case of Czechoslovakia is less well studied. Czechoslovakia is also a rare case of peaceful secession, which the statistical analysis in this book, as well as many others, does not fully capture as a result. The case of Czechoslovakia, thus, warrants a separate analysis of its own.

I selected Spain as my second case study as it provides an example of decentralization in an economically advanced country. Spain, in particular, is larger and less well studied than many other potential examples, such as Belgium and Switzerland. The small size of these often-studied examples of decentralization raises questions about their generalizability. Spain's large and diverse population makes it more likely to be generalizable and allows for within-country comparisons as well. Additionally, the existing literature touts Spain as one of the most successful cases of decentralization in the world. Despite significant ethnic and economic diversity among its regions, Spain has remained united, with violence confined to a single terrorist organization in the Basque Country, which has been responsible for more than 800 deaths since the 1970s. Yet, the particular reasons for decentralization's success in Spain are not well studied.

Finally, I selected India as my third case study to incorporate an example of decentralization in an economically developing country in order to examine the generalizability of my findings to these types of countries. India stands out as the most important of these developing countries to study because it is the most populous democracy in the world and its peace and stability has important consequences for all of Asia as well as the world. India's large and diverse population, like Spain's, also allows for interesting within-country comparisons. The sheer magnitude of intrastate violence in India is far greater than the two other cases in this study, with thousands of lives lost to intrastate conflict compared to the hundreds lost in Spain. This violence has been confined, however, to only certain regions of the country at different periods of India's history. India, moreover, unlike Czechoslovakia, has averted state collapse.

1.6.2. *Quantitative analysis*

The statistical analysis examines the effect of decentralization on intrastate conflict more generally, drawing on an original dataset of election results for fifty democracies around the world between 1944 and 2002, known herein as the *Constituency-Level Elections* (CLE) dataset (Brancati 2007). The sheer lack of systematic data on regional parties presented the greatest obstacle to this analysis. To rectify this problem, I amassed a large dataset on election results at the constituency level of government (i.e. the level at which seats are distributed in a country). This dataset allows me to classify parties according to the geographic basis of their electoral support and to measure this support consistently across countries over time. This dataset permits a very comprehensive analysis of regional parties, providing data on all parties regardless of how many votes or seats they win and on national legislative elections (upper and lower houses), as well as regional elections. I present further details about the CLE dataset in Chapter 6 of this book.

The analysis also draws on the *Minorities at Risk* dataset, which I have corrected for both group-based and country-based selection bias, to measure ethnic conflict and secessionism.[10] The dataset provides information on these phenomena on a yearly basis from 1985 to 2000. It offers a more refined measure of ethnic conflict and secessionism than most other datasets because it distinguishes between the two, and captures different intensities of conflict, whereas most other datasets generally only determine whether or not a civil war has occurred in a country (Fearon and Laitin 2003; Collier and Hoeffler 2004). Originally, the dataset was collected to identify incidents of conflict in the world. Therefore, to apply it to this project, I had to collect data on all groups excluded from the dataset because they did not meet the dataset's selection criterion. Combined, these two datasets allow for a strong test of the generalizability of the ideas presented in this book over a long period of time and across a large number of countries.

1.7. Plan of the book

This book is divided into three parts. In Part I, I develop the argument introduced here. In so doing, I first explain why regional parties are more likely than statewide parties to intensify ethnic conflict and secessionism in countries. I also explicate the ways in which they promote both, and the conditions under which they are most likely to do so. I further expand upon the role that statewide parties play in reducing ethnic conflict and secessionism, and in reigning in regional parties. I also illustrate how decentralization increases the electoral strength of regional parties to different degrees depending on the structure of decentralization. To elucidate my claims, I draw on examples from the case studies and many other countries as well.

The case studies comprise Part II of this book. Chapter 3 focuses on Czechoslovakia and highlights how both the proportion of seats that a region has in a national legislature, as well as the number of subnational legislatures in a country, influence the strength of regional parties and the occurrence of secessionism. Here, the division of the country into two large regions, coupled with a law granting parties from one region veto power over national legislation, created strong incentives for regional parties during Czechoslovakia's transition to democracy. In turn, the strong presence of regional parties with the ability to block national legislation prevented Czechoslovakia from agreeing on a new constitution and led to the breakup of the country.

Contrary to what some scholars argue, regional differences and regional parties did not cause decentralization or the dissolution of Czechoslovakia. Rather, it decentralized under communist rule in 1968. It also had weaker regional parties under a democratically elected centralized system of government during the interwar period than under decentralization in the postcommunist period. This is despite the fact that regional differences (e.g. economic, ethnic, and religious) were much stronger in the former than in the latter. Regional parties were also weaker in the nonautonomous region of Moravia than in Slovakia, even though Moravia was arguably as culturally and economically distinct from the rest of the country as Slovakia.

Chapter 4 is devoted to Spain. Among other things, this case study demonstrates how regional parties can promote secessionism by advocating legislation harmful to other regions and supporting extremist organizations that agitate for independence. It also demonstrates how the proportion of seats that a region has at the national level of government, as well as the method used to elect upper houses, can influence the electoral strength of regional parties. The fact that individually each of Spain's regions comprise a small proportion of the national legislature, and that people directly elect most of the country's upper house, has limited the presence of regional parties at the national level. Regional parties have had a stronger position in the part of Spain's upper house, which is indirectly elected by the country's regional legislatures, but this part constitutes only one-fifth of the national upper house.

Spain also illustrates that regional parties are not simply the product of ethnic conflict and secessionism. Regional party strength increased markedly after Spain adopted a decentralized system of government in the late 1970s, particularly in those regions of Spain where regional parties were especially weak prior to decentralization. This strength also varies considerably within the same region depending on the legislature in which parties compete. Moreover, regional parties are not necessarily stronger in those regions of Spain that are ethnolinguistically or economically distinct from the rest of the country, or that have strong regional identities according to surveys.

Chapter 5, on India, demonstrates how regional parties contribute to ethnic conflict and secessionism by adopting legislation that threatens regional minorities, and by supporting extremist groups that attack different ethnic groups and use violence to achieve regional independence. It also shows the conditions under which statewide parties are less likely to reduce ethnic conflict and secessionism. India's example further substantiates earlier findings regarding a region's share of national legislative seats and the method used to elect upper houses. The fact that India is divided into numerous regions, each with only a small proportion of seats in the lower house, reduces the strength of regional parties at the national level. The indirect election of all of India's upper house by its regional legislatures, in contrast, enhances their strength.

India also demonstrates how regional differences are important, but also insufficient, in explaining the strength of regional parties in countries, since they differ widely in strength across regions and throughout India's history, despite a lack of commensurate variation in the strength of regional cleavages. In India, the strength of regional parties varies considerably based on the decision-making authority of regions (with regional parties having weaker positions in regions without any decision-making authority) and on the legislature in which parties compete. Regional cleavages also contributed to the decision of India to decentralize after it gained independence from the United Kingdom, although regional parties did not play a role in this process.

Part III presents the quantitative analysis. I use the statistical analysis to test the generalizability of the hypotheses I derive from the case studies. The statistical analysis also offers insight into the causal relationships presented in my argument. Chapter 6, in particular, examines the effect of decentralization and regional parties on ethnic conflict and secessionism while controlling for a number of other factors that may also affect these phenomena. The analysis confirms that political decentralization is associated with lower levels of ethnic conflict and secessionism, while regional parties are associated with higher levels. Chapter 7 explores the effect of decentralization on regional parties while controlling for various factors. The analysis also confirms that decentralization is associated with electorally weaker regional parties in general and that the strength of regional parties depends on the specific institutional features of decentralization in a country.

Finally, Chapter 8 offers a forward-looking discussion of the implications of these findings for countries worldwide. In this chapter, I examine alternative methods of conflict resolution, as well as the ways in which political decentralization should be designed to maximize its effectiveness in reducing ethnic conflict and secessionism.

Part I

Theory Development

2

Decentralization: Fueling the Fire or Dampening the Flames of Intrastate Conflict?

Whether decentralized governance can effectively manage ethnic conflict and secessionism is greatly influenced by the electoral strength of regional parties. In this chapter I illustrate the central importance of regional parties in this regard by examining the ways in which regional parties intensify ethnic conflict and demands for independence. I highlight three ways, in particular, associated with identity formation, legislation, and mobilization. I also discuss the potential conditions under which regional parties are likely to intensify conflict, and those in which statewide parties are likely to reduce it.

I further demonstrate in this chapter how the electoral strength of regional parties is contingent on the institutional structure of decentralization, thus providing at least one explanation for why decentralization does not reduce ethnic conflict and secessionism equally in all countries. These features of decentralization include the share of national legislative seats that a region holds, the number of regional legislatures in a country, the method used to elect national upper houses, and the sequencing of national and regional elections. In developing my argument, I also address a number of potential alternative explanations for the effects of decentralization and regional parties on conflict and secessionism.

2.1. Deconstructing the impact of regional parties

Regional parties, I argue, can intensify ethnic conflict and secessionism through at least three different mechanisms. Regional parties can create regional cleavages, advocate legislation harmful to
other regions in a country and regional minorities, and mobilize
groups in support of ethnic conflict and secessionism besides back-
ing terrorist groups engaged in these activities. The type of ethnic
conflict at issue here is ethnic conflict involving territorially concentrated ethnic groups. This is the only type of conflict decentralization is supposed to reduce, and is often, incidentally, intertwined
with separatism. I discuss each of the mechanisms through which
regional parties promote both ethnic conflict and secessionism in
this section in turn.

2.1.1. *Identity formation*

Regional parties play an important role in transforming regional
differences into salient political identities. These differences are the
building blocks of regional identities. They are not, however, auto-
matically or necessarily translated into political identities through
which people understand, interact with, and make evaluations
of their political systems. Individuals residing in certain regions
of countries are not necessarily aware of the characteristics they
share in common, nor do they effectively associate with each other
because of these characteristics or think of themselves as members
of the same group. After all, individuals are defined by many different characteristics all of which may potentially form the basis of
people's political identities.

Instead, as a growing body of literature in political science demonstrates, identities are constructed (Laitin 1985; Kalyvas 1996;
Giuliano 2000; Herrera 2005; Posner 2004; Penn 2007a). As this
literature also points out, political leaders and the institutions in
which they interact, construct identities to enhance their political power and further their political goals. These rationally motivated leaders politicize whichever societal difference – be it ethnic,

religious, economic, or territorial – that offers them the greatest political advantage. Statewide parties, because they stand to benefit politically from uniting people across regional boundaries, generally foster national identities. Regardless of whether or not these identities include everyone within a country, these identities are national in the sense that they incorporate people across the internal borders of a state. Regional parties, in contrast, construct more narrow identities that are based on residency in a particular geographic locale.

Regional parties foster regional identities by making individuals living in the same region aware of the characteristics they have in common, and are key in explaining why decentralization is associated with mixed results in terms of minority identification with the state (Elkins and Sides 2007). Frequently, these characteristics include a common ethnicity, language, religion, history, or economic position. Regional parties can also encourage people to think of themselves as a group with shared needs and goals, distinct from those of other groups, and to conceive of their individual well-being as tied to that of their group as a whole. In encouraging people to think of themselves as part of a group, regional parties can convince people that they will gain, either psychologically or materially, by associating with other members of their region. Often, regional parties emphasize how people, in failing to think of themselves collectively as a group, are disadvantaged vis-à-vis others.

Regional parties may use many different tactics at their disposal to help create regional identities. Some invent regional symbols to create a sense of unity among people, such as flags, currency, license plates, or identification cards akin to passports or visas.[11] Other regional parties hold rallies and demonstrations of regional pride, while still others sponsor legislative initiatives that deepen people's ties with one another. These initiatives may foster regional identities in many different ways, such as spreading the use of a common language. Perhaps, the most common way that regional parties create regional identities, however, is through the dissemination of information. In framing issues in particular ways and providing people with certain information, regional parties can elicit a collective identity among people living in the same region.

Voters, for their part, may adopt regional identities because party appeals resonate with them, although voters may not yet be mobilized around these identities and these identities may not yet constitute a salient cleavage for them.[12] Whether the appeals of regional parties resonate with voters may depend, in part, on the underlying characteristics of society. Do the groups, for example, actually speak the same language or practice the same religion? Are they, or do they feel, displaced economically in a country? How much the appeals of parties resonate with voters also depends significantly on how well regional parties frame issues in terms that people understand and consider relevant (Chong and Druckman 2007).

By framing issues, regional parties can make seemingly disparate groups appear quite similar and very similar groups seem completely different. In this way, regional parties can also convince voters to align with certain groups, suggesting that by not associating with other members of their group they are incurring significant losses, a strategy that is typically more effective than presenting people with information about what they may gain through a particular action (Kahneman and Tversky 1979). The ability of parties to frame issues effectively depends not only on whether parties use available considerations, but on a number of other factors as well. These factors include, but are not limited to, the credibility of regional party leaders (Popkin 1994), their likeability (Iyengar and Valentino 2000), and the political knowledge of voters themselves (Zaller 1992; McGraw and Hubbard 1996). As members of groups they purport to represent, regional party leaders may fare particularly well in terms of credibility.

Strong regional identities do not necessarily lead to conflict. However, groups that have strong identities are easier to mobilize collectively toward a given end than those that do not – regardless of whether this end is conflict and secessionism, or something else. Identities that are premised on certain beliefs are also more likely to lead to conflict than others. Those most likely to spark conflict are generally rooted in beliefs that a group is threatened or disadvantaged in some way, either politically, socially, or economically vis-à-vis the state or other groups in the country. Politically, groups that engage in conflict or seek independence may do so because they believe that they have less political influence than they are owed. Socially or culturally, they may do so because they believe that their language is undervalued or that their religion is unprotected, while economically, they may do so because they feel burdened with a disproportionate share of taxes in their countries (Buchanan and Faith 1987; Bookman 1991; Bolton and Roland 1997; Hug 2005). Economically, they may also engage in conflict or seek independence because they do not receive sufficient national services, such as education, or an equitable share of the profits generated by natural resources in their regions – as was the case in the Independent Republic of the Congo in the 1960s, Papua New Guinea in the 1980s, and Iraq and Nigeria today (Ross 2004).[13]

Strong regional identities may also form the basis for ethnic conflict and secessionism because people, as psychological studies show, tend to be biased toward those belonging to their own group (Tajfel and Turner 1979; Gibson and Gouws 2000). People are also supposed to cooperate and resolve differences with members of their own groups more easily than with members of other groups (Fearon and Laitin 1996; Habyarimana et al. 2007). Finally, people are supposed to feel less threatened by those who share the same identity as them compared to those who do not (Rousseau and García-Retamero 2007).

The most common explanation for regional parties is that they are the result of regional differences, which are inadequately represented by the political system (Lipset and Rokkan 1967; Levi and Hechter 1985; Hearl et al. 1996; de Winter and Türsan 1998; Fearon and van Houten 2002). Regional differences are neither necessary nor sufficient to explain the rise of regional parties, however. Inconsistencies between the electoral strength of regional parties within countries over time and patterns in regional differences lend credence to this conclusion. As the case studies will demonstrate, regional differences are largely constant over time while the strength of regional parties fluctuates significantly within countries over time and across different institutional contexts. Additionally, some regions of countries do not have distinct ethnolinguistic characteristics or economic features, and yet, have electorally strong regional parties and vice versa. The relationship between regional differences and regional parties is much more complex and mediated by institutions, which provide politicians with incentives to exploit certain cleavages over others, as I will elucidate subsequently in this chapter.

2.1.2. Legislation

Regional parties can also promote ethnic conflict and secessionism through the legislation they advocate. Typically, regional parties are believed to decrease ethnic conflict and secessionism by advocating legislation representing regional interests that otherwise would not be addressed by the government (Rokkan and Urwin 1982; de Winter and Türsan 1998; Meguid 2002). By not only addressing, but also protecting the interests of particular groups, legislation espoused by regional parties should eliminate the reasons why groups fight each other or demand independence in the first place. As such, regional parties, or parties representing minorities in general, are best able to address regional interests and, hence, reduce conflict and secessionism when they are politically empowered (O'Leary and McGarry 1995). As Brendan O'Leary and John McGarry relate, "Federal failures primarily occur because minorities continue to be outnumbered at the federal government" (281). If regional parties do not have significant legislative authority, some scholars suggest they may have a beneficial effect on governance by pressuring statewide parties to accommodate regional interests (Meguid 2002).

While the legislation regional parties typically sponsor may make significant strides toward satiating the regions in whose name this legislation is advocated, it may nonetheless stimulate ethnic conflict and secessionism in other ways. This legislation, for example, may not only foster regional identities, as suggested in the previous section, but it may also threaten other regions in a country and prompt a reaction from them. Regional parties often sponsor legislation that threatens other regions because they draw their support from a particular geographic locale. By virtue of drawing their electoral support from a single region, regional parties advocate legislation, which they perceive to be in the best interests of their own region.

Regional parties do not take into consideration how their legislation may negatively affect another region, nor do they necessarily take into consideration what is good for the country as a whole. Legislation on behalf of wealthy regions, for example, which seeks to reduce one region's tax contributions to the national government, can threaten poor regions that rely on subsidies from the national government. Similarly, legislation on behalf of one region demanding the diversion of a major riverway to improve irrigation in that region may harm another region that depends on this river to irrigate crops and supply industries with water.

In turn, regions negatively affected by legislation favoring other regions may seek more autonomy from the national government to forestall future threats and even independence. In postcommunist Czechoslovakia, the Czech Lands initiated the dissolution of Czechoslovakia in response to Slovak demands for a level of regional autonomy that Czech regional parties considered unreasonable. In response to threatening legislation, regional parties may also attack other regions or members of another region residing within their own borders. Serbian political parties in the early 1990s encouraged Serbs in Croatia to rebel and supported them militarily after Croatia declared independence from the former Yugoslavia, an act that Serbia claimed threatened Serbs living in Croatia.

Statewide parties can also incorporate into their agendas the interests of particular regions, especially at the subnational level. They have an incentive to do this in order to win votes in regions and remain competitive with regional parties (Chandler 1987).

35

Because statewide parties draw electoral support from multiple regions, however, they are more likely than regional parties to consider how policies in support of one region may negatively affect that of another. As a result, statewide parties tend to advocate policies that are more moderate and regionally balanced than do regional parties. In order to balance the interests of different regions against each other, statewide parties may offer regions side payments to compensate one region for harm caused to them by policies favoring another, and may make concessions to the former along a different dimension.

Regional members of statewide parties at either the national or the subnational level of government may not have the interests of other regions in mind when they advocate particular legislation. However, the upper echelons of a party, which set policy for the party as a whole and seek to maintain a cohesive party label, can strongly influence, to the point of control, the legislative behavior of particular regional party members. They may do this in a number of different ways, including controlling the nomination of candidates to electoral lists and the distribution of campaign money among party members. If regional members of statewide parties want to get on their party's ballot in future elections, or rise through their party's ranks, they will need to tow the party line. Statewide parties may also overcome regional factionalism in more subtle ways, such as by refusing to endorse or make campaign appearances with party rebels. While statewide parties have many channels through which they can maintain party unity, statewide parties may be best equipped to avert potential factionalism in parliamentary systems. In these systems the vote of confidence requires parties to be very cohesive in order to keep governments in power.

Statewide parties can also regulate or modify regional parties when in coalition with regional parties. Prior to forming a coalition, statewide parties can compel regional parties who want to join the coalition to adopt policies that are more moderate. This may involve regional parties giving up demands for independence or reducing support for separatist organizations. In this regard, statewide parties will be more effective if they form coalitions without the support of particular regional parties and seek out alternative coalition partners. If, however, regional parties are pivotal to the formation of these coalitions, statewide parties may hold less bargaining power over regional parties, and may be less likely to compel regional parties to relinquish certain demands.

Once statewide parties have formed a coalition with regional parties, both must negotiate to produce policies – failing to do so may lead to government collapse (Brancati 2005). Typically, statewide parties are the more powerful members of these coalitions, which gives them more bargaining leverage. Barring collapse, a coalition of statewide and regional parties should, therefore, produce policies that address the interests of regional parties, but that are much more moderate than these parties' ideal policies. Statewide parties are prevented from going too far in the direction of one region's interests by the need to keep in mind constituents in other parts of the country. At the same time, statewide parties may demand that their regional coalition partners moderate their policies in different ways in exchange for concessions on certain issues.

Another way in which regional parties can promote ethnic conflict and secessionism through legislation is by advocating legislation that is harmful to regional minorities in ethnically heterogeneous regions. In trying to win votes in a heterogeneous region that has a dominant ethnolinguistic group, regional parties may attempt to build a cohesive majority by targeting a regional minority group and blaming it for the majority group's problems (Gagnon 1994, 1995; Wilkinson 2004). Obviously, the regional party will lose the support of the minority in doing so. However, if the minority is small, the gains to the regional party from the majority group may outweigh losses from the minority group. Statewide parties may do this as well, but are less likely to behave in this fashion if a regional minority has a strong position in other parts of the country. In doing so, statewide parties may risk losing the support of this minority in other areas of the country. Regional parties do not face similar countervailing pressures.

The ways in which legislation advocated by regional parties can threaten regional minorities, particularly at the subnational level where regional parties are electorally strongest, are manifold. This legislation may protect, for example, the dominant language of a region by banning that of another. On the other hand, it may establish a legal system that requires obediance to certain religious principles regardless of whether all citizens are members of that religion or not. Or, it may divert money needed for education and vital services, such as transportation and waste removal, from districts in which regional minorities reside. Such legislation can incite retaliation from minorities or from other regions where these minorities constitute a sizeable portion of the population.

Finally, regional parties may sponsor legislation that demands outright independence, or perhaps just as influential, the right to independence. While it is rare that regions actually have the legal right to secede unilaterally from a country, legislation declaring independence may nevertheless become a rallying cry around which regional parties mobilize groups in support of independence. A declaration of independence, in turn, may incite a reaction from the national government or from other regions in a country. Statewide parties are unlikely to agitate for regional independence because one region's independence may not only weaken a country as a whole, but also harm other regions in a country and prompt them to declare independence (Walter 2006). Although some regional members of statewide parties may seek independence, statewide parties can prevent them from initiating legislation to this effect (even at the subnational level of government) for the same reasons that statewide parties tend to promote legislation that is more moderate in general.

2.1.3. Mobilization

Finally, regional parties can promote ethnic conflict and secessionism by mobilizing society at large to engage in these activities, although social mobilization, as the case of Czechoslovakia illustrates, is not necessary for secession to result. Ethnic conflict and secessionism do not arise spontaneously (Olson 1971; Hardin 1997). Rather, individuals must be organized to engage in ethnic conflict and secessionism even if they have clear grievances against the government and/or each other (Laitin 1985; Gagnon 1994/1995; Malcolm 1996; Hardin 1997; Mueller 2000; Snyder 2000). The strong regional identities, which regional parties foster, may facilitate mobilization along these lines.

Regional parties can also mobilize groups to engage in ethnic conflict and secessionism by issuing public calls to arms, as in Yugoslavia, and encouraging individuals of one ethnic group to attack those of another or prompting groups to fight for independence. In pursuit of these ends, regional parties may employ a variety of different tactics, including public rallies and appeals through the media, flyers, etc. Regional parties can also provide funding for these activities through membership fees and donations collected from domestic and international supporters. In some countries regional parties have even trained and supplied militia forces with needed weapons and ammunition.

Decentralization provides regional parties with many resources at the subnational level, which they may utilize to mobilize groups to engage in ethnic conflict and secession, including legislatures, media, and police forces (Roeder 1991; Kymlicka 1998; Bunce 1999; Leff 1999; Snyder 2000). Regional parties can use regional legislatures and forms of media to appeal to people, while at the same time, they can use regional police forces to intimidate people of different ethnic groups or fight for regional independence. These resources in and of themselves do not lead to conflict and secessionism. All decentralized systems of government possess at least some of these resources. Yet, not all of these systems end in ethnic conflict and secessionism. It is the combination of these resources and regional parties that comprise the potentially lethal mix.

Very often, regional parties also support extremist organizations that contribute to ethnic conflict and secessionism by publicly defending their policies, financing their activities, collecting protection money through extortion, and even stockpiling guns and ammunitions for them at their own party headquarters. Because of these activities, Spain outlawed Herri Batasuna, a regional party in the Basque Country in 2003, closing its offices, sequestering its funds, and denying it the right to compete in future elections, while the United States placed the party on its terrorist watch list. Even regional parties that are not actually associated with extremist organizations often hesitate to crack down on them out of fear of either becoming targets themselves and/or appearing like sellouts to the local population. However, support is often mutual, with extremist organizations rigging subnational elections in favor of regional parties. In India extremist organizations have done just this by threatening and intimidating voters into casting their ballots for regional parties.

2.2. The when question

While regional parties have a tendency to promote ethnic conflict and secessionism in the ways described above, certain contexts make them more likely to do so. At the same time, certain circumstances can also make statewide parties less likely to reduce the potential for ethnic conflict and secessionism. Some of these factors have already been suggested, including the heterogeneity of regions and the location of regional minorities throughout a country. There are a number of other factors, however, which influence not only the incentive but also the opportunities for regional parties to seek these ends. While perhaps not an exhaustive inventory of all the conditions that may affect the behavior of these parties, they nonetheless, touch on a number of important issues and themes that may affect their political behavior.

Arguably, the most important factor in this regard is whether countries are undergoing democratic transitions (Snyder and Mansfield 1995; Snyder 2000). During transitions, regional parties can also exert considerable influence on the preferences, as well as identities of citizens. Identities may be more malleable at this juncture than at others since old political identities constructed by outgoing regimes are no longer relevant. At the same time, competition among new political parties to attract electoral support is intense, giving parties an incentive to construct new identities in ways that maximize their electoral advantage. The openness of political systems during transitions to new parties and the weakness of preexisting partisan ties can also promote regional parties in the first place.

During transitions, the media is also not completely free, which allows regional parties to construct identities along regional lines without very many checks on the validity of their appeals (Snyder and Ballentine 1996). Experimental evidence confirms that leaders are very effective in influencing people's preferences in these contexts; that is, situations where there is a single, unchallenged political frame (Iyengar 1991). In these situations political leaders may even be effective in using weak frames that draw on unavailable considerations if individuals are unmotivated and rely on accessible beliefs without regard to their applicability (Chong and Druckman 2007). Finally, parties are also thought to mobilize voters along ethnic lines during transitions because ethnic characteristics are highly visible and provide stable informational cues to voters (Birnir 2007).

In periods of transition, political systems are also in flux and subject to question. As a result, regional parties are more likely to question the position of their regions during these periods than in others. They are also more likely to demand a maximum amount of authority from the national government since governments tend to be weak in these periods and need to bargain with their constituents for support. Weak states are also vulnerable to mobilization executed by regional parties and may not be able to rely on the state military to quell conflict or secessionism. The military can be an unreliable partner because it opposes democratic transitions, as in Spain. In robust, stable democracies, in contrast, regional parties are less likely to mobilize groups toward conflict and secessionism, while national governments are more capable of fending off regional party demands. Regional parties are also less likely to pass legislation harmful to regional minorities in these countries since democracies generally enshrine political and civil rights.

Electoral competition among regional parties may also influence the potential for regional parties to increase conflict and secessionism by encouraging electoral outbidding. Scholars have shown formally that when two ethnic parties compete for the support of a single group, they tend to adopt increasingly extreme positions on issues to steal votes from each other (Rabushka and Shepsle 1972; Horowitz 1985). While only a subset of regional parties are ethnically based, outbidding may also occur among regional parties because they seek support from groups that likewise have defined boundaries (i.e. the regional border).

The essentialist assumptions of outbidding models have been thoughtfully critiqued by scholars for taking preferences as uniform, shared, and fixed, in contrast to the constructed understanding of identity that underpins the argument of this book (Giuiliano 2000; Chandra 2005). However, even if identities are constructed, once parties identify individuals along regional lines, competition from other parties along these same lines can also lead to outbidding. This is consistent with the work of Pieter van Houten (2008) on European regional parties. Van Houten (2008) finds that when electoral competition among regional parties is intense, regional parties demand more fiscal autonomy from the state. Electoral competition, in turn, is not necessarily driven by the underlying regional differences in countries, but by features of electoral systems, such as proportional representation and high district magnitude, which increase fractionalization.

Leadership style is another important factor that may affect the strategy through which regional parties pursue their goals. Some leaders at the helm of regional parties may perceive violence as the best or only means through which to achieve their goals, while others, even those from the same region, may not. The fact that regional parties alter their tactics over time as leadership changes is strong evidence of this effect. While leadership style may play a less influential role than other factors that affect the amount of discretion leaders possess, it is nonetheless an interesting factor that may help explain why regional parties from the same region adopt different strategies.

The ability of regional parties to attain their goals effectively depends on their ability to control a legislature's agenda, as well as the specific powers of this legislature. Legislative control is determined principally by the proportion of seats a region has in a legislature and the specific rules by which that legislature makes decisions (i.e. how much support legislation needs to become law). Typically, legislation only needs the support of a majority of the legislature in order to become law. Yet, in different systems it can require much greater support. In general, the higher the required threshold of support, the more difficult it is for regional parties to pass legislation. If regional parties need the assistance of a statewide party to govern, the policies they adopt are likely to be much more moderate, as previously described.

In some cases, however, decision-making rules, like those in Northern Ireland and postcommunist Czechoslovakia, can actually increase the strength of regional parties by requiring legislation to have the support of particular territories or groups in order to become law. In Northern Ireland representatives self-designated as either nationalists or unionists must both approve key legislation (e.g. the budget, standing orders, and elections of the Speaker and First Minister) in order for it to pass. This invariably downgrades the influence of nonaligned legislators and discourages candidates from declaring themselves as such. Decision-making rules in postcommunist Czechoslovakia had a similar effect, as I will detail in the next chapter of this book. The extreme case of this is consociationalism, which requires grand coalition governments and minority vetoes (Lijphart 1977).

The authority of the legislature that a regional party controls can also heavily influence a party's ability to pass conflict-inducing legislation. In other words, having a strong position in a subnational legislature with little power to legislate (or where decisions are easily overridden) will leave a regional party hamstrung. If national governments oversee and actively enforce political and civil rights, regional parties will have particular difficulty in passing legislation harmful to regional minorities. Alternatively, a strong showing in a subnational legislature with wide-sweeping powers can give regional parties boundless opportunity to pass legislation, especially if a legislature has constitutional veto powers. Also important in this regard is the relative power of national lower and upper houses of government. Regional parties tend to have stronger positions in upper houses than in lower houses for reasons described later. Yet, upper houses typically have fewer powers, diminishing the impact of regional parties on legislation as a result.

Many of the themes and issues identified above are also relevant to explaining the likelihood of statewide parties in reducing conflict and secessionism. Statewide parties may not necessarily reduce conflict among ethnic groups dispersed throughout a country, and may even increase it, particularly if the party represents a single ethnic group within a country. This fact does not pose a challenge to the argument presented here, however. This analysis seeks to understand the conditions under which decentralization is more or less effective in reducing ethnic conflict and secessionism among territorially concentrated groups. Decentralization is not purported to affect ethnic conflict among widely dispersed groups and the party system is, thus, not relevant to explaining the relationship between the two. Decentralization, moreover, does not provide statewide parties with any more or any fewer incentives than centralized systems of government to incorporate ethnic groups based on ethnicity when groups are dispersed throughout a country.

In addition to the ethnic composition of a country, an important factor influencing the effect of statewide parties on ethnic conflict and secessionism is the extent to which statewide parties need the support of a particular region or group in order to govern. This, in turn, depends on a number of issues, including the proportion of seats that a region has in a national legislature, the size of ethnic groups both inside and outside of a region, as well as the type of electoral system in a country. Statewide parties are more likely to need the support of regions that control a large proportion of seats in a national legislature than regions that do not. As a result, statewide parties are more likely to incorporate the interests of the former rather than the latter into their agendas.

Some regions, even though they may not have many seats in a legislature, may still offer statewide parties a pivotal number of seats. Whether or not these regions are pivotal can depend on how competitive an election is – the more competitive it is, the more likely a region with a small number of seats is critical to a party's ability to govern. Steven Wilkinson (2004) makes this case for India, where electoral competition, he argues, increases the propensity for parties to incorporate minorities within their agenda and, hence, reduces communal conflict in India. A region may also be pivotal if it is a swing region; that is, if it is a region that does not consistently vote for particular parties or parties of a particular ideological bent.

Related to this issue is the type of electoral system in a country and the incentives electoral systems provide to parties to incorporate multiple ethnic groups into their agendas (Horowitz 1991). Statewide parties are more likely to incorporate regional minorities into their agendas when the electoral system within a region – either for national or subnational elections – requires parties to win a large proportion of the vote within that region. Single-member district systems require parties to earn more votes to win seats than proportional representation (PR) systems. Within PR systems, higher electoral thresholds increase the number of votes parties must receive in order to win seats. Besides the type of method used to distribute seats, electoral laws requiring parties not only to compete in every region of a country, but also to compete in a certain number of districts within these regions, like those that exist in Indonesia and Turkey, can encourage statewide parties to incorporate minority interests into their agendas.

In addition to pivotalness, whether statewide parties incorporate the interests of a particular region into their agenda depends on the ideological leaning of that party and the region in which it seeks to win support. If a statewide party is politically conservative and a region is left-leaning (perhaps because it is home to large industries with powerful unions), a statewide party is less likely to incorporate this region's interests into its agenda. It is less likely to win votes within this region as well.

Of course, as in the case of regional parties, legislative voting rules determining how much support bills need in order to become law can also affect the incentives for statewide parties to incorporate the interests of particular regions into their agendas. Obviously, statewide parties have little incentive to reach out to certain groups or regions in weakly democratic states, where these groups are excluded from electoral competition entirely. The same is true in countries where statewide parties can circumvent genuine electoral competition in other ways. However, if legislative voting rules require statewide parties to have significant support within a legislature to adopt laws, statewide parties have more incentive to incorporate particular regions' interests into their agendas.

The internal structure of statewide parties, as well as the leadership style of their top players, is also key to explaining the extent to which statewide parties incorporate regional issues into their agendas. Parties that are very centralized perform poorly in this respect, while ones that are decentralized perform much better. Broadly defined, centralized parties are parties in which the top leadership formulates political policies, selects candidates for electoral office, and controls the distribution of funds with little input from the party at large (Janda 1980). In decentralized parties where the opposite is true, the rank-and-file have a much greater voice in the direction of the party, as do regional members of the party. According to Riker, decentralized parties as such maintain the integrity of decentralization by preventing political systems from becoming centralized (1964). Riker's views are echoed by Filippov et al. (2004), who contend that integrated parties, which maintain a close relationship between politicians at the national and subnational levels of government, are conducive to federal stability.

The extent to which parties are centralized may be a function of the leadership style of different party leaders, and thus, vary significantly over time. Alternatively, it may result from particular party structures or institutions and, therefore, vary less often and more gradually over time. The different ways in which parties are internally decentralized present regions with different opportunities to exert their influence. If parties are decentralized because the top leadership exerts little control over candidate selection, voters may choose candidates for electoral office through regional primaries, as voters decide presidential candidates in the United States (Lundell 2004). In the absence of primaries, regional or local party organizations may select a slate of candidates for national executive or legislative office. Thresholds requiring regional diversity on standing committees or national caucuses on issues such as fundraising, the budget, and policy can likewise increase the influence of regions within statewide parties.

Related to the issue of party centralization is the strength of party discipline; that is, the extent to which party members support their party's positions on issues whether or not they agree with them. Party discipline, in turn, is associated with the type of political system in a country. All parties tend to be more disciplined in presidential systems than in parliamentary systems. Party discipline also works in conjunction with party structure. The more disciplined centralized parties are, the less able regional members of statewide parties may be to influence their parties' direction. Party discipline is a function not only of the type of executive system in a country, but also the type of electoral system, with party discipline being weaker in candidate-focused systems (Carey and Shugart 1995). A number of scholars suggest that decentralization also encourages less-disciplined political parties because of the mechanisms through which presidential candidates are chosen within them, among other things (Truman 1955; Wildavsky 1967; Chandler 1987; Desposato 2004). Having delineated the ways in which regional parties can promote ethnic conflict and secessionism, I turn my attention, in the remainder of this chapter, to explaining how decentralization promotes regional parties and how particular features of decentralization encourage regional parties more than others.

2.3. Political parties in a decentralized context

Before developing my argument about the effect of decentralization on regional parties, I situate it within the existing literature
on decentralization and political parties in this section. Most studies, which have previously examined this topic, focus on decentralization's effect on the organization and cohesion of statewide
political parties (Truman 1955; Wildavsky 1967; Chandler 1987;
Desposato 2004). David Truman and Aaron Wildavsky claim, for
example, that decentralization, in combination with presidential
systems, discourages cohesion among statewide parties because
decentralized systems lack clear lines of succession when presidents are nominated through regionally based primaries, as in the
United States (Truman 1955; Wildavsky 1967). Meanwhile, Scott
Desposato (2004) argues that in Brazil decentralization reduces
party cohesion because subnational conflicts are common and
because national politicians are tied to subnational interests.
Finally, William Chandler (1987), who introduces the notion of
regional parties into his argument, claims that in decentralized
systems of government, statewide parties have strong regional
branches because they must react to pressures from regional parties (Chandler 1987: 152). Chandler's argument seems to assume,
although it does not make explicit, a link between decentralization
and regional party strength.

Only a few scholars have looked specifically at decentralization's
effect on the electoral strength of regional parties (Montero et al.
1998; Brzinski 1999; Linz and Montero 1999). By and large, these
scholars argue that decentralization *allows* regional parties to win
office more easily, but that it does not *encourage* politicians to form
regional parties, or people to vote for them. Instead, they suggest
that social cleavages determine the types of parties that politicians
form and voters elect, in contrast to my own argument. Pradeep
Chhibber and Ken Kollman (1998, 2004) have a more nuanced
understanding of the relationship between decentralization and
political parties. While they also believe that ascriptive characteristics, such as ethnicity and caste, shape the party system, they

do not believe that these are the only relevant factors in this regard. Chhibber and Kollman propose that political and fiscal decentralization foster "denationalized" party systems in which the votes for parties are not evenly distributed throughout a country. Decentralization, they argue, does this by distributing political authority to subnational legislatures and giving parties fewer incentives to merge with each other in order to control the national apparatus.

While I share Chhibber and Kollman's larger perspective on decentralization, my argument differs from theirs in a number of respects. In addition to focusing exclusively on regional parties rather than the distribution of all parties' votes throughout a country, I emphasize the institutional structure of decentralization over the distribution of power among levels of government. These institutional features, I argue, encourage politicians to form regional parties by increasing their likelihood of governing. In contrast, Chhibber and Kollman focus on the payoffs associated with governing as determined by the political authority of national versus subnational legislatures. I, nevertheless, contend that subnational legislatures must have some decision-making authority for politicians to have a reason to form regional parties. If they do not, politicians have no incentive to form regional parties because they could not influence policy through them at this level of government.

Further, I argue in contrast to Chhibber and Kollman that political and fiscal decentralization are distinct phenomena and should be analyzed separately. Fiscal decentralization refers to the division of authority between different levels of government regarding revenues and expenditures (Rodden 2004), and is not as closely associated with political decentralization as it may seem. Many politically decentralized countries are more decentralized fiscally than politically, and vice versa. This disconnect can result from national governments granting subnational governments fiscal powers in centralized systems precisely to avoid extending political powers to them (Falleti 2005). It may also arise from national governments undermining subnational governments in decentralized systems by denying them the financial powers needed to implement their policies (Chhibber 1999). The statistical results presented in this book, which show that political, more than fiscal decentralization, affects regional parties as well as ethnic conflict and secessionism, lend credence to this argument.

2.4. Unpacking the relationship between decentralization and regional parties

Political decentralization, I argue, encourages regional parties because politically decentralized systems of government have regional legislatures through which regional parties have a much greater opportunity to govern than they do in national legislatures.[14] Governing refers to the ability of parties to control a legislature's agenda and maximizes a party's influence over policy. Only parties that have a legislative majority can independently control a legislature's agenda. Lacking one, parties may still govern as part of coalitions, but within these coalitions, they must bargain with each other in order to pass legislation.

In national legislatures, a party's ability to govern is constrained by the number of votes it receives in a country overall. As a result, parties that compete in only one region of a country can win only as many seats as that region holds in the national legislature. Thus, the proportion of seats that a region has in the national legislature strongly determines a regional party's strength and its political influence. At the regional level, regions typically have their own legislatures so that parties competing in only one region can, in theory, win all of the seats in that region's legislature. Politicians have a greater incentive, therefore, to form regional parties to compete in regional legislatures than in national legislatures, and voters have more incentive to vote for them as well.

Very populated regions tend to have more seats in national legislatures than less populated ones. In national upper houses, though, the latter often have more seats than their size warrants to protect them against political impotence (Patterson and Mughan 1999; Stepan 1999). For this reason, politicians are more likely to form regional parties in regions that command a large share of a national legislature. At the same time, voters are more likely to vote for them as well. The proportion of seats that a region has in a legislature is largely a function of size, with the one exception noted above, and is not a function of regional party strength or ethnic conflict and secessionism.

Regional boundaries are largely constant over time. Only rarely have regional parties sought to enlarge regions by merging with other territories, and most of these cases have been fruitless attempts at irredentism. If anything, regional parties are likely to be associated with smaller, less populated regions in contrast to the hypothesis outlined above. This is because regional parties representing minorities within large regions may demand their own regions, as they have in India, where the national government has responded to regional minority demands by subdividing existing regions into multiple, smaller ones. In most countries, however, with India being an exception, internal state borders are largely constant over time.

Although regional parties face the same constraints at the national level of government in both decentralized and centralized systems, regional parties tend to have stronger positions at this level of government in the former rather than in the latter. For regional parties, the costs of participating in national legislative elections are smaller in decentralized systems than in centralized ones because regional parties already exist in large numbers to compete at the regional level. In centralized systems, however, the costs are much greater because regional parties must be created from scratch to do so. Among many other things, these costs entail renting office space, hiring staff, and publicizing candidates. As a result, regional parties are much more likely to toss their hats into the national ring in decentralized systems of government than in centralized ones.

In decentralized systems of government, regional parties may also compete at the national level with an eye toward improving their regional level performance. Regional parties may gain attention and respect among regional voters by competing at the national level since national elections generally garner much more attention than regional elections, even in the region where they occur. As a result, regional parties that compete in national elections may increase their notoriety within their own regions, which may lead to greater returns in regional elections. In competing at the national level, regional parties may also win points among their regional electorates by challenging statewide parties at the highest level of government and appearing as strong defenders of their region's interests. Additionally, as I will detail in the next section, regional parties tend to have stronger national legislative positions in decentralized systems than in centralized ones when regional legislatures elect upper houses at the national level.

One may challenge the argument presented here on the grounds that regional parties cause countries to decentralize, not vice versa.[15] Regional parties can influence a country's decision to decentralize (Rokkan and Urwin 1982; de Winter and Türsan 1998; Meguid 2002). Their effect, however, is more indirect and diffuse than is hypothesized. Countries are often reluctant to agree to regional party demands for autonomy for a number of reasons. In many cases, countries fear that if they make concessions to regional parties in one region, similar demands for autonomy or independence will follow in others (Walter 2006). Similarly, some countries fear that extending autonomy to one region will eventually result in that region demanding complete independence (Nordlinger 1972; Gleason 1990; Kymlicka 1998; Hechter 2000).

Countries possess significant discretion in deciding whether or not to accede to regional party demands because regional parties generally lack the political power to compel countries to decentralize and often cannot credibly commit to secession if their demands are not met. The latter is true because regions are generally too small to be economically viable and physically defensible on their own, and often simply fare better across the board as part of a larger country (even a centralized one) than as an independent state (Alesina and Spolare 1997; Bolton and Roland 1997). As a result, many countries have simply ignored regional party demands. Regional parties in Northern Ireland, Scotland, and

Wales have adamantly demanded either autonomy or independence from the United Kingdom for decades. Successive Labour and Conservative governments, however, repeatedly disregarded these demands—until 1997 that is, when the Labour Party seized an opportunity to improve its own electoral support by embracing decentralization. The Labour Party also suspended Northern Ireland's legislature in 2001 despite pressure from regional parties, illustrating the limitations regional parties face not only in causing countries to decentralize, but also in preventing already decentralized ones from centralizing.

As previously mentioned, when national governments choose to decentralize in the face of regional party demands or otherwise, it is ultimately because statewide parties see an opportunity to aggrandize, or at least maintain, their own power by doing so (Escobar-Lemmon 2003; O'Neill 2003; Eaton 2004). Evidence from the United States suggests that national governments are more likely to extend autonomy to subnational governments when they are assured that these governments share their own policy preferences (Krause and Bowman 2005). By this logic, decentralization is much less likely to result if statewide parties dominate at the national level and regional parties do so at the subnational level, which is generally the case.

Thus, not all countries with strong regional parties have decentralized systems of government (e.g. Mauritius or Trinidad and Tobago), just as not all decentralized countries have strong regional parties (e.g. Australia, the United States, and India pre-1990s). Furthermore, as Daniel Ziblatt (2004) shows, even when state leaders desire decentralization, as did leaders in nineteenth-century Germany and Italy, they may not be able to implement it. According to Ziblatt, leaders in Germany achieved decentralization because the territories they sought to incorporate not only had constitutions, but also parliamentary systems and modernized administrations that allowed for the effective delivery of public goods.

One may also counterargue that ethnic conflict and secessionism cause countries to decentralize and not vice versa. Both conflict and secessionism present countries with good reasons to decentralize and many countries have considered these reasons in deciding whether to decentralize. This fact does not preclude decentralization, however, or regional parties from exerting an independent effect on conflict and secession. Moreover, the threat of conflict and secessionism does not predestine countries to decentralize and, in fact, political leaders exhibit a significant amount of discretion in deciding whether or not to decentralize. In the face of conflict and secessionism, many countries do not decentralize, believing that decentralization intensifies ethnic conflict and secessionism. Sri Lanka, Madagascar, the United Kingdom, and Uganda have all been reluctant at times to adopt decentralization for this reason.

Additionally, in some countries, including Spain and the United Kingdom, governments have explicitly refused to negotiate with groups demanding decentralization unless they end the conflicts in which they are engaged and renounce support for independence. In the United Kingdom, Westminster has suspended Northern Ireland's assembly on more than one occasion because the IRA failed to fulfill its promise to disarm completely. Further, in many post-civil war situations, warring factions have been unwilling to accept decentralization in peace settlements because it can elevate the political power of a weaker, or seemingly weaker, opponent in a country's new political system (Walter 2002). In general, decentralization is associated with a lower level of ethnic conflict and secessionism rather than a higher one (as Chapter 6 makes apparent), in contrast to expectations that ethnic conflict and secessionism cause decentralization.

These issues, moreover, are just one of many factors that countries consider when deciding to decentralize, and often are not the determining factor. Countries decentralize for many different reasons, which are unrelated to the potential for conflict and secessionism. Typically, decentralization is the product of a confluence of several factors. Canada and the United States, for example, adopted decentralization to unite many distinct territories into a single country, not to prevent a united country from breaking apart. At the same time, the United States favored decentralization to protect itself against foreign invasion, to minimize conflict among states, and to establish a common market to improve its economy (Hamilton et al. 1987).

In other countries, like Nigeria and South Africa, decentralization is a product of UK colonialism. The United Kingdom used decentralization to maintain control over its colonies, many of which remained decentralized once they had achieved independence because entrenched regional elites refused to relinquish power (Young 1994; Herbst 2000). Other colonial powers, including France and the Netherlands, did not use decentralization to maintain control over their colonies even though they were very heterogeneous and had fissiparous tendencies. As a consequence, French and Dutch colonies are not generally decentralized today.

Still other countries have decentralized simply because they are too large territorially to be managed from a single central government located far from most of their constituents (Panizza 1999; Treisman 2002). All of the world's largest democracies have decentralized systems of government (e.g. Argentina, Australia, Brazil, Canada, India, Mexico, Russia, and the United States). Pressures from globalization (Alesina and Spolare 1997; Bolton and Roland 1997), democratization (Diamond and Tsalik 1999), and market-oriented reforms (Campbell 1997) can also contribute to a country's decision to decentralize. Finally, it is not decentralization per se that is important in this study, but rather the particular features of decentralization, which are not associated with ethnic conflict and secessionism, and how these features determine the strength of regional parties in countries. In the next section, I will describe how these features of decentralization promote regional parties more than others.

2.5. The importance of structure

Decentralization does not increase the strength of regional parties equally in all countries. Rather, certain institutional features of decentralization increase the strength of regional parties more than others, which helps to explain why decentralization, in turn, does not reduce ethnic conflict and secessionism equally in *all* countries. In addition to the regional distribution of national legislative seats as already described, I argue that three other features of decentralization influence the strength of regional parties. These features are the number of regional legislatures in a country, the upper house election procedure, and the sequencing of national and regional elections.

2.5.1. *Regional legislatures*

Regional parties have stronger overall positions in countries with greater numbers of regional legislatures. Even in decentralized systems, regional legislatures do not exist in every region of a country. Finland, for example, only grants autonomy to the Åland Islands. Portugal only extends it to the Azores and Madeira Islands, while Denmark only offers it to Greenland and the Faeroe Islands. India, moreover, only grants decision-making authority to states and not union territories, which by definition have only administrative powers. Having a greater number of regional legislatures increases the electoral strength of regional parties in countries overall because it creates more opportunities for regional parties to participate in government. And, parties that compete at the regional level often compete at the national level for reasons described in the previous section. Obviously, within particular regions the presence of regional parties is stronger in those that have their own regional legislatures with decision-making authority than those that do not.

The electoral strength of regional parties cannot fully explain why some regions have autonomy while others do not for the same reasons that regional parties cannot explain why countries decentralize. Moreover, some countries offer autonomy to all regions regardless of whether they demand autonomy initially or have strong regional parties. These countries, of which Spain is one, provide an excellent opportunity in which to test the effect of decentralization on regional parties. In the late 1970s, Spain extended autonomy to nineteen regions, of which three were ethnically or linguistically distinct, namely the Basque Country, Catalonia, and Navarra, and which demanded autonomy initially. Following decentralization regional parties emerged in all regions and are now as strong in some of the distinct regions of Spain as in the nondistinct ones.

2.5.2. Upper house election procedures

Regional parties also have stronger positions in upper houses of government directly elected by regional legislatures than in upper houses directly elected by citizens. In most countries, whether decentralized or not, citizens directly elect upper houses of government (Patterson and Mughan 1999).[16] In many countries with decentralized systems, however, regional legislatures elect or appoint upper houses of government, either in part or in full (e.g. Austria, Bosnia-Herzegovina, Germany, India, South Africa, and Spain). In Indonesia, which is also decentralized but does not have an upper house, regional legislatures elect almost 25 percent of the country's national legislature. This method of electing upper houses is likely to increase the electoral strength of regional parties because these parties tend to have strong positions in regional legislatures and are likely to elect regional parties to upper houses of government as a result.

The method used to elect upper houses is not, moreover, a function of regional party strength. Often, regional legislatures elect upper houses of government because countries desire to integrate national and subnational levels of government, and not to increase the strength of regional parties, which can divide the two levels of government. This is true of countries with strong regional parties and autonomy movements as well as those without. Many countries in which regional legislatures elect upper houses of government have weak regional parties (e.g. Austria and Germany), while many countries that have strong regional parties do not elect their upper houses (e.g. Belgium and Canada). Other countries, such as Spain, moreover, only elect their upper houses in part. This provides an excellent opportunity to examine the effect of upper houses within regions that elect representatives to both aspects of the upper house. Incidentally, as Chapter 4 clarifies, the presence of regional parties is much greater in the part of Spain's upper house, which regional legislatures elect, than in the part that the people directly elect.

2.5.3. *Electoral sequencing*

When national and regional elections occur at the same time, regional parties may have stronger positions in regional legislatures than when they occur at different times. The extent to which sequencing comes into play hinges on the coat tails effect (Shugart and Carey 1992). According to the so-called coat tails effect, elections to higher offices influence elections to lower offices because the former garner more public attention and funding than the latter.[17] As a result, parties that win elections to higher offices tend to win the lion's share of the seats in lower offices – but only when both elections occur at the same time. Since statewide parties are stronger than regional parties in national elections, the coat tails effect suggests that statewide parties should have stronger positions in regional elections when national and regional elections occur at the same time. From this, it also follows that regional parties should also have very strong positions in regional elections when the first democratic elections in a country occur at the regional level.

The sequencing of elections is not endogenous to the strength of regional parties. In other words, elections do not occur at different times because regional parties make demands on governments for nonconcurrent elections. There are numerous reasons why national and regional elections do not occur at the same time, which are unrelated to regional parties. Very often, they do not occur at the same time because national and regional legislatures have different terms of office. Some terms last four years and others five. As a result, even if national and regional elections are initially held at the same time, eventually they are delinked. Initially, however, many countries do not hold national and regional elections at the same time because national legislatures create regional legislatures and do not wait until the next national elections to hold regional elections in these newly created regional legislatures. In other instances, national governments have worked together with regional governments, headed by regional parties, to synchronize national and regional elections to increase turnout within the latter.[18]

Another important reason that national and regional elections are not synchronized is because of the type of executive system in a country. Presidential systems of government are more likely to have concurrent national and regional elections than parliamentary systems because executive and national legislatures have fixed terms in presidential systems unlike in parliamentary systems, where legislatures can throw executives out of office before they complete their full terms in office. However, presidential elections do not always occur at the same time as legislative elections in the first place.

When presidential and national legislative elections occur at the same time, regional parties should also have weaker positions in national legislative elections than when presidential and legislative elections are held at different times (Cox 1997). Again, this is attributable to the coat tails effect and the fact that statewide parties are more likely than regional parties to control the office of the presidency since presidents need significant cross-regional support in order to be elected. Some countries even constitutionally require presidents to have significant cross-regional support. In the United States, presidential candidates need the support of a large number of states in order to be elected because they must have a majority in the Electoral College in order to win office. In Nigeria, presidential candidates need the support of at least two-thirds of all states and the capital of Abuja to be elected, although they do not have to win more than a quarter of the votes in these states in order to be elected.

2.6. Conclusion

Regional parties are the linchpins that connect decentralization to ethnic conflict and secessionism, and are not simply a function of the underlying regional differences in society. Regional parties tend to promote ethnic conflict and secessionism by creating regional identities, supporting legislation harmful to regional minorities and other regions of a country, and, ultimately, mobilizing groups to engage in ethnic conflict and secessionism. Statewide parties, for their part, tend to discourage conflict among territorially concentrated ethnic groups, as well as secessionism, by promoting national identities and incorporating regional interests into their agenda while balancing the interests of competing regions against each other.

Regional parties also have a greater incentive to promote both conflict and secessionism in weakly democratic states and in periods of transition, depending on the leadership style of party elites and the amount of competition they face from other regional parties. Similarly, statewide parties are more likely to quell conflict and secessionism depending on the distribution of ethnic groups throughout a country, the importance of a particular region to a party's electoral prospects, and the competitiveness of the overall electoral system. This may also depend on the extent to which a party is internally decentralized. Ultimately, the ability of regional parties to carry out their goals depends largely on whether they can govern within a legislature and whether this legislature has significant decision-making capabilities.

Decentralization, in turn, promotes regional parties. Decentralization encourages regional parties by creating subnational legislatures endowed with real decision-making authority in which regional parties have a much greater opportunity to govern than they do at the national level. While regional parties in certain circumstances may contribute to decentralization, the degree to which they may is overstated. The extent to which decentralization encourages regional parties depends on the structure of decentralization, which regional parties do not dictate, and how this structure affects the potential for regional parties to govern. The differential strength of regional parties, in turn, explains why decentralization does not reduce ethnic conflict and secessionism equally in all countries.

In the chapters to follow, I examine the generalizability of my argument through statistical analysis and explore the nuanced ways in which my argument plays out in each of my case studies. I also revisit the issue of endogeneity in the statistical analysis, as well as the case studies, bringing to bear methodological techniques, such as instrumental regression in the former and process tracing in the latter. While the statistical analysis takes advantage of issues that affect either decentralization or regional parties, but not conflict and secessionism in order to do so, the case studies exploit variation in decentralization and regional party strength over time to disentangle the relationship between both decentralization and regional parties and ethnic conflict and secessionism.

Part II

Case Study Analysis

3

Czechoslovakia

Czechoslovakia's dissolution in 1993, and the failed attempts to keep the country united in the years preceding it are puzzling both to outside observers, as well as Czechs and Slovaks themselves. After all, the objective differences between Czechs and Slovaks were small at the time of the dissolution, with Czechs and Slovaks sharing similar histories, speaking mutually intelligible languages, and practicing the same religion. Public opinion was also staunchly opposed to the breakup and all major political parties in the postcommunist period sought to maintain the country's unity. Yet, in the end, these same political parties partitioned Czechoslovakia into separate states against the tide of public opinion.

Few would disagree that regional parties played a major role in the breakup. Shortly after Czechoslovakia democratized, regional parties from the Czech Lands initiated the dissolution in response to demands from Slovak regional parties regarding the political system, which they considered unreasonable. Most also assume that the shape of the party system was due to the underlying differences between Czechs and Slovaks. I argue, in contrast, that it was due to the existing structure of decentralization. Czechoslovakia was highly decentralized at the time it democratized. Not only did regional legislatures wield a veto power over the national constitution, but the country's two national legislatures were also divided almost evenly between the Czech Lands and Slovakia, and decision rules within the latter allowed parties from either region to thwart that of the other.

Regional differences, while they formed the basis around which regional parties mobilized people, cannot fully account for the dissolution of Czechoslovakia or the existence of regional parties in this period. Historical and cross-regional comparisons of Czechoslovakia support this account. During the interwar period under a democratically elected, centralized system of government, regional parties had a much weaker presence than in the postcommunist period, despite stronger regional differences in the former than in the latter. In the postcommunist period, Moravia – a territory of the Czech Lands (Bohemia is the other) which lacked political autonomy – had much weaker regional parties and a smaller secessionist movement than Slovakia, even though differences between Bohemia and Moravia were as strong as those between the Czech Lands and Slovakia.

In order to illustrate this argument, the remainder of this chapter proceeds as follows. In Section 3.1, I evaluate the strength of ethnic conflict and secessionism in Czechoslovakia. In Sections 3.2 and 3.3, I lay the groundwork for my argument, describing the structure of decentralization in Czechoslovakia and existing views of this system. In Sections 3.4 and 3.5, I depict the shape of Czechoslovakia's party system and discuss the most common explanations for this system. In Sections 3.6 and 3.7 of this chapter, I describe the extant criticisms of Czechoslovakia's party system and its effect on the country's dissolution. Finally, in Section 3.8, I discuss the influence of decentralization on the development of Czechoslovakia's party system.

3.1. Brief history of intrastate conflict in Czechoslovakia

By all accounts, the level of ethnic conflict and popular support for secessionism in Czechoslovakia was low at the time the country broke up in 1993. Prior to the dissolution, Czechoslovakia was composed of two major ethnic groups – Czechs and Slovaks. While

Czechs and Slovaks were members of different ethnic groups, they spoke mutually intelligible languages. They also practiced the same religion, Catholicism, although Slovaks tended to be more religious than Czechs, and supposedly were more family- and community-oriented, and less cosmopolitan than Czechs (Kusý 1995; Musil 1995; Příhoda 1995).

Czechs and Slovaks resided primarily into two separate regions of the country – the Czech Lands (which formed the Czech Republic) and Slovakia. The Czech Lands were themselves divided into two areas – Bohemia and Moravia. The latter includes the area of Silesia. At the time of the transition, 95 percent of the people in Bohemia considered themselves to be ethnically Czech, but only 61 percent of those in Moravia did.[19] The next largest group in Moravia, constituting 34 percent of the population, considered themselves to be ethnically Moravian. Slovakia at the time was more heterogeneous – 86 percent of this region considered themselves ethnically Slovak while the next largest group, making up 11 percent of the population, considered themselves Hungarian.[20]

At the time, there were no incidences of ethnic conflict between Czechs and Slovaks and no parties encouraging violence between them.[21] A number of political parties did, however, endorse Slovak independence, including the Slovak National Party (SNS) and the Christian Democratic Movement (KDH), although KDH only demanded independence in the long term. For the short term, it demanded a confederation and eventually only a loose federation. The two parties earned a moderate share of the vote cast in Slovakia in the postcommunist period, and SNS was notably smaller than KDH. Together the two won about 20 percent of the vote cast in Slovakia for lower and upper house elections held in 1990 and 1992, and less than 25 percent of Slovakia's regional legislature in this period.

Political surveys also suggest that relations between Czechs and Slovaks during the country's transition to democracy were amicable. According to one survey taken by the *Institute for Public Opinion Research* in May 1990, 73 percent of people polled considered relations between Slovaks and Moravians to be either "friendly" or "rather friendly" (Mišovič 1990).[22] Thirty-nine percent of respondents shared this view of relations between Bohemians and Slovaks while an additional 20 percent thought that the two groups were indifferent to each other.[23] Incidentally, the survey also revealed that relations between the two Czech regions, Bohemia and Moravia, were amicable with 81 percent of survey respondents reporting that relations between Bohemians and Moravians were either "friendly" or "rather friendly."[24]

Public opinion surveys also indicate that support for secessionism in Czechoslovakia was low prior to the country's dissolution.[25] Early on, in September 1990, only 11 percent of people surveyed in the Czech Lands and 12 percent of those surveyed in Slovakia supported dividing the country into two independent republics (Tomek and Forst 1990). Over time, support for independence grew, principally in Bohemia and Moravia, but still remained relatively low. By July 1992, 20 percent of people surveyed in Bohemia and 11 percent of those surveyed in Moravia supported independence (Hampl 1992). Meanwhile, 16 percent of Slovaks surveyed backed independence. Table 3.1 depicts the results of the 1992 survey.

Table 3.1. Public opinion on the optimal political system in Czechoslovakia, July 1992

	Bohemia (%)	Moravia and Silesia (%)	Slovakia (%)
One state with one government	40	36	14
Federation of the Czech Republic and Slovak Republic	20	19	27
Federal republic	12	29	8
Confederation	4	2	30
Independent states	20	11	16
Do not know	4	3	5

Note: The table depicts the percentage of total respondents in Czechoslovakia viewing each of the above political systems as the optimal one for Czechoslovakia. The response for a "Federation of the Czech Republic and Slovak Republic" represents the current level of regional autonomy in Czechoslovakia at the time, while the response for a "Federal republic" is indicative of more autonomy for the republics.

Source: Hampl (1992).

Not only did more people advocate independence in 1992 than two years prior, but the attitudes of Czechs and Slovaks were also more polarized. More people, that is, demanded independence in 1992, and more supported the opposite extreme of a completely centralized state. In September 1990, only 22 percent of people surveyed in the Czech Lands favored a centralized state while 7 percent of those in Slovakia did (Tomek and Forst 1990). By contrast, of those surveyed in 1992, 40 percent in Bohemia, 36 percent in Moravia, and 14 percent in Slovakia supported a centralized state (Hampl 1992).

3.2. Structure of decentralization in Czechoslovakia

Although decentralization was toothless under communism, Czechoslovakia emerged from communist rule with the structures of decentralized system already in place, having established them in 1968. Under this system, the national government was divided into two legislative bodies – the House of People (Sněmovna Lidu) and the House of Nations (Sněmovna Národů). Each region also had its own legislature, known as a National Council (Národní Rada), and the division of authority between the national and regional legislatures was extensive. This institutional arrangement formed the basis for future negotiations over the country's new political system.

3.2.1. *Division of political authority in Czechoslovakia*

As a first step in this process, the national government redefined the country's division of political power through the power-sharing law in December 1990. This law granted the national government exclusive control over several political issues (e.g. defense, war and peace, foreign affairs, currency, national material resources, and the protection of the national constitution). It also allowed the country's regional legislatures to assume singular or joint control over any area that the national government did not have exclusive jurisdiction. Eventually, the National Councils also gained the right to approve all legislation pertaining to the country's new constitution, as a consequence of which four distinct legislative bodies had to approve the constitution before it could become law (i.e. House of People, House of Nations, and the Czech and Slovak National Councils). This law only established a basic framework for decentralization in Czechoslovakia. The country's new constitution was to further delineate the distribution of powers.

3.2.2. *Division of fiscal authority in Czechoslovakia*

The division of fiscal authority in Czechoslovakia at the time was extensive. Thanks to a 1990 budgetary law, the Czech Lands and Slovakia raised their own revenue while the national government allocated to the regions a share of the revenue it generated based on their population. As a result, in 1991 the national government distributed 40 percent of its total revenue to the Czech Republic and 25 percent to the Slovak Republic. The remaining 35 percent the national government reserved to finance its own programs (Svitek 1992: 35). The law also abolished the country's system of national subsidies, although in 1992 the government made a one-time subsidy of 5 billion crowns to the Czech Lands and Slovakia. After taking into account funds transferred from the Czech Lands to Slovakia for Slovaks working in the Czech Republic, this subsidy amounted to 3.3 billion crowns for the Czech Lands and 1.7 billion crowns for Slovakia (Svitek 1992).

By abolishing this system, the 1990 budgetary law forced the Czech Lands and Slovakia to rely more heavily on their own sources of revenue. As a result, the proportion of revenue generated in Czechoslovakia at the subnational level of government increased from 52 percent in 1989 to 77 percent in 1991 (Havel 1991: 149). The percentage of expenditure made at this level decreased slightly from 83 to 78 percent (Havel 1991: 149). This was largely at the expense of the municipal level since the percentage of subnational expenditure allocated at the regional level increased from 46 to 59 percent in this period (Havel 1991: 149). Despite an already extensive division of political and fiscal authority in the country, the struggle over how to further divide powers plagued the country's brief postcommunist existence.

3.3. Perspectives on decentralization in Czechoslovakia

A number of politicians and scholars have blamed decentralization for contributing to Czechoslovakia's dissolution, launching three major criticisms against the system. The first contends that decentralization encouraged secessionism by strengthening regional identities in the country (Rychlik 1995; Bunce 1999). According to Jan Rychlik (1995), decentralization reinforced regional identities from the outset by employing Slovaks in the national government. Valerie Bunce (1999) likewise suggests that decentralization bolstered regional identities under communism. For Bunce, decentralization fostered regional identities among everyday citizens, as well as elites, by recognizing minority languages, naming regions according to the largest ethnic group they contained and declaring people's ethnicity on official government documents, among other things.

While decentralization may have strengthened regional identities in Czechoslovakia, as these scholars highlight, strong regional identities cannot fully explain the breakup. Regional identities among everyday Czechs and Slovaks did not cause the dissolution. Regional parties divided Czechoslovakia into separate states against the tide of public opinion even though the parties themselves were initially opposed to the division. Regional leaders, thus, played a major role in the dissolution of Czechoslovakia, as Rychlik and Bunce suggest. However, most political leaders that came to power after 1989 were not members of the former communist regime, but instead were members of the scientific community, attorneys, professionals, workers, and members of the anticommunist movement (Kroupa and Kostelecký 1996). Undoubtedly, decentralization influenced the orientation of these leaders. But, as I will demonstrate in the last section of this chapter, this is due to the specific institutional design of decentralization in postcommunist Czechoslovakia, which provided politicians opportunities to win office and influence decision-making as members of regional parties.

The second major criticism of decentralization is that it encouraged secessionism by giving Czechs and Slovaks broad political powers, which they used to prevent the government from adopting a new constitution. Two different features of Czechoslovakia's political system provided Czechs and Slovaks with broad political powers at the time. The first was the prohibition of the majority, which gave Czechs and Slovaks the ability to veto legislation at the national level of government (Henderson 1995; Kroupa 1996; Leff 2000; Wolchik 2000). This requirement, scholars claim, contributed to the dissolution of Czechoslovakia by making it very difficult for the national legislature to agree on a new constitution.

According to Carol Leff, "The fact that either party could veto a constitutional settlement and block a decision was particularly important to the logic of the breakup.... Doing nothing and deciding nothing was the death sentence of the common state" (2000: 45). Daniel Kroupa of the Christian Democratic Party-Czechoslovak People's Party (KDU-CSL) also believes that the "prohibition of the majority" contributed to the dissolution of Czechoslovakia. However, unlike Henderson and Leff, who claim that regional differences were the underlying reason Czech and Slovak politicians failed to agree on a constitution, Kroupa argues that differences between Czechs and Slovaks played no role in the breakup. According to Kroupa, "The prohibition of the majority gave a crucial position to a small group of representatives on which building progress depended. In the beginning of 1990, the far-reaching unity of opinions was reduced and an increasing number of representatives did not form an opinion on political evolution and concentrated instead on questions mainly on national matters of Slovakia.... Eventually it became completely unworkable" (1996: 32).

As these scholars and politicians suggest, the prohibition of the majority played a significant role in the breakup of Czechoslovakia by requiring a high level of consensus on the country's new constitution. Like Kroupa, however, I do not believe that parties failed to reach a consensus because of the underlying regional differences between Czechs and Slovaks. Instead, I argue that they were unable to agree on a new constitution because the dominant political parties in Czechoslovakia at the time were regional parties, which were not simply a function of these differences, as I will demonstrate later in this chapter. Moreover, the prohibition, as I will likewise discuss later in this chapter, gave politicians a significant incentive to form regional parties in the first place.

The second aspect of the country's political system, which gave Czechs and Slovaks broad political powers, was the existence of two separate regional legislatures in the Czech Lands and Slovakia. Scholars suggest that these legislatures contributed to the breakup by giving politicians platforms from which to promote secessionist ideas and defeat drafts of the constitution (Dorff 1994; Leff 1999). As Robert Dorff relates, "The processes of federalism were inadequate to overcome the use of federalist structures by local, national leaders to promote their own causes and agendas" (1994: 40). In 1991, regional leaders used these legislatures to establish separate, regional media outlets through which they disseminated their political views. Vladimir Mečiar notoriously propagated his views in weekly television spots on Slovak television (Vadas 2000; L. A. 1994).

Like the prohibition of the majority, regional legislatures and regional forms of media contributed to the breakup of Czechoslovakia, as other scholars have argued. However, I argue that in the case of the prohibition, they only had the effect that they did because of regional parties. Had regional parties not controlled the regional legislatures, I suspect that these legislatures would not have rejected the constitutional drafts presented to them, and would not have created regional media organizations from which regional leaders could disseminate their views.

A third criticism of decentralization in Czechoslovakia is that it consisted of only two members – the Czech Republic and Slovakia – and that two-member states are inherently unstable because they cannot resolve deadlocks between members (Dorff 1994; Macek

2000; Stanger 2000). According to Petr Pithart, former Prime Minister of the Czech Republic (1990–1992), "talks of two partners are difficult. When there are only two partners, voting is impossible; one can only break the other."[26] In the face of opposing opinions, having only two regions, as Pithart points out, can make agreement difficult. However, as with the other features of decentralization already discussed, one must ask why the positions of parties in the Czech Lands and Slovakia were conflicting in the first place. I submit that it was a result of the type of parties in power at the time, and not the underlying differences in society. The division of the country into two large regions, nevertheless, played a role in promoting regional parties, the evolution of which I will discuss in the final section of this chapter.

3.4. Party system in postcommunist Czechoslovakia

Before explaining the role that regional parties played in the dissolution of Czechoslovakia, and the origins of these parties, I first need to provide context for this argument by presenting an overview of the electoral strength of regional parties prior to the dissolution. At the national level, the presence of regional parties was overwhelmingly strong following the country's first two elections held in 1990 and 1992. Figure 3.1 depicts the performance of regional parties in these elections.

In 1990, only one statewide party won seats at the national level, namely the Communist Party of Czechoslovakia (KSC), which was well positioned to win seats in both the Czech Lands and Slovakia as it had established a strong organizational network throughout the country during the communist era (Grzymala-Busse 2002). Following these elections, regional parties from the Czech Lands and Slovakia formed a coalition with each other at the national level. The government was composed of the Civic Forum (OF) in the Czech Lands and Public Against Violence (VPN) in Slovakia, which were democracy movements in the communist era. Despite winning enough seats to constitute a government on its own, OF formed a grand coalition with VPN to enable the latter to play a

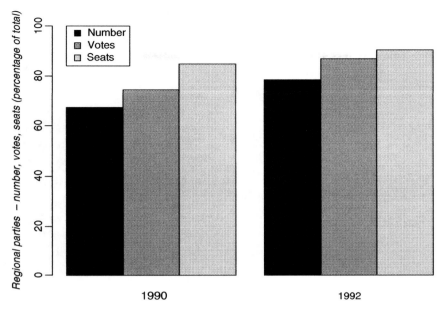

Figure 3.1. The electoral strength of regional parties in Czechoslovakia's two national legislatures, 1990–2

Source: Český Statistický Úřad, http://www.volby.cz/ and Štatistický Úrad Slovenskej Republiky, http://www.statistics.sk/ Accessed: January 20, 2007.

role in creating the democratic institutions that it had fought for under communism (Honajzer 1996).

Overall, regional parties had an even stronger presence at the national level in 1992. By then, however, OF and VPN had splintered into several different parties. In the aftermath, the Civic Democratic Party (ODS) emerged as the strongest party in the Czech Lands, while the Movement for a Democratic Slovakia (HZDS) emerged as the strongest in Slovakia. Unable to form a government on its own, ODS formed a coalition at the national level of government with the largest regional party in Slovakia, HZDS, and its preelection coalition partner in the Czech Lands, the Christian Democratic Party (KDS).

In 1992, only two statewide parties – the Association for the Republic-Republican Party of Czechoslovakia (SPR-RSC) and the

Hungarian Coalition (MKDH-ESWS) – won seats in these elections. While these parties competed in both the Czech Lands and Slovakia, they only won seats in one region. SPR-RSC earned all of its seats in the Czech Lands while MKDH-ESWS won all of its seats in Slovakia. Only one moderately successful cross-regional coalition existed in 1992, which consisted of ODS in the Czech Lands and the Democratic Party (DS) in Slovakia. ODS competed on its own in the Czech Lands but aligned itself with DS in Slovakia. DS, like ODS, supported a rapid transition to a market economy involving extensive privatization and the removal of all restrictions on foreign investment. The coalition, though, did not win enough votes in Slovakia to pass the region's 7 percent threshold for two-party coalitions.

Regional parties had a slightly stronger presence in Czechoslovakia's regional elections in 1990–2 than its national elections, the results of which are presented in Figure 3.2.

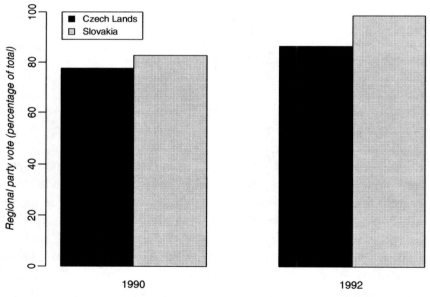

Figure 3.2. The electoral strength of regional parties in Czechoslovakia's National Councils, 1990–2

Source: Český Statistický Úřad, http://www.volby.cz/ and Štatistický Úrad Slovenskej Republiky, http://www.statistics.sk/ Accessed: January 20, 2007.

3.5. Origins of regional parties in Czechoslovakia

The general understanding of Czechoslovakia's party system is that it developed along regional lines because of the ethnolinguistic and economic differences dividing Czechs and Slovaks. According to Karen Henderson, "The saliency of nationality in Czechoslovak politics is demonstrated by the existence of Czech and Slovak parties" (1995: 115). Similarly, Karel Vodička argues that, "the gradual differentiation of the Czech and Slovak parties was based on the distinct political cultures of both republics" (Vodička 1996: 79). Finally, Eric Stein claims that the lack of statewide parties in Czechoslovakia was "a factor symptomatic of different political cultures" in the Czech Lands and Slovakia (2000: 94).

Several scholars and policy-makers also attribute the breakup of Czechoslovakia to the underlying differences between Czechs and Slovaks. According to Carol Leff, the disintegration of Czechoslovakia was not "merely bad luck; the possibility of deadlock was foreshadowed in the long history of previous conflict and history" (2000: 45). Likewise, Jan Čarnogurský of KDH claims that Czechoslovakia broke up because "[i]t has never been possible to weaken the will for self-realization, which lead to the culmination of these aspirations."[27] Finally, expressing similar fatalism, Václav Klaus, the second president of the Czech Republic, declares that "[t]here was no other solution... [i]t is clear we were not destined to live together in one state."[28]

Definite differences existed between Czechs and Slovaks during the country's transition to democracy, as already described. The most salient differences between the two were in terms of the economy. The Czech Lands, much richer than Slovakia, wanted to make a rapid transition to the market economy and halt state subsidies to Slovakia (Jozífková 1990; Slavíková 1990, 1992; Elster 1995; Kopecký 2000). Slovakia, in contrast, wanted to maintain the system of state subsidies and slow down the pace of the market transition. Strapped with the country's arms industry, which suffered a fatal blow when President Václav Havel ceased arms exports abroad, Slovakia experienced a slightly higher rate of inflation than the Czech Lands and a much higher rate of unemployment. In 1992, the unemployment rate in the Czech Lands was 2.6 percent while the unemployment rate in Slovakia was 10.4 percent (Dědek 1997: 54).

While important, these differences cannot fully account for why Czechoslovakia's party system developed along regional lines, nonetheless, for at least three different reasons. First, the objective differences between Czechs and Slovaks were not very large at the time Czechoslovakia broke up, and certainly not greater than many other countries that have remained intact. They had also decreased considerably since the first time Czechoslovakia held democratic elections in the interwar period. Yet, there were fewer regional parties in the interwar period than in the postcommunist period. Regional parties had a weaker presence in the interwar period because Czechoslovakia had a centralized system of government at the time, in contrast to the decentralized one in the postcommunist era. The lack of decentralization encouraged parties in Czechoslovakia to compete in both the Czech Lands and Slovakia.

During the interwar period, regional parties accounted for an average of 13 percent of the vote in the country's lower house, earning between 0 and 37 percent in the four democratic elections held in this period. In the postcommunist period, in contrast, regional parties made up an average of 81 percent of the vote in the lower house, earning between 75 and 87 percent in the two elections held in this period. Figure 3.3 illustrates the percentage of votes that regional parties received in interwar Czechoslovakia.

Most of the regional parties present in Czechoslovakia during the interwar period were regional parties representing the German, Hungarian, and Ruthenian minorities in the country. The principal Slovak regional party at the time was the Hlinka's Slovak People's Party (HSLS), which demanded political autonomy for Slovakia, but not independence. It received no more than 7 percent of the vote in national elections held between 1925 and

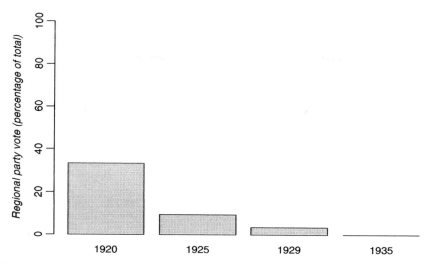

Figure 3.3. The electoral strength of regional parties in interwar Czechoslovakia, 1920–35

Note: The original data includes an "other" category, totaling 17 percent, 19 percent, 11 percent, and 6 percent of the vote in 1920, 1925, 1929, and 1935 respectively. This category may contain regional parties.

Source: Figures calculated by the author based on data reported in Český Statistický Úřad http://www.czso.cz (Accessed January 21, 2006) and Rothschild (1974).

1935 (Rothschild 1974). Like some Slovak regional parties in the postcommunist period, HSLS wanted a confederation in which the national government retained control over only a few issue areas, including defense, foreign affairs, finance, and the election of the president. It also advocated laws demanding the exclusive use of the Slovak language in Slovakia.

Differences between the Czech Lands and Slovakia were greater, moreover, in the interwar period than in the postcommunist period because Czechoslovakia was more ethnically diverse in the former. There were fewer ethnic groups in Czechoslovakia during the interwar period because the Nazis had exterminated the Jews during World War II, and the Czechoslovak government expelled the Sudetenland Germans after the war for their apparent support of Hitler's invasion. Communism also reduced differences between

Czechs and Slovaks (Kučera and Pavlík 1995; Průcha 1995; Svejnar 2000). In the interwar period, Slovaks were more religious than Czechs. Communism, however, minimized these differences because it did not permit Czechs or Slovaks to practice their religion publicly. Communism also reduced the economic differences between the two by building up Slovakia's industry and improving its economy more generally.

The second reason that regional differences cannot fully account for the rise of regional parties in postcommunist Czechoslovakia is that differences between Bohemians and Moravians were just as great as those between Czechs and Slovaks. Yet, there were not as many regional parties dividing Bohemians and Moravians from each other, as there were regional parties dividing Czechs and Slovaks. Moravians, like Slovaks, constituted their own ethnic group. Moravians were also poorer and more religious than Bohemians, although both were predominantly Catholic.

A strong movement for autonomy also existed in Moravia. According to a survey taken by the *Institute for Public Opinion Research* in February 1991, 35 percent of the people polled in Moravia and Silesia wanted Moravia and Silesia to be "a land" or "a republic" within Czechoslovakia (Hampl 1991). Another 26 percent wanted it to be "a land" within the Czech Republic, while 21 percent wanted it to be elevated to the status of "a region." Only 14 percent supported the status quo and 4 percent "did not know."

The views of Daniel Kroupa of KDU-CSL strongly support this argument. Kroupa once stated that, "I must emphatically reject the notion that it was the different characteristics of the Czech and Slovak nations that led to the dissolution of Czechoslovakia. I dare say that within the Czech Republic there are far greater differences between some of its constituent parts than those that exist between the Czech and Slovak Republics. What I have in mind are the differences, for example, between southern Bohemia and northern Moravia, which are great, even though they are both Czech regions" (2000: 237).

The third reason that regional differences cannot explain the rise of regional parties in Czechoslovakia is because political parties were not formed in Czechoslovakia around different social groups. Instead, they were formed around different cliques of elites although different social groups in both the Czech Lands and Slovakia tended to support some parties more than others (Gregor and Caha 1993; Kostelecký 1994; Krejči 1994; Řeháková 1999).[29] In other words, political parties were not formed from the bottom up, but from the top down. As Dvořáková and Kunc relate, "parties did not form from certain social groups around some collection of winning interests or program – but around several small personalities drawn from society, absent of their own historical legitimacy" (1996: 58). Ultimately, these parties dictated policy from the top down, dissolving the country against the tide of public opinion.

The electoral strength of regional parties in Czechoslovakia is largely a result of the specific structure of decentralization in the country. However, before discussing how decentralized governance contributed to the strength of regional parties in the final section of this chapter, I describe the role regional parties played in precipitating the dissolution of Czechoslovakia.

3.6. Role of the party system in the breakup of Czechoslovakia

Politicians and scholars have widely criticized Czechoslovakia's party system for contributing to the country's dissolution. According to some scholars, the parties were too rigid and uncompromising (Cox and Frankland 1995; Wightman 1995; Žak 1995; Kopecký 2000). In Václav Žak's view, the dissolution of the country hinged on "the foresight of the political élite, their ability to differentiate the common good from their own assertion of power, their ability to judge the intention of partners who lacked foresight, and a certain generosity," which Žak suggests was significantly lacking at the time (Žak 1995: 266). Other scholars have criticized Czechoslovakia's party system for being too nationalistic (Pehe 1993; Wolchik 1995), and for not representing well the views of Czechs and Slovaks, because the country was dissolved against the tide of public opinion without a referendum to decide the matter (Cox and Frankland 1995; Innes 1997).

Some scholars have also criticized party leaders for having very few personal interactions with politicians from the opposing region (Henderson 1995: 130) and little experience in politics and the art of negotiations (Wolchik 2000: 98-99; Kopecký 2000: 79). A number of others have blamed particular leaders for the dissolution; many scholars attribute the breakup to Vladimir Mečiar for refusing to compromise with the Czechs and heightening tensions between Czechs and Slovaks. According to Petr Tatar, a former member of the Slovak Constitutional Committee, the split occurred because "Mečiar was the massive winner and nobody can live with Mečiar, not even [Václav] Klaus."[30] According to Tatar, Mečiar contributed to the breakup because he was a populist with an autocratic personality, more fond of criticizing others and the reforms initiated, than of developing his own program. Mečiar's party, Public Against Violence, Tatar said, asked nine other people to be the leader of the party before they asked Mečiar. "All of which," he claims, "would have been better than Mečiar."[31]

Vladimir Mečiar, not surprisingly, blamed Václav Havel for the breakup. According to Mečiar, "It was not possible to find a definition of common interests. Václav Havel is to blame for it.... Václav Havel initiated the process of separation.... He made great promises to the Slovaks, of which nothing has been left."[32] Roman Zelenay (HZDS) has also criticized Czech politicians for the breakup of Czechoslovakia. Zelenay claims that the breakup was due to the Czechs' failure to recognize that "sovereignty was for Slovak citizens a basic attribute that they were not willing to surrender" (Valko et al. 1992: 10).

Consistent with these authors, I argue that the rigid, narrowly focused nature of the party system in Czechoslovakia was the primary cause of the breakup of Czechoslovakia. I do not believe, however, that one person or one party in particular was responsible for the breakup of the country. Instead, I assert that the primary reason for the breakup was the structure of the party system, which was dominated by regional parties. Given this structure, I propose that different leaders would have yielded the same result, but more importantly, I argue that the structure of the political system would have produced similar leaders.

3.7. Reconsidering the role of the party system in the breakup of Czechoslovakia

Regional parties, I argue, contributed to Czechoslovakia's dissolution – independent of the underlying regional differences within the country – because Slovak regional parties advocated legislation regarding the country's new constitution, which prompted Czech regional parties, viewing these demands as unreasonable, to dissolve the country. Regional parties were able to dissolve Czechoslovakia because they had strong positions in the country's national and regional legislatures, which both had to agree on the country's new constitution in order for it to become law.

Regional parties in the Czech Lands agitated for a federation in which the national government would retain considerable authority over a number of political, social, and economic issues. They initiated various proposals along these lines, the principal one of which the Civic Forum (OF) initiated.[33] In contrast, Slovak regional parties supported a confederation under which the national government would retain very few responsibilities and the Czech Lands and Slovakia would be independent states. Czech regional parties opposed the Slovak plans, fearing that, among other things, a dual political and economic system would delay the country's entry into international organizations, such as the European Union and the North Atlantic Treaty Organization.

Regional parties from both the Czech Lands and Slovakia initiated and also defeated numerous proposals on the design of the country's new constitution, including those of Prague native, President Václav Havel, who did not belong to any political party.[34] The straw that broke the camel's back, however, was the defeat of the Milovy Draft Treaty, the government's last serious attempt at writing a new constitution.[35] On February 12, 1992, Slovak regional parties rejected the Milovy Draft Treaty by one vote in the presidium of the Slovak National Council. Having failed to pass the Slovak National Council, the bill was not submitted to the national legislature for a vote.

The Milovy Draft Treaty represented a significant compromise between the Czech and Slovak sides. The treaty proposed that Slovakia would be able to maintain independent relations with other countries, as long as these relations were in harmony with Czechoslovakia's foreign policy, and that Slovakia would be able to sign treaties with other countries and receive foreign representation. Milovy also required the Czech and Slovak National Councils to ratify the constitution and any amendments to it. To satisfy Czech concerns about having dual economies, the treaty also proposed that there be a single market and a single central bank, and that the national government have control over legislation regarding borders and customs.

Unfortunately, statewide parties lacked a strong enough presence in the country to bridge regional differences over this treaty and any others. President Havel was unsuccessful in this regard and was viewed by Slovaks as partial to Czech interests. The Communist Party, which competed in both the Czech Lands and Slovakia, broke up shortly after the first elections in Czechoslovakia – a fact that Miloslav Ransdorf of the Communist Party of Bohemia and Moravia (KSCM) laments. According to Ransdorf, "The federal structure of the Communist Party was an obstacle for the split of the federal state."[36] When the Communist Party split up into two parties, Ransdorf argues that "[t]he problem was that this federal political force represented formerly by the Communist Party was not replaced by a strong political force as a guarantee of freedom."[37]

The Communist Party broke up because of internal differences over the direction of the party.[38] Decentralization, however, facilitated the party's breakup by making it easier for regional parties to govern at the national and regional levels of government.

Failing to reach an agreement on a new constitution, regional parties in the Czech National Council approved an initiative in July 1992 preparing the Czech Republic for independence, one month after the country's general elections. That same month the Slovak National Council declared its own sovereignty. The Slovak Council tried twice before to declare sovereignty, once in September 1991 and once in March 1992, but failed by a narrow margin both times. Eventually, the national government agreed to dissolve itself in November 1992 by a narrow three-vote margin.

At the same time that the party system contributed to the breakup of Czechoslovakia, the party system mitigated tensions between the two Czech territories of Bohemia and Moravia. Many people in Moravia demanded regional autonomy and supported a regional party known as the Movement for Self-Governing Democracy-Association for Moravia and Silesia (HSD-SMS). In the Czech National Council this party won about 10 percent of the vote in 1990 and about 6 percent in 1992. The party had a much smaller presence at the national level of government in these years and did not earn any seats. HSD-SMS demanded a tripartite federation made up of Bohemia, Moravia, and Slovakia, in which each region would have the same level of autonomy, and threatened to secede from the country if its demands were not granted.

The party system mitigated tensions in Moravia because Czech parties competed in both Bohemia and Moravia. In fact, all political parties that competed in Moravia also competed in Bohemia, including HSD-SMS. Additionally, Czech political parties competed in both regions, and also incorporated Moravian interests into their political programs – a fact that led Petr Pithart to declare that "[s]ome Moravians are assiduously pushing at a door that is already open."[39]

Many, though not all, Czech parties supported giving Moravia some form of self-government. The strongest Czech advocates of Moravian self-government were OF and KSC, which drew substantial support from Moravia. Marian Čalfa, Prime Minister of the national government and member of the Communist Party, once declared, for example, that "Moravia and Silesia have so many important regional differences that they deserve to be reflected in a form of the territorial set up within the Czechoslovak federation."[40] The strongest individual Czech supporter of Moravian autonomy was Petr Pithart. Pithart, advocated a tripartite federation for Moravia. Pithart believed that "[t]he Czech state is not something that can be built from above.... The Czech state can come about only as a sum total of living, self local and regional autonomies."[41]

For its part, HSD-SMS was willing to work with Czech parties in order to achieve its goals of a tripartite federation. According to Rudolf Opatřil, "We [HSD-SMS] have a strategy that we work with whatever partner is the most important – in ČR [Czech Republic] ODS prevailed and in Slovakia HZDS."[42] In turn, the Czech government attempted to accommodate the interests and demands of Moravia in a number of different ways. Not only did the government transfer funds to Moravia to improve infrastructure and complete a new hospital, but it also set up a commission to devise different proposals to extend autonomy to Moravia, of which four took precedence (Obrman and Mates 1994).

The first proposal restored the system of Lands, which dated back to the Medieval Ages, and gave Bohemia, as well as Moravia and Silesia, their own regional legislatures. The second proposal called for a tripartite federation in Czechoslovakia in which Moravia (combined with Silesia) would have the same status as Bohemia and Slovakia. The third proposal redesigned the country's political system based on provinces, but did not address the autonomy concerns of Moravia, and the fourth plan was based on a combination of the first and third proposals, but was eventually jettisoned because it was too complicated. None of these plans was ever adopted, though, because Czechoslovakia dissolved into two separate states in 1993. The Czech Republic eventually extended a limited form of self-government to Moravia later in the decade.

3.8. Impact of decentralization on the party system in Czechoslovakia

Decentralization had a major influence on the development of Czechoslovakia's party system, which scholars have largely overlooked, with one notable exception (Olson 1993).[43] Several features of this system encouraged the presence of regional parties in the country, namely the size and distribution of national legislative seats among Czechoslovakia's regions and the number of regional legislatures in the country. It is not possible to examine the effect of election timing on the strength of regional parties in the Czech and Slovak National Councils, since national and regional elections occurred simultaneously in both Councils.

The principal feature that encouraged regional parties in Czechoslovakia was the division of Czechoslovakia's national legislatures into two large political regions with extensive decision-making authority and rules granting the Czech Lands and Slovakia legislative veto powers. Czechoslovakia's lower house, the House of People, was divided between the Czech Lands and Slovakia based on population, so that the Czech Lands constituted about 60 percent of the country's two national legislatures and Slovakia comprised about 40 percent. Designed to protect the rights of Slovaks outnumbered by Czechs in the country's lower house, Czechoslovakia's upper house, known as the House of Nations, distributed seats equally between the Czech Lands and Slovakia. This gave politicians strong incentives to form regional parties to compete at the national level by allowing regional parties from the Czech Lands and Slovakia to have a significant impact on legislation produced at this level, although based on size alone, regional parties from the Czech Lands had a legislative majority.

Rules governing how the national legislatures made decisions increased the incentive politicians had to form regional parties in Slovakia, and voters to vote for them, because they augmented the legislative power of Slovak regional parties. The House of Nations and the House of People had to approve all bills in order for them to become law and the House of People could not override the

House of Nations. Most bills required a simple majority in both legislatures, which gave Czech regional parties a lot of power in the national government. Issues related to the constitution, however, required a three-fifths majority of the Czech and Slovak sections of the House of Nations, as well as a three-fifths majority of the lower house, according to the prohibition of the majority.

As a result, both the Czech Lands and Slovakia wielded a veto power over the new constitution. The Czech Lands' veto power rested squarely in Bohemia's hand since Bohemia constituted about 60 percent of the seats in the House of Nations, while Moravia made up the remaining 40 percent. Parties, therefore, which competed in only Bohemia could veto the national constitution. This meant that parties had few incentives to compete in only Moravia, leading all parties that ran in Moravia to run in Bohemia as well.

Another feature of decentralization that contributed to the shape of the country's party system was the number of regional legislatures in Czechoslovakia. While the Czech Lands and Slovakia had their own regional legislatures, Bohemia and Moravia did not. They shared control of the Czech National Council of which Bohemia comprised 60 percent and Moravia 40 percent, as they did at the national level. Regular bills needed the support of a majority of the legislature in order to become law, whereas bills relating to the constitution needed a three-fifths majority of the Czech National Council. However, since Bohemia constituted a three-fifths majority on its own, the impact of parties competing in only Moravia was very limited. This likewise discouraged parties from competing only in this region.

3.9. Conclusion

Czechoslovakia's dissolution suggests an important mechanism through which regional parties instigate ethnic conflict and secession. Czechoslovakia dissolved because regional parties from the Czech Lands and Slovakia advocated legislation that regional parties from the opposing region viewed as less preferable than dissolution. Regional differences did not preordain the dissolution of Czechoslovakia. Regional parties transformed these differences into salient political cleavages around which they mobilized the electorate. Comparisons with interwar Czechoslovakia and the Moravian region of the Czech Lands make this apparent.

Decentralization was critical to the dissolution of the country, providing politicians with incentives to mobilize Czechs and Slovaks along regional lines and to form regional parties. The structure of decentralization was conducive to regional parties because it divided the country into two, very large political regions with veto power over the national constitution and control over their own regional legislatures with significant decision-making authority. These features of decentralization not only encouraged politicians to form regional parties, but also gave regional parties significant authority within the country.

At the same time that the structure of decentralization made it difficult to keep Czechs and Slovaks united, it helped quell secessionism in the Czech Lands. Although Moravia was arguably as different from Bohemia as Slovakia was from the Czech Lands, regional parties did not have a hold on Moravia, and most parties that competed in the Czech Lands supported some form of autonomy for Moravia. Czechoslovakia's system of government discouraged politicians from competing in only Moravia by preventing parties that did from governing at either the national or regional level of government. Institutional design thus played a major role in the dissolution of Czechoslovakia and, simultaneously, the unity of the Czech Lands.

4

Spain

At the time Spain embarked on a transition to democracy in the late 1970s, the potential for ethnic conflict and secession was high. Not only were economic and ethnolinguistic differences substantial, but support for independence was also considerable. Violent separatist organizations were widely active at the time as well. Yet Spain, unlike Czechoslovakia – where the potential for conflict and dissolution was much lower – remained unified. Since the transition, secessionist sentiment has stayed relatively stable and violence has been confined to separatist organizations in which public support has waned.

Critical in explaining the success of decentralization in this regard is the strong presence of statewide parties in the country and the willingness of these parties to incorporate regional issues into their agendas. Statewide parties have single-handedly controlled the national government since the first democratic elections were held in Spain after General Franco died in 1975.[44] At the regional level, statewide parties have governed alone or in coalition with regional parties in every region of the country, and in most regions they have done so quite frequently. During the country's critical transition period, regional parties were especially weak at this level of government because the national government appointed Spain's first regional legislatures based on national-level representation.

Statewide parties, using their dominant position in the country at the time, established a decentralized system of government and delicately balanced the regions' competing interests. Since the transition, statewide parties have continued to play this balancing role and have prevented regional parties from adopting legislation threatening other regions in the country and from declaring independence. At the same time, statewide parties have encouraged some regional parties to sever ties with separatist organizations, although a number of regional parties continue to support extremist organizations in the Basque Country, rhetorically as well as financially.

The structure of decentralization in Spain has helped shape the country's party system while two features, in particular, have limited the extent to which decentralization encourages regional parties, namely the regional distribution of seats in Spain's lower house and the direct election of most of Spain's upper house. Both features diminish the legislative impact of regional parties at the national level and discourage politicians from forming regional parties in the first place. The presence of regional parties is much greater at the regional level of government, however, since every autonomous community in Spain has their own regional legislature. Regional legislatures, though, have limited national influence because they cannot veto the national constitution, unlike in Czechoslovakia. Ethnolinguistic and economic differences in Spain, while substantial, cannot fully account for the presence of regional parties in the country. Inconsistencies between these differences and the strength of regional parties over time and across regions in Spain make this apparent.

In order to illuminate this argument, this chapter proceeds as follows. In Section 4.1, I briefly depict the evolution of ethnic conflict and secessionism in Spain from the time Spain embarked on a transition to democracy in 1976 up to the present. In Sections 4.2 and 4.3, I describe the structure of decentralization in Spain and how scholars regard this system more generally. In Section 4.4, I depict the strength of statewide and regional parties in the country, and in Section 4.5, I discuss existing explanations for the strength of regional parties in Spain. In Section 4.6, I explain why Spain was able to adopt a decentralized system of government in the late 1970s and the role that statewide and regional parties have played in the country ever since. Finally, in Section 4.7 I describe the effect of decentralization on the shape of Spain's party system.

4.1. Brief history of intrastate conflict in Spain

Spain is comprised of five major ethniclinguistic groups (i.e. Basques, Catalans, Galicians, Valencians, and Spanish speakers). For the most part, all five groups practice Catholicism and live in different regions of the country. There are seventeen regions in Spain, known as autonomous communities, as well as two Spanish city-states in Africa – Ceuta and Melilla. Basques reside largely in two of these regions (i.e. the Basque Country and Navarra), as do Catalans (i.e. Catalonia and the Balearic Islands). Valencians, whose language is similar to Catalan, live principally in Valencia while Galicians, whose language is similar to Portuguese, live primarily in Galicia. Spanish speakers make up the largest of Spain's ethnolinguistic groups and are dispersed throughout the country's eleven remaining regions (i.e. Andalusia, Aragon, Asturias, Canary Islands, Cantabria, Extremadura, Castilla-La Mancha, Castilla-Leon, Madrid, Murcia, and La Rioja).

Post-Franco, there has been no significant incidence of conflict in Spain among the country's major ethnolinguistic groups.[45] Relations among these groups are largely amicable as well. According to one survey conducted by the *Center of Sociological Investigations* (CIS), respondents in almost every region of Spain expressed friendly views toward people living in every other region of Spain (CIS 1996). On a 1–10 point scale, where 1 indicates complete antipathy and 10 indicates complete sympathy toward people living in other regions, the mean level of sympathy expressed for every region in Spain is 6.5 or above, except for the Basque Country and Catalonia. For these regions, the mean is between 5.0 and 5.5. In other words, all regions in Spain are moderately sympathetic toward all other regions in Spain, except the Basque Country and Catalonia. To these regions, they are more indifferent. Importantly, however, the mean level of sympathy expressed by the Basque Country and Catalonia toward all other regions in Spain is 6.8 or above.

Secessionism is much more prevalent in Spain. In the 1970s a number of violent separatist organizations were active in the Basque Country, the Canary Islands, Catalonia, and Galicia.[46] Today, only one organization, Euskadi Ta Azkatasuna (ETA), is still active. ETA seeks an independent Basque state but its activity has declined since the World Trade Center attacks. This tragedy propelled the Spanish government to crack down on terrorists within its own borders and prompted the United States to support the Spanish state in this regard. Public support for ETA has also declined over time. In the 1970s, the Basque people widely backed ETA not just for its views on Basque independence, but for its opposition to Franco as well. In 2001, however, 93 percent of Basques surveyed said that ETA's actions "greatly" or "somewhat" concerned them (CIS 2001).[47] According to the same study, 62 percent of Basques said that they supported social movements opposed to ETA "a lot" or "somewhat."[48]

Public support for political parties seeking independence has also diminished in the Basque Country and Galicia, but not Catalonia. In the Basque Country numerous regional parties have advocated independence over time, but today only two of these parties still demand Basque independence – Basque Solidarity (EA) and the United People, known more commonly as Herri Batasuna (HB). Electoral support for these parties has always been confined to the subnational level of government and has declined over time. Together EA and HB captured fewer votes in 1998 than they earned in the first elections they ever competed in within Spain.[49] Outlawed in 2003, HB no longer participates in elections.

Support for independence-seeking parties has also existed in Galicia, but political parties advocating independence have not been active in this region for decades.[50] In Catalonia, however, electoral support for independence-seeking parties still exists. Support for these parties has remained stable over time, and has not been confined entirely to the subnational level of government. Today, the largest party advocating independence in Catalonia is the Republican Left of Catalonia (ERC).[51] This party, which once supported the use of violence to achieve independence, won 16 percent of the vote in Catalonia's last regional elections in 2003.

Finally, public opinion surveys suggest that support for independence in Spain has remained low since Spain democratized. Surveys administered in 1979 indicate that 6 percent of Spaniards believed that the autonomous communities should have the right to become independent states even if they do not exercise this right (García et al. 1994). The same percentage of Spaniards shared this view in 2003 (CIS 2003). The extent to which people share this view differs by region. In the 2003 survey, 28 percent of people in the Basque Country, 18 percent of those in Catalonia, and 10 percent of those in Navarra said that they believed that their regions should have the right to be independent, even if they did not exercise this right (CIS 2003), which is notably higher than in other regions of Spain, as Figure 4.1 depicts.

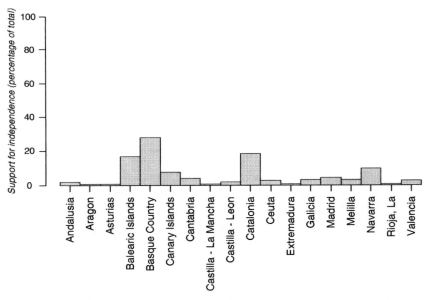

Figure 4.1. Public support for the right to be independent in Spain, 2003

Note: The question depicted in the graph asks: "Of the following alternative formulas for the organization of the state, which are you in most agreement?" The figures represent the percentage of people who responded: "A state that recognizes the possibility of the autonomous communitities converting into independent states." Murcia is excluded from the figure because no respondents in this region supported independence.

Source: CIS (2003).

Additional studies conducted at different moments in Spain's history reach similar conclusions (García 1982; CIS 1998).

Together each of these different ways of measuring ethnic conflict and secessionism suggest that overall the intensity of both phenomena is moderate in Spain. Not only do people express friendly relations toward people living in other regions of the country, but in most regions they provide only limited support to independence-seeking parties and separatist organizations as well. In a number of regions of Spain, this support has declined over time, and at no point in Spain's post-Franco history have the country's major ethnic groups clashed violently. Decentralization has made a major contribution in this respect. In order to understand why, it is first necessary to understand the structure of decentralization in Spain, which I turn to next.

4.2. Structure of decentralization in Spain

During its transition to democracy in the late 1970s, Spain adopted a decentralized system of government that divided decision-making authority between a national and subnational level of government. Then and now, national level authority is divided between a lower and an upper house of legislature, known respectively as the Congress of Deputies (Congreso de los Diputados) and the Senate (Senado). At the subnational level, every autonomous community in Spain has their own regional legislature and multiple local ones. This division of political and fiscal authority is asymmetric, but extensive, although a number of scholars have argued that the regional legislatures should have more political and fiscal powers (Fossas 1999; Requejo 1999).

4.2.1. Division of political authority in Spain

The national government in Spain has exclusive control over 32 political, social, and economic matters.[52] All powers not exclusively reserved for the national government fall under the purview of the regions. In practice, regions share control over most of these powers with the national government. Those over which regions have exclusive control include the following: associations, casinos and gambling, cooperatives, energy, entertainment, foundations, industry, meteorology, order, publicity, as well as weights and measures.

The distribution of power between these levels of government is asymmetric, which a number of scholars have objected to on the grounds that all regions in Spain should have as much authority as the most powerful regions in the country (Tornos Más 1991). Today, there are seven regions in Spain that have greater political powers than the rest of the country (i.e. Andalusia, the Basque Country, Catalonia, the Canary Islands, Galicia, Navarra, and Valencia). The issues over which these regions have control and other regions do not include: banks, credits and securities, education, health and justice, as well as public order and police.

This asymmetry is a result of two different processes. The first is Article 151 of the Spanish Constitution.[53] It granted regions, which had autonomy prior to the Franco regime, more decision-making powers than the rest of Spain for the first five years after Spain decentralized. These regions include the Basque Country, Catalonia, Navarra, and Galicia. The second relates to the bargaining process between the national government and the regions. As part of this process, regions demand more autonomy from the national government in exchange for their support of the national government, among other things. Regions have made notable gains in the Basque Country, Catalonia, and the Canary Islands in this way. Generally, though, regions receive much less autonomy through this process than they actually demand from the government, as I will detail subsequently in this chapter.

4.2.2. Division of fiscal authority in Spain

Spain also divides fiscal authority between the national and subnational levels of government. In 1980, the year Spain elected its first regional legislatures, the national government accounted for 89 percent of total government expenditure, while the regional and local levels of government accounted for only 11 percent. Since the 1990s, the regional and local levels have accounted for approximately 35–40 percent of Spain's total government expenditure, as Figure 4.2 depicts. Subnational expenditure is based primarily on national government transfers, with large regions receiving more money from the national government than smaller ones.

Autonomous communities can also raise their own taxes, but only a small fraction of their resources are derived from these taxes, thereby, in the views of many scholars emasculating the autonomous communities (Perulles 1991; Agranoff and Ramos 1998; Bañón and Tamayo 1998). The Basque Country and Navarra rely more heavily on their own tax bases than other regions. Both have a distinctive financial system,

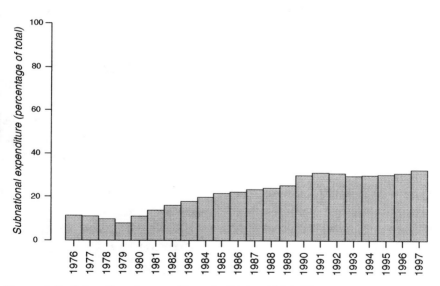

Figure 4.2. Subnational expenditure in Spain, 1976–97

Source: IMF (2001) The Spanish government reports very similar figures for the period 1980–93. See MAP (1994).

known as the Foral System, which allows the Basque Country and Navarra to levy their own taxes. In exchange, these regions cede only enough money to the national government to cover the costs of services that the national government provides.[54] The Basque Country and Navarra, though, must follow certain economic guidelines within their regions, which prevent them from establishing biases or privileges in the system, distorting the distribution of resources within the country, or hindering the free movement of capital. The Basque Country and Navarra must also negotiate with the national government regarding the amount of money they cede to the national government each year.

Regional economic disparities have increased over time due to the ability of prosperous regions to raise more revenue than less developed ones (Perulles 1991; Aznar and López 1994; Braña and Serna 1997). In order to rectify this situation, the national government established a fund, called the Interterritorial Compensation Fund (FCI), which transfers money from the wealthy regions of Spain to the poor ones. The government makes these transfers in inverse proportion to the size and wealth of regions for the purpose of infrastructure development, public works, territorial management, housing, and communication. Figure 4.3 depicts the percentage of all FCI transfers that each autonomous community in Spain received between 1997 and 2008. Autonomous communities that do not receive funding from the FCI, such as the Basque Country and Catalonia, are excluded from this graph.

As this graph makes apparent, Andalusia, which accounts for a large share of Spain's total population and is poor, receives the most money from the FCI. Galicia, which is poor but less populated than Andalusia, receives the next largest amount, followed by Castilla-La Mancha. Regions that do not account for much of Spain's population, such as Cantabria, and are economically more developed, receive the least amount of money from the FCI.

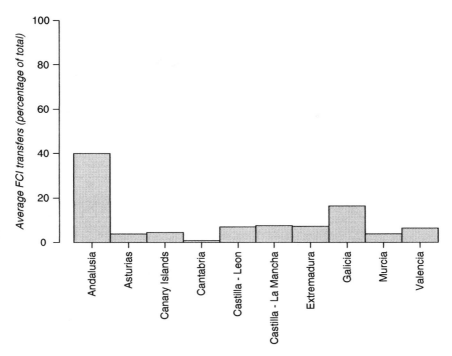

Figure 4.3. FCI transfers to Spain's autonomous communities, 1997–2008
Source: See Ministerio de Hacienda (1997–2008). The graph excludes regions that did not receive funds from the FCI in this period.

4.3. Perspectives on decentralization in Spain

Decentralization is widely credited for establishing democracy in Spain and reducing ethnic conflict and secessionism in the country (Shabad 1986; Brassloff 1989; Beramendi 1995; Moreno 1997; Fossas 1999; Requejo 1999; Fusi 2000; Beramendi and Máiz 2004). Juan Pablo Fusi claims, for example, that decentralization has been "an essential and necessary instrument for the establishment of democracy" (2000: 279), while Eliseo Aja believes that decentralization is "a cornerstone of Spanish democracy" (1991: 111). At the same time, Luis Moreno claims that decentralization has "transcended the traditional cultural patterns of ethnic confrontation in Spain" (1997: 65). Finally, Goldie Shabad contends that "the process of autonomy served to moderate public opinion with respect to the question of the state structure in those regions in which the demands for autonomy were most explicit and persistent in 1979" (1986: 537).

However, not all scholars' praise of decentralization has been unbridled. Juan Pablo Fusi cautions that people should not fall victim to "the illusion of autonomy" and to "the belief that the approval of the autonomous communities could put an end to the problem of nationalism (and the terrorism of ETA)" (2000: 275). Meanwhile, Justo G. Beramendi (1995) claims that decentralization has institutionalized nationalism in Spain. According to Beramendi, "by partly satisfying the demands of the alternative nationalisms, it has helped to moderate their potential radicalism...and to neutralize the pro-independence tendencies which are inherent in movements of this kind" (1995: 94). But, at the same time, "it has also created an institutional framework, which is favorable to the consolidation of these alternative national identities, thereby reducing the level of national conflict but also contributing to the stabilization of this conflict" (Beramendi 1995: 94).

Finally, Xosé-Manoel Núñez (1999) claims that decentralization has not only institutionalized nationalist tensions in some regions of Spain, but has also created similar sentiments in regions that previously did not have them. Núñez argues that decentralization created a situation where "[r]egional elites now encounter greater opportunities for achieving power and controlling resources" so that "regional administrations imposed from above, which very often did not correspond to any regional consciousness by the majority of the respective populations, caused regionalism to be promoted by both" (1999: 127). Moreover, Núñez claims that "the more power regional institutions have, the more they will consciously promote the territorial loyalty of the citizens in order to reinforce their own legitimacy" (1999: 127).

Although a few scholars have their reservations, most scholars credit decentralization for reducing ethnic conflict and secessionism in Spain, believing that decentralization reduces both phenomena by giving groups control over their own political, social, and economic affairs.

In studying this issue, however, scholars have not fully explored the role that the party system has played in facilitating decentralization's ability to reduce ethnic conflict and secessionism, and the influence of decentralization on the party system in Spain. In order to understand these issues, it is first necessary to examine the shape of Spain's party system and the strength of regional parties in particular.

4.4. Party system in post-Franco Spain

At the national level of government, regional parties, competing by definition in one autonomous community of Spain, accounted for nearly 15 percent of the vote on average between 1977 and 2000. Figure 4.4 illustrates the average vote cast for regional parties during

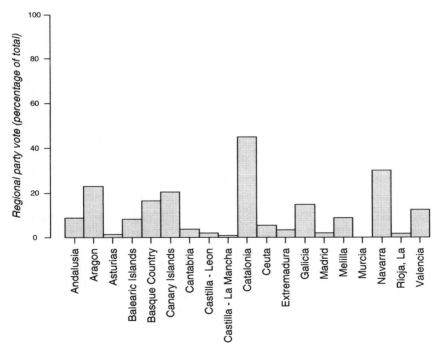

Figure 4.4. Regional party vote in Spain's national legislatures, 1977–2000
Source: Ministerio del Interior (2000, 2001).

101

this period. Not surprisingly, regional parties have had a stronger presence in certain regions of Spain at the national level of government than in others. Their presence is strongest in Aragon, the Basque Country, the Canary Islands, Catalonia, Galicia, and Navarra. Their presence in the Basque Country is even greater if the Basque National Party (PNV) is included in these figures for the years it maintained a minor presence in Navarra while also competing in the Basque Country.[55] Including PNV for these years, the average vote for regional parties is just shy of 40 percent, making the Basque Country second to Catalonia in terms of regional party strength.

Regional parties have never participated in the national government although on two occasions the national government invited regional parties from the Basque Country, Catalonia, and the Canary Islands to participate in the government. They summarily refused, choosing to support the national government from outside in exchange for a number of concessions from the government. By forming agreements with statewide parties instead of joining the government directly, regional parties, according to some scholars, captured benefits for their autonomous communities while maintaining their images as true defenders of their communities (Linz and Montero 1999; Guerrero 2000).

At the regional level of government, regional parties accounted for over 35 percent of the vote between 1980 and 1999. Figure 4.5 depicts the average vote cast for regional parties during this period. Prior to the first regional elections in Spain, the national government appointed regional legislatures based on political representation at the national level. As a result, the strength of regional parties in these legislatures matched that of the national legislatures.

Over time, regional parties have had stronger positions in certain regional legislatures than in others. Their presence has been strongest in Andalusia, Catalonia, Navarra, and Valencia.[56] In these regions and others, regional parties, such as the Spanish Socialist Workers' Party of Andalusia or the Socialist Party of Catalonia, have competed jointly with statewide parties at the national level, but individually as regional parties at the regional level. At the regional level, these parties are independent of statewide parties. At the national level,

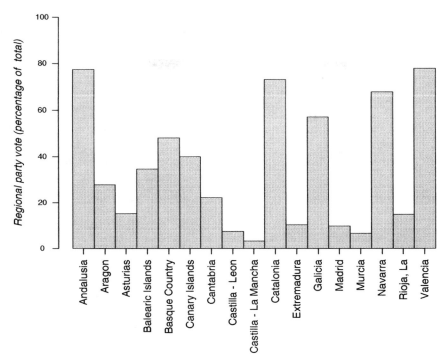

Figure 4.5. Regional party vote in Spain's autonomous community elections, 1980–99

Source: Data depicted in the graph are drawn from numerous sources provided by political institutions within each region. The figures for Extremadura reflect elections held in 1999 only.

they are not. Here they adhere to the agendas of the statewide parties. Even though regional parties are stronger overall at the regional level of government than at the national level, statewide parties have still controlled most of Spain's regional governments since the first autonomous community elections held in the country.

4.5. Origins of regional parties in Spain

Regional differences are the most common explanation for the existence of regional parties in Spain (de Esteban and López 1982;

Garmendia et al. 1982; Buse 1984; Llera 1984, 1995; Gunther et al. 1986; Shabad 1986; Pérez 1987; Cotarelo 1992; Padró-Solanet and Colomer 1992; Chueca and Montero 1995; Martinez 1995; Montero et al. 1995; Alcántara and Martínez 1998; Pérez-Nievas and Fraile 2000). In *Spain After Franco*, Gunther et al. (1986) claim, for example, that "[t]he linguistic and cultural distinctiveness of the Basque, the Catalan, and Gallego electorates, the widespread sense of belonging to the regional group and the generalized desire for autonomy have all resulted in the emergence of regional party systems in Spain" (385).

Similarly, de Esteban and López (1982) argue that "the incidence of a regional fact in Spain is the cause of the excessive atomization of political parties and the preeminence of regional bonds over national ones. The consequence of which has been that innumerable parties emerged, which are born, structured and actuated in an extreme parochialism" (46). Finally, Michael Buse (1984) claims that regional parties exist in Spain because "a very notable part of the electorate that defends the political, cultural and economic independence of its region considers that these desires are adequately represented by the large nationalist parties....This electorate cannot integrate themselves in the central system of parties" (317).

Recently, several scholars have argued that regional differences are only relevant to the discussion of regional parties in the ethnolinguistically distinct regions of Spain (Montero et al. 1998; Hamann 1999; Linz and Montero 1999; Grau 2000). In the nondistinct regions, they attribute regional parties to decentralization. As Juan Linz and José Montero assert, "[t]he nationalists in Catalonia and the Basque Country had developed their own identity some time before and there was little question that they would not vote for statewide parties" (1999:14). In the other regions, however, "the political opportunity structure offered by the decentralization process" led to the growth of regional parties (Linz and Montero 1999:96).

Regional differences are important. They are the basis around which regional parties mobilize voters and an important reason why statewide parties decided to decentralize Spain in the first place. Decentralization, however, is an equally important component in explaining regional party success in Spain. Decentralization did not cause all regional parties in Spain. A number of regional parties existed in the country prior to decentralization, particularly in the Basque Country and Catalonia. Decentralization, however, has helped sustain these regional parties and encouraged new ones to arise both in the distinct and nondistinct regions of Spain.

Regional parties exist in both the distinct and nondistinct regions of Spain and do not necessarily have stronger positions in the former than in the latter. Regional parties have strong positions in Catalonia and Navarra at the national level of government, but not in the Balearic Islands, Galicia, and Valencia – even though these regions have distinct ethnolinguistic identities. Regional parties have also earned more votes in two of the nondistinct regions of Spain, namely Aragon and the Canary Islands, than in some of the distinct regions. They have also earned fewer votes in some of Spain's poorer regions, such as Andalusia, Extremadura, and Galicia, than in some of its wealthier or middling regions.

Regional identities, which scholars theorize result directly from ethnolinguistic differences, are not, moreover, overwhelmingly strong in the distinct regions of Spain. According to a CIS survey taken in 2003, only 29 percent of the people surveyed in the Basque Country, 16 percent of those in Catalonia, and 12 percent of those in Navarra and the Balearic Islands identify with only their region (CIS 2003). Figure 4.6 depicts the results of this survey. Regional identities are even weaker in Galicia and Valencia. Accordingly, only 7 percent of people in Galicia and 1 percent of those in Valencia identify with only their region. People's regional identities are stronger in the Canary Islands than in a number of these regions, even though people in the Canary Islands are not ethnolinguistically distinct from the rest of Spain. As a basis for comparison, I show the results of an earlier 1996 survey on the same question (CIS 1996).

Finally, the electoral strength of regional parties has grown most dramatically in those regions of Spain that did not have strong

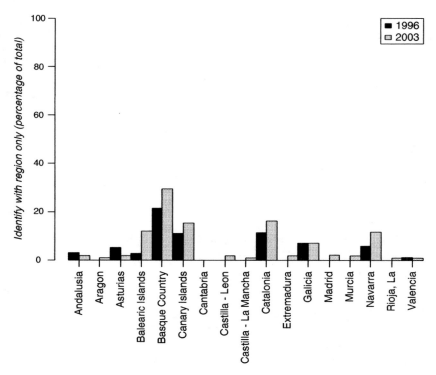

Figure 4.6. Regional identities in Spain's autonomous communities, 1996 and 2003

Note: The question depicted in the graph asks: "Which of the following phrases/terms do you identify with the most?" The figures in the graph represent those who responded "only their community." The results for Ceuta and Melilla are not presented because comparison data for 1996 are not available. The results for 2003 are as follows: Ceuta (3 percent) and Melilla (6 percent).

Source: CIS (1996, 2003).

regional parties prior to decentralization, and did not demand autonomy during Spain's transition to democracy. Before Spain decentralized, regional parties had very strong positions in the Basque Country and Catalonia, but not really anywhere else. Regional parties in these two regions adamantly demanded autonomy during the transition and prior. Spain, though, extended autonomy to every region in the country, not just the Basque Country and

Catalonia. As a result, regional parties have grown significantly in these other regions. The most dramatic growth in regional parties has occurred in Andalusia, Balearic Islands, Canary Islands, Galicia, and Melilla. Between 1982 (the first post-transition period election) and 2000, the average vote for regional parties at the national level has grown from 9 percentage points in Andalusia to 25 percentage points in the Canary Islands.[57] Of these regions, only the Balearic Islands and Galicia have distinct ethnolinguistic identities. In the final section of this chapter, I describe the particular features of decentralization that most influence the strength of regional parties in Spain.

4.6. Explaining the success of decentralization in Spain

The ability of decentralization to manage intrastate conflict in Spain hinges on the electoral strength of regional parties. Where present, regional parties have reinforced regional identities and advocated legislation harmful to other regions in the country. At times, they have also demanded the right to be independent and supported violent separatist organizations, such as ETA. Fortunately, statewide parties have dominated most legislatures in Spain and have kept regional parties in check, either blocking or moderating the legislation regional parties advocate, and incorporating regional interests into their agendas while balancing the competing ones against each other.

4.6.1. The transition period

During transitions, regional parties pose significant challenges to countries trying to maintain unity because political systems are open to redefinition in these periods. The weakness of democracy and preexisting political ties also facilitate the construction of identities along regional lines in these periods. Spain, though, during its transition, successfully navigated the challenges posed by regional parties, which had a rather limited presence in the country at the time. Spain designed its new political system in this period in two stages – the success of which some leaders attributed to the limited presence of regional parties. According to Adolfo Suárez, "The task of creating a new state... required the existence of very strong parties at the national level. If there had been small parties, we would have run the risk of instability and polarization."[58] Suárez was the leader of the largest political party in Spain during the transition period, the Union of the Democratic Center (UCD).

The first stage involved the adoption of Spain's new constitution, which established a general division of powers between the national and subnational levels of government, but did not delineate the latter's powers. Regional parties had a limited role in this process because they had a small presence in the country's national legislatures, which, unlike in Czechoslovakia, had the sole power to approve the constitution. The constitution passed despite the concerns (and abstentions in some cases) of regional parties that sought a more explicit delineation of subnational authorities.

The second phase of the process involved the adoption of the regional autonomy statutes, which defined the specific responsibilities of each region in Spain. Regional legislatures were charged with drawing up the statutes, but both houses of the national legislature had to approve them before they could become law. Regional parties had a limited involvement in this stage of the process as well, since Spain appointed its first regional legislatures based on representation at the national level. Regional parties were not excluded from this process entirely, though, because statewide parties invited regional parties to participate. Within a span of a couple of years, the national government had approved every region's autonomy statute.

During the transition era, regional parties advocated legislation that threatened other regions in the country. Regional parties, speaking for regions that had autonomy prior to Franco (i.e. the Basque Country, Catalonia, Galicia, and Navarra), demanded a high level of autonomy from Spain. They also wanted their level of autonomy to be greater than any other region in Spain. Regions that had not previously had autonomy opposed this system because it would diminish their stature within the country. The historically distinct regions were not able to impose this system on Spain given their minor position in the country.

Statewide parties, though, balanced the two types of regions' conflicting interests against each other through Article 143 and Article 151 of the Spanish Constitution.[59] These articles gave the historically distinct regions of Spain more power than the nondistinct ones for a period of five years. In practice, the nondistinct regions did not acquire the same powers as the distinct ones until 1992, thanks to an agreement signed by two statewide parties, the Spanish Socialist Workers Party (PSOE) and the Popular Party (PP).[60]

Regional parties in the Basque Country, Catalonia, and Navarra, which are much wealthier than other regions in Spain, also demanded a high degree of fiscal autonomy from the national government. Able to raise enough revenue from their own taxes to finance projects, these regions did not want their taxes to finance the development of other regions. Less prosperous regions in Spain, such as Andalusia and Galicia, however, could not raise enough tax revenue on their own to finance all of their projects. Relying on the assistance of the wealthier regions, these regions were greatly threatened by the demands of their wealthier counterparts for a high degree of fiscal autonomy.

The wealthier regions did not fully achieve their goal either. Statewide parties and, in particular, the UCD and PSOE, conceded to some of the regions' demands, but not all of them, instead balancing the interests of Spain's wealthier regions against those of its poorer ones. Statewide parties, for example, granted a high level of fiscal autonomy to the Basque Country and Navarra by restoring their Foral systems, but it did not grant the same to Catalonia. Statewide parties, nonetheless, agreed to base Catalonia's share of national tax receipts on its population and income, which favored Catalonia not only as one of the wealthiest regions in Spain, but also as the second most populous region behind Andalusia.[61] Statewide parties also mandated that Catalonia's share of national tax receipts would be based on other factors as well, which were not specified at the time. This formula, the UCD believed, was preferable to others because it gave Catalonia real financial autonomy and was applicable to the rest of the autonomous communities.[62] Conceding more fully to the demands of the Catalan parties would have created "a disunited result" according to PSOE. To address the poorer regions' concerns that they would suffer as a result of this system, statewide parties created the Interterritorial Compensation Fund (FCI), as previously described.

Finally, regional parties in the Basque Country also threatened the interests of neighboring Navarra. These parties demanded that Navarra be incorporated into the Basque Country and even threatened to reject the Basque Country's statute of autonomy if Navarra was not.[63] Desiring its own autonomous community, Navarra was threatened by the aggressive demands of the Basque parties, which were ultimately not heeded. Statewide parties balanced the competing interests of the Basque Country and Navarra against each other by placing a clause in the country's constitution requiring Navarra to hold a referendum to decide this matter. Navarra subsequently did in favor of its own autonomous community.

Even though the structure of decentralization did not satisfy every autonomous community's desires fully at the time, the communities nonetheless supported the political system because it satisfied at least some of their demands. In explaining why the Catalan regional party CiU, accepted Catalonia's statute of autonomy, Jordi Pujol stated that "[t]his statute does not totally or definitively vindicate the national liberty of Catalonia. We would be deceiving ourselves and we would be deceiving the nation to say or to make believe that we obtained all that we wanted, that we obtained all that Catalonia needs. But, we would also be deceiving ourselves saying or making believe that what we have obtained isn't a lot."[64]

Similarly, Carlos Garaikoetxea, president of the Basque Parliament during the transition period, said that his party, PNV, supported the statute because it was "the hope of a better future and of living and coexisting, versus the emptiness and anxiety of not knowing where we will be taken."[65] The regions also expressed hope that they could modify the system more favorably in the future. As Heribert Barrera of the ERC said, "No one believes that this is the final solution to the Catalan problem. It is only one step in a long march."[66]

All the major statewide parties supported decentralization in Spain, albeit to different degrees. They were at least in part motivated by ideological, as well as strategic reasons. PSOE and the Spanish Communist Party (PCE) supported decentralization because they viewed it as an extension of socialism and the class struggle.[67] Others conceded that, in order to be competitive electorally, statewide parties had to support some form of decentralization.

The importance of electoral incentives is well illustrated by the Popular Alliance (AP) party, the predecessor of PP. AP was initially very antagonistic toward decentralization because it was a conservative political party composed of many former members of the Franco regime who were averse to democracy, let alone decentralization, and feared that decentralization would lead to the disintegration of Spain. According to internal party documents, AP eventually supported a limited form of decentralization in order to be competitive in regional elections (Lagares 1999). In one such document, AP confided that "we will have to study the problem of the introduction of the regions, although it will be only by means of a strategic support, because each time it will be more difficult to obtain a correct provincial politics without an adequate regional mark and it will be practically impossible to accede to the regional organizations of representation through the actuation of a single province."[68] Here AP reveals explicitly that it supported decentralization strategically because it needed a regional marker to compete successfully at the regional and provincial levels of government.

At the time, statewide parties also had to overcome internal pressures from members of their own party to balance the competing interests of regions against each other. In most cases, statewide parties were successful in this regard. In some cases, they were not. Several members of the UCD in Andalusia defected from the party. They formed their own party, the Social and Liberal Party of Andalusia (PSLA), because UCD did not support the accession of

Andalusia through Article 151 of Spain's Constitution.[69] According to Manuel Clavero, the leader of this new party, it was a difficult decision to resign from UCD, which he ultimately did, because he "felt more loyalty to the electorate, which since 1977 came offering compromises to full autonomy, than to a party that was still in power and that had become incompatible with Andalusia" (136). While PSLA initially had some support in Andalusia, the party no longer exists today.

One of the more significant cases of statewide party defections involved the UCD in Navarra. Several members of UCD resigned from the party in Navarra and formed the Union of the Navarran People (UPN) because they opposed UCD's position on the referendum to incorporate Navarra into the Basque Country (UPN 2000). UCD supported holding a referendum to decide the matter. Voicing his discontent with UCD, Jesús Aizpún, the founder of UPN, relates that "they [UCD] speak as if Navarra has to join the Basque Country and no one in the Congress listens to the opinion of Navarra.... They absolutely condemn us to join the Basque Community and it is not possible to raise a voice to the contrary. This is when a few of us thought of the possibility of forming our own party" (UPN 2000: 13). Despite these few incidences of fissures, the statewide parties generally created a strong consensus within their own parties during the transition period regarding the country's political system, as well as within the country as a whole.

4.6.2. The post-transition period

Statewide parties have also kept regional parties in check during the post-transition period. For their part, regional parties have attempted to strengthen regional identities in Spain and have done so in various ways. In the Basque Country, they have strengthened identities by popularizing the Basque flag (la Ikurriña), which PNV's founder, Sabino Arana, created and which is depicted on the front cover of this book. Regional parties have also tried to foster a sense of community among Basques by frequently making reference to the *fueros*, the Medieval laws extending sovereignty to the

Basque Country, Catalonia, and Navarra, and by promoting the Basque language, which only a small percentage of Basques speak, but which is widely used on public signs throughout the region. In Catalonia, street signs are also in Catalan. To further the use of Catalan, regional parties have offered free language classes to immigrants in Catalan (not Spanish) and encouraged the use of Catalan in public spaces through the CAT campaign. Regional parties have even gone so far as to describe Catalonia as a "nation" in its most recent autonomy statute.

Regional parties seem to have had some success in this regard. Although one cannot causally link regional parties to regional identities through survey responses, surveys show that over time regional identities have increased in Spain. They have increased commensurate with the growth in regional parties, at least, that is, in those regions of Spain where regional parties are strongest. Comparing the results of surveys taken in 1996 and 2003, shows that the percentage of people who identify with only their region has increased the most in the following four regions: Balearic Islands (9 percent), Basque Country (8 percent), Catalonia (5 percent), and Navarra (6 percent) (CIS 1996, 2003). Of the seventeen regions in Spain depicted in Figure 4.6, regional parties have also grown the most in these four regions between 1996 and 2000, which are the two elections that fall between the 1996 and 2003 surveys.[70] Notably, prior to decentralization, regional parties had a very weak presence in the Balearic Islands, which was not a fervent advocate of autonomy during the transition period, even though the region is linguistically distinct.

Regional parties, particularly those from the Basque Country and Catalonia, have also demanded a significant amount of autonomy from the government in the post-transition period. In a few instances, they have even demanded outright independence. The chief demand of regional parties in the Basque Country and Catalonia has been for more fiscal autonomy, which has invariably threatened the poorer regions in the country. They have also demanded more political authority over the legal system and immigration, among other issues.

Statewide parties, for their part, have conceded to some of the regional parties' demands, but not all of them, and have tried to offset the negative consequences of greater fiscal autonomy for Spain's poorer regions with transfers and subsidies. In 1993, for example, PSOE signed an agreement with CiU at the national level of government. In exchange for its support of the government, PSOE agreed to cede 15 percent of the state's personal income taxes (IRPF), which is much less than CiU demanded. PSOE also formed an agreement with the Basque regional party PNV in 1993, which did not receive any concessions from the national government in return for its support.

In 1996, PP, the conservative rival to PSOE, signed an agreement with CiU and PNV in exchange for their support of the government elected in this year. As part of this agreement, the government raised the level of income taxes ceded to the regions to 30 percent and lowered the value-added tax (IVA) to 7 percent.[71] To counterbalance demands of the Basque Country and Catalonia with those of the poorer regions in Spain, PP did not grant the regional parties' original demand of 40 percent, and at the same time, granted additional subsidies to Andalusia to compensate for the financial losses it incurred as a result. PP also signed an agreement with the Canary Coalition (CC) this year in exchange for CC's support. In the agreement, PP promised to transfer to the Canary Islands all of the competencies it was due and to reduce unemployment and improve infrastructure on the islands.[72]

At times, regional parties in the Basque Country and Catalonia have also demanded the right to self-determination or independence. In 2004, regional parties revised the Basque Country's statute of autonomy to encompass the right to self-determination. The statute also established a completely separate legal system for the Basque Country, expanded its financial autonomy, and assumed the right to have direct foreign representation in the European Union. Statewide parties rejected the plan in the Spanish parliament although many of these same parties expressed a willingness to accept a more moderate reform of the Basque statute.

In 2005, Catalonia, led by the regional party ERC, also revised its statute of autonomy. In the statute, Catalonia not only referred to itself as a nation, but also assumed the right to self-determination. This statute also enlarged the competencies of the Catalan regional legislature, including control over tax collection. Ultimately, the national government, led by PSOE, passed a modified version of this statute in 2006, which enhanced Catalonia's authorities over taxation and judicial matters, as well as airports, ports, and immigration.

Some regional parties in the Basque Country have posed a further threat to the integrity of the country by supporting the separatist organization ETA in its campaign for Basque independence. The largest regional party in the region, PNV, does not explicitly support ETA today, though, and advocates building a dialog with the group to foster peace in the region. PNV broke off all official ties with ETA in 1987 and signed an agreement calling for an end to violence in the region. It did so, however, only after PSOE threatened to dissolve its coalition with PNV in the Basque regional parliament if PNV did not sign this agreement. This is yet another example of the moderating influence statewide parties have in Spain. Despite breaking off official ties with ETA, PNV has been reluctant to oppose ETA publicly. In 2004, for example, PNV along with EA and Ezker Batua-United Left (EB-IU) refused to support a monument dedicated to ETA's victims in the town of Llodio.

Today, the regional party Herri Batasuna is the party most closely associated with ETA. Batasuna has publicly defended ETA's actions. It has helped finance the organization by collecting the proceeds of a "revolutionary tax" businesses must pay if they do not want ETA to attack them, and has even used its party headquarters to store guns and ammunition for ETA. Due to Batasuna's association with ETA, the Spanish government temporarily suspended Batasuna in 2002 and banned the party permanently in 2003 – closing its offices, freezing its assets, and denying the party the right to compete in future elections. In 2002, three regional parties (i.e. PNV, EA, and EB-IU) passed an agreement rejecting the law suspending Batasuna. Prior to the ban, electoral support for Batasuna was also rather weak.

4.7. Impact of decentralization on the party system in Spain

Decentralization has played an important role in shaping Spain's party system. Although decentralization has encouraged the growth of regional parties, two features of decentralization have limited the extent to which decentralization has produced strong regional parties. The first is the distribution of seats among regions in Spain's national legislatures. The second is the method used to elect the upper house. It is not possible to study the effect of electoral sequencing in Spain since most national and regional elections are held nonconcurrently in the country.

Each of Spain's regions constitutes a relatively small proportion of the seats at the national level. Between 1977 and 2000, the average percentage of seats that a region comprised in the country's two national legislatures was 5 percent. The largest region in Spain over this period was Andalusia, which accounted for 16 percent of national legislative seats. Catalonia and the Basque Country made up about 10 and 6 percent, respectively. This aspect of decentralization discourages regional parties because it prevents them from governing on their own at the national level of government, although regional parties may still participate in the national government through coalitions.

The significant amount of vote splitting that occurs in Spain between national and regional elections speaks of the importance of governing with regard to regional party strength. It is very common for voters to cast their ballots for a regional party at the regional level of government and a statewide party at the national level. The prevalence of vote splitting is most dramatic in Andalusia and Valencia. Between 1980 and 1999, regional parties received slightly more than 50 percent of the vote on average in regional elections held in Andalusia and Valencia than in national elections held in these regions. Rarely does the reverse occur. The left-leaning United Aragon (CHA), however, won more votes in national elections than in regional ones held in 1996 and again in 1999, the same two years that the conservative PP triumphed in congressional elections.

Regional parties themselves have recognized the importance of governing to their electoral success. According to Manuel Silva, a CiU deputy, a key reason why his party wins more votes in regional elections than in national ones is "the *voto útil* in Catalonia."[73] Silva describes this as the belief that at the national level "the only useful vote is a vote for the PSOE or the PP" – the largest statewide parties in Spain.[74] Similarly, according to Iñaki Txueka of PNV, the reason that PNV wins more votes in Basque elections than in national elections is that "people feel that we have a tremendous responsibility to govern there [at the regional level], and give us the necessary strength to govern there. But, when one speaks of elections at the national level, the people know we are not going to govern there."[75]

The second feature of decentralization that has limited the presence of regional parties at the national level of government is the method used to elect Spain's national upper house. Citizens directly elect four-fifths of the Senate while regional legislatures elect the remaining one-fifth.[76] As expected, regional parties are weaker in the former than in the latter. Between 1980 and 2004, the percentage of seats that regional parties held in the indirectly directed part of the Senate is 4 percentage points greater than in the directly elected part. Figure 4.7 depicts the percentage of seats regional parties have won in each region of Spain over this period and in each aspect of the Senate. In only three regions have regional parties won more seats on average in the directly elected aspect of the Senate than the regionally elected one. The most dramatic differences between the two have occurred in the ethnolinguistically distinct region of the Balearic Islands, as well as the Canary Islands, which despite not being ethnically distinct has strong regional parties.

Given the fact, however, that regional legislatures elect only a small part of the Senate, this alternative method of electing the Senate has made little difference to the overall strength of regional parties at the national level of government in Spain.

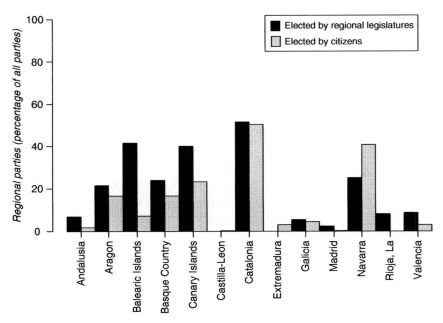

Figure 4.7. The percentage of seats held by regional parties in Spain's Senate by aspect, 1980–2004

Note: The graph excludes the following autonomous communities because they did not elect regional parties to the Senate in this period: Asturias, Cantabria, Castilla-La Mancha, and Murcia. The graph also omits Cueta and Mellila, which do not appoint Senators.

Source: http://www.senado.es/ Accessed: April 10, 2006.

The Senate is also less powerful than Spain's lower house, which further limits the influence of regional parties at this level. The Senate may initiate legislation on any matter and, together with the Congress, must approve all legislation in order for it to become law. When the two legislative bodies do not agree on a particular law, they create a joint commission that develops a new law on which both chambers vote. If both chambers still do not agree on the bill, the Congress can pass the bill or reject it without the approval of the Senate, as long as a majority of the Congress votes in favor of the bill (*Constitución Española de 1978*, Artículo 74.2).

The Senate also has a special committee dedicated to discussing matters related to the autonomous communities, known as the General Commission of the Autonomous Communities. The Commission, which is comprised of the heads of the regional governments, does not have any legislative power, however, and only meets once a year. This has sparked considerable criticism from scholars claiming that the government lacks an effective mechanism for integrating the autonomous communities within the national government (Gavela 1980; de Burgos 1983; Armet et al. 1988; Alberti 1991; Subirats 1998; Fossas 1999; Grau Creus 2000). Regardless, the Commission's lack of decision-making powers also limits the influence of regional parties within the national government.

4.8. Conclusion

The case of Spain further illustrates the role that regional parties play in promoting ethnic conflict and secessionism. This analysis, like the previous one of Czechoslovakia, highlights the ways in which regional parties promote regional identities and secessionism through legislation. It also demonstrates two additional mechanisms through which regional parties encourage secessionism, namely fostering regional identities and supporting separatist organizations – rhetorically as well as financially. This analysis also suggests a number of conditions under which regional parties are more likely to promote secessionism.

In this regard, the analysis, like that of Czechoslovakia, highlights the importance of democratic transitions. It also addresses the relevance of electoral competition among regional parties and legislative authorities. However, unlike in Czechoslovakia, in Spain regional parties could not block legislation on the country's new political system because regional legislatures had no veto power over the national constitution and were appointed based on national level representation. While regional parties have a stronger position in Spain's upper house than in its lower house, the legislative authority of the former is much weaker than that of the latter, further stressing the importance of legislative authority to regional party influence.

At the same time, this analysis of Spain sheds light on the role that statewide parties play in decentralizing countries, keeping regional parties in check and balancing the competing interests of regions against each other. In the transition era, statewide parties were particularly pivotal, balancing the demands of the historically distinct and wealthier regions for greater autonomy against the nondistinct and poorer regions. In the post-transition period, statewide parties have continued to play this role, and have even enticed regional parties to moderate their support for separatist groups. The analysis also demonstrates two reasons why statewide parties incorporate regional interests into their agendas, namely political ideology and electoral imperatives.

The Spanish case further demonstrates the importance of decentralization and the particular structure of decentralization in encouraging regional parties. The division of the country into many regions, each comprising only a small proportion of national legislative seats, inhibits regional parties. The indirect election of part of the upper house has the opposite effect. However, only one-fifth of the upper house is elected in this way. With so few regional elections occurring concurrently with national elections, it is difficult to tease out the effects of election concurrency in Spain.

While regional differences may be helpful in explaining why some regional parties have arisen in Spain, they cannot fully account for the structure of decentralization or the electoral strength of regional parties in the country. The national government, under the direction of statewide parties, extended autonomy to all regions in Spain whether or not they had strong regional parties. Regional parties and regional identities are not necessarily stronger, moreover, in those regions of Spain that have distinct ethnolinguistic identities and economic interests. The most significant growth in regional parties over time has occurred in regions where regional parties had very weak positions prior to decentralization. Even within the same region, regional parties have had stronger positions depending on the legislature in question. In the next chapter, I further develop these hypotheses about the structure of decentralization and the electoral strength of regional parties, and suggest why statewide parties in India have not reduced conflict and secessionism as well as statewide parties have done in Spain.

5

India

Decentralization has been neither an unabashed success in India, nor a resounding failure. Instead, India has experienced intermittent bouts of violence throughout its more than fifty-year history. These bouts have been more virulent in some regions of India than in others and more intense in certain periods of history than in others. Yet, throughout, India has remained united. In many ways, the relative stability of India is extraordinary given the hundreds of different ethnolinguistic and religious groups residing in the country, the sizeable economic disparities among them, and the presence of a rigid caste system dividing the country.

Decentralization's mixed track record is, I argue, due in large part to the country's party system and the behavior of statewide and regional parties within this system. In India, regional parties have promoted ethnic conflict and secessionism by passing legislation threatening other regions as well as regional minorities in the country. They have also mobilized groups to engage in ethnic conflict and secessionism and have supported extremist organizations involved in these activities. Statewide parties, for their part, have helped to reduce ethnic conflict and secessionism, although at times their actions have provoked them as well. Their behavior is attributable, in large part, to the weakness of certain conditions in India that encourage statewide parties to incorporate regional interests into their agendas. These conditions relate to how politically pivotal certain regions and groups are within India, the distribution of ethnolinguistic and religious groups throughout the country, the internal organization of statewide parties, and the leadership style of particular political leaders in the country.

Historically, regional parties have had a relatively small presence at the national level of government. Their presence has been increasing, however, since the collapse of the Congress Party in the 1990s and has always been greater in India's upper house than in its lower house. The position of regional parties at the national level is due largely to the division of India into many regions drawn along linguistic lines, each lacking the ability to control the national government on their own, and to the indirect election of India's upper house by its regional legislatures. Regional parties have a much stronger position at the subnational level, although the sequencing of national and regional elections does not seem to influence the strength of regional parties at this level. Lastly, while regional differences contribute to our understanding of regional parties, they cannot fully account for the strength of regional parties in India over time and within different contexts.

By way of elaborating on this argument, this chapter proceeds as follows. In Section 5.1, I briefly outline the most prominent examples of ethnic conflict and secessionism in India since the country's independence from the United Kingdom in 1947. In Section 5.2, I describe the institutional makeup of decentralization in India, and in Section 5.3, I present existing views about the utility of this system. In Section 5.4, I describe the shape of India's party system, and in Section 5.5, I discuss current perspectives on regional parties in India. In Section 5.6, I describe the impact of both statewide and regional parties on intrastate conflict, and in Section 5.7, I discuss the impact of decentralization on India's party system. In the final section, I present the implications of these findings for my argument about decentralization and political parties more generally.

5.1. Brief history of intrastate conflict in India

India is by far the largest country examined in depth in this study. Presently, India is divided into thirty-five regions, known as states or union territories, and is comprised of hundreds of different ethnolinguistic and religious groups.[77] Hindus are the largest religious group in India totalling about 81 percent of the population. Muslims are the next largest at about 13 percent.[78] Unlike many other groups in India, Muslims are widely dispersed throughout the country and form a majority in only one state, Jammu and Kashmir. Since 1956, India's internal borders have been drawn along linguistic lines so that one linguistic group forms a majority in each state or union territory. As a result, there are sizeable ethnolinguistic and religious minorities within each region. Differences along these dimensions are also crosscutting, meaning that people who belong to the same ethnolinguistic group in India often belong to a different religious group.

In India, the intensity of ethnic conflict and secessionism involving these groups has varied considerably over time.[79] In the following section, I briefly sketch the most prominent cases of these phenomena to provide a general picture of the strength and pervasiveness of both over time. I focus on conflict involving territorially concentrated groups because these are the only groups for which decentralization is theorized to reduce conflict. The cases presented herein are so complex that they merit books of their own.[80] I only describe the basic details of each case, however, to provide a backdrop for my argument regarding the effects of decentralization and regional parties on intrastate violence in India.

A number of conflicts erupted in India soon after the country gained independence from Great Britain in 1947. When India declared independence from the United Kingdom, the Nagas in the North East desired an independent state, but agreed to join India as long as they could become independent after ten years, or at least reevaluate their position within the state after this period. Rejecting this demand, the Indian government forcibly incorporated Nagaland into India. After several failed negotiations to resolve this issue, the conflict turned violent. The catalyst was a visit by Jawaharlal Nehru in 1952, which made it apparent that India was never going to grant Nagaland independence. Although the creation of a state of Nagaland within India in 1963 quelled violence in the region to a certain extent, the conflict is still raging today with more than 1,000 violent incidents occurring in the region between 2000 and 2004.[81] In 2006, the government made considerable headway toward reaching an agreement with the Naga insurgents, however.

The conflict in Tamil Nadu also arose immediately after India gained independence. It grew out of a series of failed attempts by the Indian government to impose Hindi on the country. Unlike the conflict in Nagaland, the conflict in Tamil Nadu is no longer active today. The Tamil separatist movement lost much of its support when India created the state of Tamil Nadu after reordering its internal borders along linguistic lines. Forming a majority in this newly created state, Tamils were able to pass laws protecting their language and other interests. The conflict flared up in the 1960s, but only temporarily, when the government declared Hindi the only official language of India. Today, the Indian government maintains two official languages, Hindi and English, and constitutionally recognizes a number of other languages, of which Tamil is one.

The Mizo conflict, in contrast, did not emerge until the 1960s. It arose out of concerns that the Assamese government did not provide adequate relief to the Mizo people during the 1959–60 famine, and threatened the distinct ethnic and religious identity of the Mizos, who are predominantly East Asian Christians. Under the Mizo Accord (1986), the government gave the Mizos their own state, known as Mizoram, with extensive financial subsidies from the government. Although the accord largely resolved the conflict between the Mizos and the Assamese, the new state of Mizoram is currently embroiled in a new conflict between the Mizos and Reangs. The Reangs, who belong to a tribe of Kau Bru-speaking Hindus, have accused the Mizos of trying to assimilate Reangs into the Mizo culture and of executing brutal attacks against them. Despite this conflict, Mizoram is relatively peaceful today.

Conflicts occurring in four other regions in India, namely Assam, Tripura, Punjab, as well as Jammu and Kashmir, erupted much later in India's history. Violence in Assam arose in the 1970s due to a massive influx of Bangladeshi Muslims into the region, which threatened the cultural and political power of the Assamese. These immigrants spoke a different language than the Assamese and supported different political parties than them as well. In response, the Assamese government declared Assamese the only official language in the region. It also made Assamese mandatory in schools and excluded immigrants from voting. The government's policies ignited conflict not only between the Muslim immigrants and the Assamese, but also between the Assamese and the Bodos, who are a non-Assamese speaking minority in the region. Similar concerns precipitated a violent secessionist movement in Tripura in 1980s. Tripuras are a group of Tibet-Burma tribes who speak the Kok-Barak language and felt threatened by Bengali immigrants who displaced Tripuras from their lands. Assam and Tripura are two of the most war-torn regions in India today, with nearly 2,000 violent incidents occurring in each between 2000 and 2004.[82]

In contrast to the Assamese and Tripuran conflicts, the conflict in Punjab, which emerged in the 1980s, has largely been resolved. Prior to its emergence, Sikhs demanded more autonomy for Punjab and a redrawing of the region's borders along linguistic lines to enhance their representation within India. Sikhs did not demand independence or use violence to achieve their goals, that is, until the 1980s, when a number of separatist groups demanding an independent Sikh state called Khalistan arose. Violence in Punjab culminated in the Indian Army storming the Golden Temple in Amritsar in 1984. The Army raided the temple in order to expel Sikh insurgents seeking refuge within the temple's confines. Following this event, the Indian government and Punjab signed an agreement to resolve the situation, known as the Rajiv–Longowal Accord. Although the government never actually implemented this agreement, violence in Punjab effectively ended in the 1990s because the Indian government used its superior military power to suppress the insurgents.[83]

The most virulent conflict in India, which is still active today, is the conflict in Jammu and Kashmir. It is distinct from those in the rest of the country because it involves another country, Pakistan. India and Pakistan have gone to war with each other several times over competing claims to the region. Despite these wars, conflict did not erupt among the people of Jammu and Kashmir until 1989. The precipitating event was the rigging of elections in Jammu and Kashmir in 1987, which resulted in the defeat of the Muslim United Force (MUF) and has since sparked demands for an independent Kashmiri state (or the reunification of Kashmir with Pakistan).[84] More than 30,000 people are estimated to have died in Jammu and Kashmir since 1989. Over time, the conflict in Jammu and Kashmir has worsened progressively both in terms of the level of violence in the region as well as the number of people immersed in the conflict. Interestingly, although Muslims in Kashmir support this conflict, Muslims in the rest of the country do not, fearing that the Kashmiri conflict may intensify Hindu nationalism in the rest of the country.

5.2. Structure of decentralization in India

India has been decentralized since gaining its independence in 1947. Its national level of government is comprised of an upper house, known as the Council of States (Rajya Sabha), and a lower house, known as the House of People (Lok Sabha). India's regional level of government is comprised of two types of regions – states and union territories. The former have decision-making authorities while the latter have only administrative authorities. Election timing varies at this level as well, with some regions holding certain elections concurrently with national elections and others not. Between levels of government, decision-making authority is divided somewhat extensively, although a number of features of decentralization undermine subnational authority in practice.

5.2.1. Division of political authority in India

India's national government has exclusive control over ninety-seven political issues while the regional legislatures (Vidhan Sabhas) have exclusive or joint control over sixty-six issues that address the political, social, and economic concerns of the states.[85] According to India's Constitution, the national government has authority over issues that the state governments do not control either exclusively or jointly with the national government.[86] Today, however, the national government no longer has jurisdiction over residuary powers. Following the recommendation of the Sarkaria Commission, convened in 1983, the national and state governments now share control over residuary powers.[87] Prior to accepting this recommendation, the two shared control over forty-seven issue areas.[88]

This division of decision-making authority is asymmetric, meaning that not all regions in India have the same decision-making powers. Besides the fact that union territories, unlike states, have no decision-making power, several states in India have authority over more issues than other states. In addition to the authorities guaranteed to all states, some states (e.g. Assam, Andhra Pradesh, Arunachal Pradesh, Goa, Gujarat, Maharashtra, Manipur, Mizoram, Nagaland, and Sikkim) have authority over other issues, such as education, civil service, justice, law and order, land ownership, and religion, according to Article 371 of the Constitution of India.[89]

In principle, the state of Jammu and Kashmir also has special decision-making authorities. As part of its accession agreement with India, Jammu and Kashmir retained control over all political, social, and economic issues in the region, with the exception of defense, foreign affairs, and communication. Article 370 of India's Constitution solidified this agreement, allowing Jammu and Kashmir to legislate on any matter over which states have either exclusive or joint control, as long as the President of India believes that this matter corresponds to the region's Instrument of Accession.[90] The Indian government, though, has significantly curtailed Jammu and Kashmir's autonomy over time in ways that I will describe subsequently in this chapter.

Besides directly reducing state authorities, the national government exerts influence over all states in India through President's

Rule and gubernatorial appointments. Under Articles 356 and 357 of India's Constitution, the President of India may suspend India's regional legislatures if they do not comport themselves in accordance with the constitution, a practice known as President's Rule.[91] The national government also controls gubernatorial appointments through which it can exert influence over state legislatures. Regional governors have considerable power in India. Not only can they appoint the chief ministers of their states, but they can also dismiss regional assemblies at their own discretion, approve bills into law, send bills for consideration to the President of India (who has the power to promulgate ordinances), and recommend the invocation of President's Rule.

5.2.2. Division of fiscal power in India

Fiscal authority is also divided between India's national and subnational levels of government. Almost half of India's total government expenditure is spent at the subnational level of government, as Figure 5.1 illustrates. Most of this expenditure is derived from national government transfers to the regions in the form of grants and loans. These transfers are based predominantly on the population and income of the regions. As a result, richer regions tend to receive more transfers from the national government than poorer ones (Bhargava 1984; Chhibber 1995, 1999; Rao 1998). One of the two agencies responsible for allocating national grants and transfers, namely the Planning Commission (the Finance Commission is the other), also takes into consideration the ability of regions to meet national objectives.[92] In this way, fiscally prudent regions tend to receive more grants from the national government than fiscally imprudent ones. India, unlike Spain, does not have a system to equalize regional disparities.

The subnational level of government may also generate its own revenue as is evident from Figure 5.2. The amount of revenue generated at this level (as a percentage of total revenue) has hovered between 30 and 40 percent since 1963. According to some scholars, the somewhat limited revenue generating abilities of

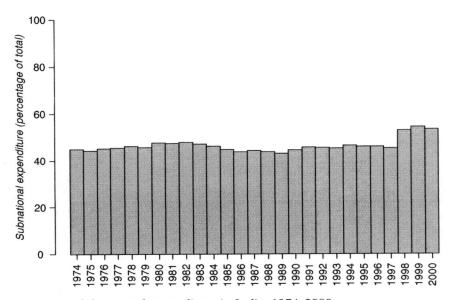

Figure 5.1. Subnational expenditure in India, 1974–2000

Source: For 1974–97, see IMF (2001). For 1998–2000, see Ministry of Finance (1998–2000).

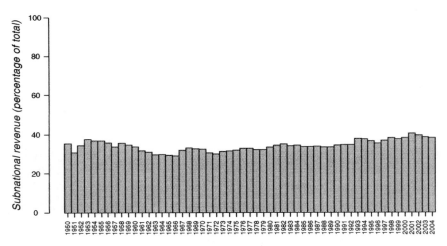

Figure 5.2. Subnational revenue in India, 1950–2004

Source: Ministry of Finance (2006–7).

these legislatures have undermined their independence from the national government (Pal 1984; Narula 1999).

5.3. Competing views of decentralization in India

Perspectives on how effective decentralization is in reducing ethnic conflict and secessionism in India are greatly divided. In part, this may be due to India's mixed track record in reducing both phenomena. A number of scholars claim that decentralization reduces ethnic conflict and secessionism (Lijphart 1996; Manor 1998) and suggest that decentralization could reduce both even further were it more extensive (Pal 1984; Ganguly 1996; Tremblay 1996, 1997; Manor 1998; Widmalm 1998; Narula 1999). They argue that decentralization has achieved this result by creating state legislatures that engage groups in politics and offer them control over their own political, social, and economic affairs. In the words of James Manor, "the existence of so many opportunities to capture at least some power persuades parties and politicians to remain engaged with elections and logrolling, even when they are defeated in some arenas" (1998: 23). Only certain ethnolinguistic groups, however, are able to manage their own affairs because they constitute a majority within a particular state.

Some scholars also claim that decentralization reduces intrastate violence by preventing conflicts from spilling over from one area of a country to another (Hardgrave 1994; Manor 1998). Decentralization is supposed to quarantine conflicts by directing the demands of groups to the regional level of government instead of the national level. This, in turn, allows the national government to maneuver between opposing groups while seeming to stand outside of the conflict (Manor 1998). Decentralization's utility in this respect is limited, however, since many important and contentious issues in India are not directed at the states but at the national government, including demands for more political and fiscal autonomy. Conflicts between Hindus and Muslims are not, moreover, confined to the states since Hindus and Muslims are dispersed throughout India.

Many other scholars argue, in contrast, that decentralization actually contributes to intrastate violence in India. They suggest that decentralization has this effect by reinforcing regional identities and whetting the appetite of groups for more and more autonomy until they finally demand complete independence (Pal 1984; Agarwal 1997; Singh 1997). Some scholars even contend that a more extensive form of decentralization would provoke conflict and secessionism even further. According to U. C. Agarwal, "if the states are made semi-independent, the country's political solidarity and national unity may greatly suffer" (1984: 34). Meanwhile, Chandra Pal believes that "overcentralisation as much as excessive autonomy would lead to fissiparous tendencies and hamper national integration" (1984: 74). The key, I argue, to reconciling these views and explaining the seemingly disparate effects of decentralization in India, rests in the shape of India's party system, which is the subject I turn to next.

5.4. Party system in postcolonial India

In order to understand why India's party system has played a pivotal role in this regard, it is first necessary to understand the shape of India's party system, both in terms of the types of parties that define the system, as well as their relative strength over time. Statewide parties have dominated national politics since India's first elections in 1952. For most of India's history one statewide party, the Congress Party, has controlled politics at the national level. With its decline in the early 1990s, the presence of regional parties at this level of government has grown. The Congress Party's hold on the country resulted from a unique confluence of factors due in large part to the party's power prior to India's independence and its ability to capitalize on its power in the post-independence period (Weiner 1967).

Still, regional parties account for only a moderate share of the vote at this level. In the first national elections ever held in India, regional parties accounted for almost 7 percent of the vote in the lower house. Almost fifty years later, they won about 11 percent of the vote. Figure 5.3 illustrates the electoral strength of regional parties in India's lower house between 1952 and 1999.

While the overall presence of regional parties in the lower house is moderate, regional parties have had a stronger presence in some regions of India than in others. To illustrate this, Figure 5.4 breaks down India's lower house election results by region.[93] As this graph demonstrates, regional parties have had their strongest showing in Sikkim, where they have won more than 60 percent of the vote on average. They have won more than 20 percent of the vote in eight other regions in India, and about 15 percent or more in four other regions. Their presence is notably smaller in the rest of India.

Although the overall presence of regional parties in the lower house is moderate, regional parties have participated in the

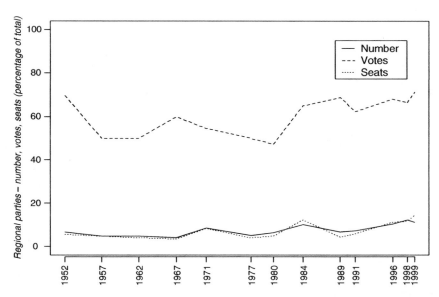

Figure 5.3. The electoral strength of regional parties in elections to India's House of People, 1952–99

Source: Singh and Bose (1986) and the Election Commission of India (1991, 1996, 1998, 1999).

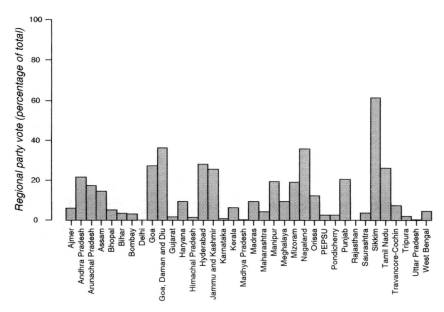

Figure 5.4. Regional party vote in elections to India's House of People by region, 1952–99

Source: Singh and Bose (1986) and the Election Commission of India (1991, 1996, 1998, 1999). The graph omits the following states and union territories because regional parties won 0 percent of the vote within them: Andaman and Nicobar Islands, Chandigarh, Coorg, Dadra and Nagar Haveli, Daman and Diu, Kutch, Laccadive, Lakshadweep, Madhya Bharat, Minicoy and Amindivi Islands, Mysore, and Vindhya Pradesh.

national government on several occasions (Nayar 1986; Singh 1998). Generally, these governments have been short-lived and on more than one occasion, they have fallen due to irreconcilable differences between statewide and regional parties. Regional parties participated in the 1989 National Front government, which was formed when the Congress Party failed to win a legislative majority because of corruption charges leveled against Rajiv Gandhi.[94] The National Front government collapsed eleven months after assuming office with the resignation of Prime Minister V. P. Singh. A new National Front government was subsequently installed and a new prime minister, Chandra Sekhar, was elected. Five months later, this government also fell when the Congress Party withdrew its support.

Regional parties also participated in the 1996 United Front government. In this year, another statewide party, the Bharatiya Janata Party (BJP), won a legislative plurality in the lower house and formed a government on its own. Lacking a majority, the BJP government resigned after only thirteen days in office. To prevent the BJP from forming a new government, a group of thirteen statewide and regional parties formed a coalition known as the United Front. This coalition, externally supported by the Congress Party, contained four regional parties: Asom Gana Parishad (AGP), Dravida Munnetra Kazhagam (DMK), Tamil Maanila Congress (TMC), and Telugu Desam Party (TDP). The government, led by H. D. Deve Gowda, was also short-lived. After seven months in office, the coalition collapsed when the Congress Party withdrew its support because the government refused to oust the DMK from the coalition. At this time, the DMK was implicated in the assassination of Rajiv Gandhi by the Sri Lankan terrorist organization, the Liberation Tigers of Tamil Eelam.

The subsequent BJP-led government composed of seventeen political parties, many of which were regional parties, lasted only thirteen months in office. It fell after a regional party from Tamil Nadu, the All-India Anna Dravida Munnetra Kazhagam (AIADMK) party, which held only one seat in the government, withdrew its support from the government. It did so because of differences between its own position on caste reservations and that of the government's, among other things. After new elections were held in 1999, the third election in little more than three years, the BJP formed a new government with twenty-four other political parties, many of which were also regional parties. The new government, known as the National Democratic Alliance (NDA), completed its full term but came close to collapsing on several occasions. In 2001 the Samata Party threatened to remove its support from the government because the BJP failed to support it in a vote of confidence in Manipur. New elections held in 2004 brought to power another coalition of statewide and regional parties, led by the Congress Party and known as the United Progressive Alliance (UPA), which has remained in power despite regional parties withdrawing support from the government.

Regional parties have had a slightly stronger presence in India's upper house than its lower house. From 1952 to 1999, almost 14 percent of the candidates elected by the regional legislatures to India's upper house were regional parties as Figure 5.5 illustrates. Their presence was strongest in Nagaland and Goa, where regional parties accounted for more than 25 percent of the representatives on average, followed by Arunachal Pradesh, Meghalaya, and Tamil Nadu. In these states, regional parties accounted for just less than 20 percent of the representatives. Their presence was weakest in Bombay where regional parties accounted for less than 1 percent of the representatives.

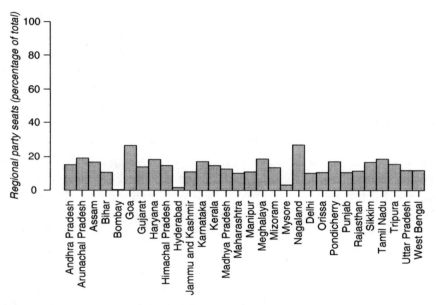

Figure 5.5. Regional parties elected to India's Council of States by the state assemblies, 1952–99

Source: Rajya Sabha. http://rajyasabha.gov.in/ Accessed April 10, 2006.

Overall, regional parties have had a much stronger presence in India's regional legislatures than either of its national legislatures. Figure 5.6 illustrates the strength of regional parties at this level of government between 1977 and 1998. Over this period, regional parties accounted for about 15 percent of the vote on average.

They garnered much more support in certain regions of India than in others, winning over 45 percent of the vote in some regions (e.g. Jammu and Kashmir, Meghalaya, and Sikkim) and a very small percentage of votes in others (e.g. Delhi, Himachal Pradesh, Madhya Pradesh, Pondicherry, and West Bengal).

Regional parties have also governed more often at the regional level of government than at the national level. Prior to 1967, the Congress Party controlled every regional legislature in India. In 1967, however, the Congress Party lost power in a number of legislatures. Despite Congress splitting in 1969, though, the party regained

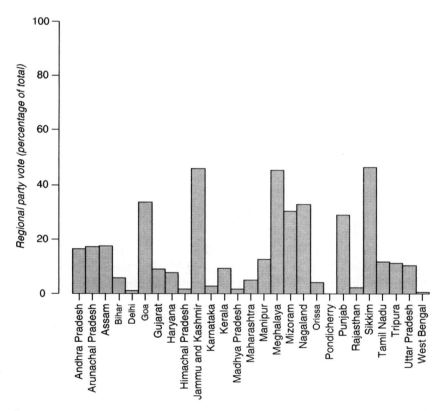

Figure 5.6. Regional party vote in elections to India's state assemblies by region, 1977–98

Source: Election Commission of India. http://www.eci.gov.in/ Accessed April 10, 2006.

power over most of India's state assemblies in 1972, due in part to India's victory over Pakistan in the Indo-Pak War of 1971.[95] Since this time, regional parties have controlled many regional legislatures in India, which has had significant consequences for the country.

5.5. Origins of regional parties in India

The role that regional parties play in Indian politics is highly debated, with some suggesting that regional parties have had a positive impact on the country – improving representation and increasing participation (Banerjee 1984; Bhatnagar and Kumar 1988a), and with others suggesting they have had a negative impact by destabilizing the national government and dividing people (Gopa 1986; Singh 1998). Despite these divergent views, scholars largely agree that regional parties are products of the underlying ethnolinguistic and religious differences in India (Bhatnagar and Kumar 1988a; Biswas 1992; Dutta 1992; Sengupta 1992; Dutta 1998; Pai 1998; Seshia 1998; Singh 1998; Thandavan 1998; Suresh 2000; Arora 2002; Hasan 2002; Sridharan 2002). Epitomizing this view, Satyavan Bhatnagar and Pradeep Kumar claim that regional parties are a "natural consequence of the operation of the democratic system based on adult franchise in a multi-ethnic, multi-racial, multi-religious and multi-linguistic society like India" (1988b: vii).

Given, however, the hundreds of different ethnolinguistic and religious groups in India, an understanding of political parties based solely on these differences would suggest that regional parties would have an even greater presence in India than they actually have. Acknowledging this, Pradeep Chhibber and John Petrocik remark that India's "salient and highly charged social divisions seem to play an insignificant role in determining party preference" (1989: 193). Regional parties do not have a larger presence in India because parties choose to politicize certain differences over others based on whichever will maximize their electoral advantage (Widmalm 1998; Hasan 2002). In this way, parties also influence whether or not cleavages are crosscutting. As Zoya Hasan notes, "India's diversity yields a variety of social differences, and these differences can form the basis of very different kinds of parties and distinct party systems at the national and state levels depending upon the patterns of political mobilization and organization" (2002: 21).

Further evidence that ascriptive characteristics do not singularly determine the strength of regional parties in India rests in the behavior of both over time and space. The ethnolinguistic and religious composition of India's regions has not changed much over time since India redrew its borders along linguistic lines in 1956. Yet, the strength of regional parties has grown considerably over time at the national and regional levels of government. Regional parties are also stronger in some regions of India than in others, even though all states and union territories in the country have been composed of a single ethnolinguistic majority group and various minority groups since 1956.

Regional parties have also won more votes in certain legislatures of India than in others, even within the same region of the country. Regional parties, for example, earned a larger share of seats in India's upper house than its lower house in Karnataka, Meghalaya, Pondicherry, and Tripura, and a much smaller proportion in Jammu and Kashmir, Punjab, and Sikkim.[96] Regional parties have also won a notably larger proportion of the vote at the regional level of government than at the national level (lower house) in Jammu and Kashmir, Meghalaya, and Mizoram, and a smaller proportion in Manipur, Sikkim, and Tamil Nadu.[97] Only by looking at decentralization, and particular features of decentralization, can one explain these phenomena more fully.

5.6. Role of the party system in intrastate conflict in India

India's party system has had a major influence on the ebbs and flows of ethnic conflict and secessionism in the country. As expected, regional parties have had a negative effect on both phenomena – threatening regional minorities legislatively, using armed conflict to fight for autonomy or independence, and supporting extremist organizations engaged in these activities. Statewide parties have had a much better, but still insufficiently good, effect on conflict and secessionism. In India, statewide parties are poorly incentivized to reduce ethnic conflict and secessionism because of the absence of certain conditions that encourage statewide parties to incorporate regional interests into their agendas. In this section, I address the role of both types of political parties on the incidence of ethnic conflict and secessionism. Since it is impossible to examine every instance of their behavior, I highlight here only some of the more significant ones, which demonstrate the different ways in which these parties have had an effect on ethnic conflict and secessionism, as discussed earlier in this chapter.

A critical way in which regional parties have undermined the effectiveness of decentralization in reducing intrastate conflict in India is by adopting legislation that threatens regional minorities. Regional parties have done so in a number of ways. They have discriminated against regional minorities by denying them certain rights or privileges in their own languages, including education, civil service examinations, and other government publications. They have also infringed on the rights of non-Hindu minorities by imposing bans on the slaughter of cows, which are sacred in the Hindu religion. They have even adopted policies that harm the economic integrity of regional minorities by unduly favoring regional majorities.

Their effects in this respect are acutely apparent in Jammu and Kashmir. Here regional parties have pursued policies harmful to regional minorities in a number of ways. The National Conference (NC) party, which has historically been the largest regional party in Jammu and Kashmir, is a major offender in this regard. NC, which draws most of its support from Kashmir, favors Kashmiri Muslims over others living in the Jammu and Ladakh districts of the region. The inhabitants of Jammu are mostly Hindus, who speak the Dogri language, while the inhabitants of Ladakh are mostly Buddhists, who speak the Tibetan language. NC has supported redistricting schemes favoring Muslims in government office and restricting the religious practices of non-Muslims. It has also supported policies that overrepresent Kashmiris in public sector employment and neglect the economic development of Jammu and Ladakh.

The People's Democratic Party (PDP), another prominent regional party in Jammu and Kashmir, has also threatened the economic well-being of non-Kashmiris in India. It has done so by preventing women who marry non-Kashmiris from passing on immovable property to their husbands and children. Known commonly as the Daughter's Bill (2004), this policy was intended to prevent an influx of immigrants into Jammu and Kashmir and preserve Muslim culture in the region. The policy was never adopted, however, because the Congress Party broke ranks with its coalition partner, the PDP, voting against the bill in the regional assembly, thus offering a glimpse into the role that statewide parties play in keeping regional parties in check.

In many cases, the actions of regional parties in Jammu and Kashmir and elsewhere have prompted violence by provoking regional minorities to action (Wilkinson 2004). In Assam, for example, attempts to declare Assamese the only official language in the region and make it mandatory in schools led to the creation of extremist groups representing the Muslim and Bodo minorities in the region. Attempts to restrict the voting rights of immigrants also prompted the rise of these groups in Assam. The general mistreatment of Bengalis, not to mention the blunt attempts to expel them from the region, has similarly given rise to terrorist organizations in Tripura.

In India, regional parties have also mobilized groups to attack others and fight for independence. The All-Parties Hurriyat Conference (APHC) has tried to mobilize public opinion in Jammu and Kashmir against Indian security forces in the region. It has also organized numerous strikes and boycotts in the region to rally support for independence. The DMK has likewise used violence to achieve its goals in Tamil Nadu. In the past, these goals included independence, but now they focus on greater autonomy for Tamil Nadu within India. The Mizo National Front (MNF) has also caused tremendous violence and destruction in Assam in its attempt to achieve an independent Mizo state, and has trained and supplied the Tripura National Volunteers (TNV), which seeks an independent Tripuri state.

In 1986, though, the MNF stopped assisting the TNV when it signed the Mizo Accord. As part of this agreement, the MNF renounced the use of violence in exchange for the creation of a Mizo state within India. TNV is now a regional party contesting elections in Tripura. It recently merged with the Indigenous People's Front of Tripura (IPFT), which is backed by the terrorist organization, the National Liberation Front of Tripura (NLFT). The NLFT has intimidated voters into supporting the IPFT in elections for the Tripura Tribal Autonomous District Council (TTADC), forced voters at gunpoint to vote for the IPFT, and entered polling booths to ensure that voters cast their ballots in favor of the IPFT. The NLFT has also threatened and kidnapped opposition candidates to prevent them from running against the IPFT.

Regional parties in Assam have similarly supported separatist organizations. Many AGP party members have been linked to the United Liberation Front of Assam (ULFA). Supposedly, members of the Assamese police forces have also been trained in ULFA camps and have tipped off ULFA members about raids on their camps. Despite political pressure from the Indian government, the AGP has been reluctant to crack down on the ULFA. In pursuit of its goal, the ULFA has bombed crude oil pipelines, freight trains, and government buildings, in hopes of achieving independence by crippling Assam's economy. It has also assassinated prominent people representing India's political and business interests in Assam and those opposed to an independent Assamese state.

The Congress Party, in contrast, as a statewide party, has helped reduce ethnic conflict and secessionism by incorporating the interests of different regions into their agenda, as well as those of different ethnicities, languages, tribes, religions, and castes, which vary from state to state (Chhibber and Petrocik 1989; Candland 1997; Heath and Yadav 2002). In so doing, the Congress Party has capitalized on the crosscutting nature of ethnolinguistic and religious differences in India, which is supposed to reduce the potential for conflict and secessionism in India and create an all-encompassing national identity (Brass 1974; Manor 1998; Seshia 1998; Varshney 1998, 2001; Singh 2000).

The Congress Party has actively incorporated regional interests into its agenda in a number of ways. The first, and perhaps the most important way, is through the creation of a decentralized system of government following India's independence from Great Britain. The Congress Party played a principal role in decentralizing India prior to the country's first elections. It rejected the United Kingdom's initial attempts to impose a limited form of freedom and decentralization on the country and established a more extensive one, although ultimately the system of government India adopted was not as decentralized as the one intended prior to Pakistan's independence. Nevertheless, the Congress Party also signed an accession agreement with Jammu and Kashmir granting it significant autonomy.[98] While regional differences may have contributed to India's decision to decentralize, regional parties did not play a role in the decentralization process. They had a very weak presence in India at the time. Regional parties did not influence the design of the political system either. The system was designed to resemble the one established in India under British colonial rule through the 1935 India Act. The British established a decentralized system of government in India at this time to efficiently administer control over its expansive colony (Bombwal 1967).

Subsequently, statewide parties, like the Congress Party, have addressed regional concerns in a number of ways. One way is by redrawing India's internal borders. In 1956, the Congress Party agreed to redraw India's regional borders along linguistic lines to improve the representation of linguistic groups in the regional legislatures. Congress did so despite its own concerns that redrawing the state borders would increase secessionism in India.[99] In 1971, the Congress Party also signed the North Eastern Areas (Reorganization) Act, which gave either union territory or state status to a number of areas in the North East. More recently, the BJP supported the creation of three new states in India to address some groups' concerns that their political influence at the regional level of government was limited. These new states are Chhattisgarh, Uttaranchal, and Jharkhand, which previously formed parts of Madhya Pradesh, Uttar Pradesh, and Bihar, respectively.

Statewide parties have also negotiated a number of agreements to end regional conflicts in India. To resolve the conflict in Assam, the Congress Party signed the Illegal Migrants Act (1983) and the Assam Accord (1985). The Illegal Migrants Act tried to eliminate the arbitrary expulsion of immigrants from Assam by establishing tribunals to decide their legal status on a case-by-case basis. The Assam Accord stated that only those people who came to Assam between 1966 and 1971 would be disenfranchised for a period of ten years after which they could become citizens, and that anyone who entered Assam after this period would be deported. In 1993, it also signed the Bodo Accord, which established a separate Bodoland Autonomous Council (BAC) in Assam. Earlier in 1985, the Congress signed the Rajiv–Longowal Accord to end the conflict in Punjab. Among other things, the agreement offered restitution to Punjabis for losses suffered during the conflict. It also called for the transfer of Chandigarh to Punjab and established a tribunal to resolve disputes over certain waterways between Punjab and Haryana. The accord has never been fully implemented.

At the national level, the Congress Party, as well as the BJP, have both formed coalitions with regional parties since the 1990s, through which they have incorporated regional interests into their agendas. The efforts of the Congress Party in this regard are most apparent in the Common Minimum Programme (CMP), which the party signed along with its regional coalition partners in 2004. In the CMP, the government made significant concessions to the regions – promising to declare Tamil a classical language, elevate other languages potentially to official languages, and affirming its commitment to state and local autonomy, especially in Jammu and Kashmir, as well as to the National Development Council (NDC), which plays an important role in development planning in India. At the same time, the coalition also pledged to combat terrorism in the North East, protect minority interests, and redress regional economic inequalities.

Some regional parties have accused the government, however, of not fulfilling its pledges. Sharing this opinion, the Marumalarchi Dravida Munnetra Kazhagam (MDMK) withdrew its support from the government in 2007. The Congress Party, as a result, has viewed the support of its regional allies with skepticism. According to Prime Minister Manmohan Singh, "Sometimes, the resolution of problems acquires an excessively political hue, and narrow political considerations, based on regional or sectional loyalties and ideologies, can distort the national vision and sense of wider collective purpose."[100] Earlier in 2006, Singh suspended privatization initiatives because of opposition from the Left Front and its regional coalition partner, DMK, in Tamil Nadu. Tamil Nadu is home to one of the major firms slated for privatization. The previous BJP-led coalition government came under similar criticism.

As the previous discussion of national-level coalitions suggests, despite its status as a statewide party, the Congress Party has not fully incorporated regional interests into its agenda, and at times, its actions have even prompted ethnic conflict and secessionism. The more fully the Congress Party has incorporated regional interests, however, the better able it has been to reduce ethnic conflict and secessionism. As Atul Kohli remarks, "[T]he more accommodating the ruling strategy, the more likely it is that self-determination movements will traverse the shape of an inverse U-curve: they will first rise because it is 'natural' for them to do so in the political context of developing country democracies…but, later, after a more or less prolonged period of power negotiation with the central state, they will inevitably decline in intensity as exhaustion sets in and some compromise is reached" (1998: 12). Along similar lines, Steven Wilkinson argues that parties are more likely to use government police forces to squelch violence against regional minorities when parties rely on these minorities for electoral support (2004).

The failure of statewide parties to better accommodate regional interests is attributable, at least in part, to the structure of India's political system, the nature of its demographic makeup, the internal organization of statewide parties, and the leadership style of particular statewide leaders. The first factor concerns how pivotal particular regions and regional minorities are in the country. With so many regions in India and so many groups within these regions, many are too small to offer a real electoral incentive to statewide parties to incorporate their interests. Many regional minorities are also confined to particular regions of India so that statewide parties can ignore the interests of these minorities at the regional level without jeopardizing their support in other regions of the country.

According to Wilkinson (2004), an important factor that increases the electoral relevance of particular minority groups in India is the competitiveness of elections. The more competitive elections are, he argues, the more pivotal minorities become and the more incentive parties have to protect minorities against violence perpetrated by others. In very heterogeneous districts, first-past-the-post systems, like India's, may facilitate this process. Since only one party can win a seat in each district of this system, parties have an incentive to incorporate multiple ethnolinguistic groups into their agendas within heterogeneous districts to secure an electoral plurality (Horowitz 1985).

If ethnolinguistic or religious groups are widely dispersed, statewide parties can compete throughout a country while representing only one group in the country, as the BJP has done. This situation is particularly prone to intrastate conflict although neither is inevitable in this context (Giuliano 2000; Chandra 2005). The BJP has promoted ethnic conflict by espousing pro-Hindu policies, razing a Muslim mosque, advocating a uniform civil code, and blocking greater autonomy in Jammu and Kashmir, among other things. This fact, however, does not pose a challenge to the argument offered here since this analysis seeks to understand the conditions under which decentralization is more or less effective in reducing ethnic conflict and secessionism among territorially concentrated groups. Decentralization is not theorized to reduce conflict among widely dispersed groups, like Muslims outside of

Jammu and Kashmir. Furthermore, regardless of whether a system of government is decentralized or not, statewide parties can promote ethnic conflict in this way. Decentralization, that is, does not provide statewide parties with any more, or any fewer incentives, than centralization to incorporate a single ethnic or religious group into their agendas when ethnic or religious groups are dispersed throughout a country.

In addition to the size and dispersion of groups throughout India, another factor that undermines the extent to which any one region in India is pivotal to the ability of statewide parties to govern is the weakness of democracy in the country. Jammu and Kashmir is not pivotal because the Congress Party suspended elections in the region until 1957 and rigged subsequent elections so that its regional ally, the National Conference (NC), could come to power. Beginning with the Application to Jammu and Kashmir in 1954, the Congress Party has also undermined Jammu and Kashmir's accession agreement. According to this law, the national government does not have to consult with the region's assembly before legislating on any matter over which it has exclusive or joint control. Today, the national government may legislate on any issue not exclusively assigned to Jammu and Kashmir.

Statewide parties have also abused certain constitutional provisions, such as President's Rule, to maintain power within regions without fully incorporating their interests. Although President's Rule was only intended for cases of internal disturbances, statewide parties have abused their authority, invoking President's Rule for partisan reasons (Dua 1985; Tummala 1992; Iyer 1999; Khanna 1999; Sen 1999). The President of India invoked this law ninety times in India between 1947 and 2001. President's Rule, as Krishna Iyer colorfully relates, "has been invoked with anathematic frequency and callous unconscionability, so much so, that state autonomy, the very life-breath of federal polity, has been the plaything of infantile adventurism and political expediency by central Moghuls" (Iyer 1999: 58).

Statewide parties have also utilized their control over gubernatorial appointments to maintain their power and influence over regional governments without fully incorporating regional interests into their agendas. At the helm of the national government, statewide parties, and the Congress Party in particular, have appointed members of their own party to governorships even if their party was not the majority party in the regional legislature. In turn, these governors have appointed chief ministers who are party loyalists. Through these governors, statewide parties have exerted influence on legislation issued at this level of government, preventing legislation from being adopted that contradicts their goals.

Sometimes these governors have even disbanded governments and dismissed regional legislatures to advance the position of their own parties. What is perhaps most alarming is that governors sometimes reported to the national government that their states were not following constitutional principles, even though they were, so that the national government could invoke President's Rule in the region. The most recent incidence of gubernatorial appointments to raise concerns in this regard is the national government's dismissal of the Bihar legislature in 2006 and its appointment of Buta Singh as governor. Singh was appointed to prevent Nitish Kumar of the Janata Dal (United) from coming to power. Public outrage at this event led Singh to resign his post the same year.

At an even more fine-grained level of analysis, another factor that influences the extent to which statewide parties incorporate regional interests into their agendas and reduce ethnic conflict and secessionism is the internal structure of parties and the leadership style of particular party leaders. Jawaharlal Nehru, by all accounts, was more supportive of regional interests than other prime ministers in India (Kothari 2002). Nehru was the prime minister who signed the accession agreement with Jammu and Kashmir, giving the region extensive control over its political, social, and economic affairs. Nehru also redrew the country's regional borders along linguistic lines despite his own reservations that this would increase secessionist sentiment in the country.

Indira Gandhi, on the other hand, was arguably the least supportive of regional interests. Gandhi had a very centralized leadership style. Under her, the upper echelons of the party made major policy decisions with little involvement from the lower levels, including those within the regions (Weiner 1967). Gandhi also exerted tight control over appointments within the party and the selection of candidates for national and regional elections. She was known to appoint Gandhi loyalists to power and oust people after they had been in power for only a short period of time to prevent them from forming alliances against her.

Rather than incorporating people's interests into the party's agenda, Gandhi used patronage to maintain the loyalty of Congress Party members and to garner support within the electorate at large (Chhibber 1995, 1999; Manor 1998). This patronage assumed many different forms including, loans, grants, food supplies, industrial licenses, etc. The effect of this patronage was only temporary, however. Gandhi and her successors had to continually extend patronage to the states to maintain their support. Gandhi also widely abused the practice of President's Rule to maintain power. Of all the prime ministers in India, Indira Gandhi invoked President's Rule more than anyone else – 41 times during her fourteen-year rule. Understanding the incentives statewide parties face in addressing regional interests, as well as those of regional parties, helps us understand more fully the impact of decentralization on the evolution of ethnic conflict and secessionism in India.

5.7. Impact of decentralization on the party system in India

Decentralization has played a pivotal role in shaping India's party system and its effect, in turn, on violence within the country. The extent to which decentralization has promoted regional parties, in particular, depends on certain key features of this institution, the first of which is the size of India's regions. Unlike Czechoslovakia, but like Spain, no region is India has enough seats in the lower house to govern on its own. Between 1952 and 1999, the percentage of seats held by each region in the Lok Sabha was 4 percent on average. Over time, this number has declined slightly due to the subdivision of some states. The fact that regional parties cannot govern discourages regional parties from competing at this level of government and voters from voting for them.

Regional parties may still participate in the national government, albeit through coalitions, as they have done since the 1990s. Generally, the influence of each region within these coalitions is small. These coalitions are also prone to instability, as alluded to earlier, because each regional party wields little bargaining power within a coalition. This is especially true in light of India's fractionalized lower house and the many alternative coalition partners present within this legislature. Regional parties, as a result, receive few concessions in return for their participation, which reduces their incentives to remain within the coalition (Brancati 2005).

The second feature of decentralization that may influence the electoral strength of regional parties is the number of regional legislatures in India. The large number of these legislatures, which presently stands at twenty-eight with one legislature for each state in India, creates many opportunities for regional parties to participate in government. While all states have their own regional legislatures, the union territories do not. As a result, the presence of regional parties in Lok Sabha elections is higher in the states than in the union territories. In the union territories, regional parties earn an average of 3 percent of the vote in lower house elections between 1952 and 1999. By contrast, they average 13 percent in the states.[101]

This pattern is consistent with my argument that the presence of regional legislatures with real decision-making authority encourages regional parties. Although one cannot exclude the possibility that union territories are not states because they have weaker regional parties, union territories that become states have stronger regional parties as states than as union territories. Between 1953 and 1999, regional parties won 8 percent more of the vote in union territories that became states (i.e. Arunachal Pradesh, Goa, Himachal Pradesh, Manipur, Meghalaya, Mizoram, Nagaland, and Tripura) when they were states than when they were union territories.[102]

The third feature of decentralization that affects the strength of regional parties is the method used to fill India's upper house.

Unlike in Spain, where regional legislatures appoint only one-fifth of the upper house, in India regional legislatures appoint all but twelve seats in the upper house. The President of India selects these twelve representatives based on their knowledge or expertise in literature, science, art, and social services. Since regional legislatures elect most of the upper house, regional parties tend to have stronger positions in India's upper house than in its lower house. In fact, the presence of regional parties in the upper house is twice as strong as it is in the lower house. The upper house in India is fairly powerful, which increases the influence of regional parties in the country. The upper house has the same jurisdiction as the lower house, except that it cannot initiate financial bills related to taxes, loans, the Consolidated Fund, or the Contingency Fund, and is not subject to a vote of confidence. It cannot veto these bills either, although it can veto all other legislation produced by the lower house.

The fourth feature of decentralization that may affect the strength of regional parties is the sequencing of national and regional elections. Regional elections are held at the same time as national elections in some regions of India, but not others. Regions that hold elections concurrently, moreover, do not necessarily hold all of their elections this way. The first two national elections in India were held at the same time as every regional election in the country, while the next two national elections were held concurrently in all but two states in India.[103] Since 1967, however, the majority of national and regional elections have not been held concurrently. Elections are no longer concurrent, mostly because national and regional legislatures have not completed their full terms of office for a multitude of different reasons.

Although nonconcurrent national and regional elections should reduce the strength of regional parties in regional elections, in India the difference between the percentage of votes that regional parties win on average in concurrent versus nonconcurrent elections is trivial. Regional parties account for about 15 percent of the vote in both types of elections. India may be unique in this respect. The effect, however, of electoral sequencing may be obscured by other

151

differences among these regions, which a simple comparison of means cannot capture, but which a statistical analysis controlling for different factors, such as heterogeneity and size, can. I explore this further in the statistical analysis in Chapter 7. This analysis supports the claim that regional parties have stronger positions in regional legislatures when national and regional elections are nonconcurrent.

5.8. Conclusion

The case of India expands our understanding of how the effectiveness of decentralization hinges on the electoral strength of regional parties. In India, regional parties have prompted ethnic conflict and secessionism legislatively by undercutting the rights and opportunities of regional minorities who have organized themselves, often violently, in response to these actions. Regional parties have also mobilized groups to attack others and fight for independence. They have even supported extremist organizations engaged in these activities and have done so on a much greater scale than regional parties have in Spain.

Additionally, this analysis helps to identify a number of conditions under which statewide parties are less likely to reduce conflict among regionally concentrated ethnic groups. These conditions include the extent to which particular regions and groups are electorally pivotal, the internal organization of statewide parties, as well as the personal management style of specific political leaders. The first condition depends, in turn, on the population of regions, the distribution of groups throughout India, and the robustness of democracy (e.g. electoral competitiveness, President's Rule, and gubernatorial appointments). In India, the weakness of democracy, at least in terms of political and civil rights, also allowed regional parties to pass legislation harmful to regional minorities to engender support among the dominant linguistic group in their regions.

India also provides further insight into which aspects of decentralization are most conducive to regional parties. It confirms the findings of the previous case studies about the importance of governing and upper house election procedures. It also suggests that administrative authority is insufficient to foster regional parties since regional parties have a much weaker presence in India's union territories, which have only administrative powers, than in the states, which have administrative and decision-making authorities. The sequencing of national and regional elections does not seem, however, to influence the electoral strength of regional parties in the latter type of elections.

Finally, the case of India helps disentangle the causal relationships between decentralization and regional parties and between both of these institutions and ethnic conflict and secessionism. Regional parties played no role in the decentralization process in India, although regional differences surely factored into India's decision to decentralize in the first place. The fact, however, that regional parties vary significantly in strength across legislatures and over time within the same regions (even though regional differences are relatively stable over time) suggests that institutions, such as decentralization, have played a vital role in fostering ethnic conflict and secessionism in India. Through statistical analysis, I test the generalizability of these arguments in the remainder of this book, and further explore the causal relationships that underpin them.

Part III

Quantitative Analysis

6

Ethnic Conflict and Secessionism

Building on the findings of the previous case studies, in this chapter I examine the effects of decentralization and regional parties on ethnic conflict and secessionism more generally, using quantitative analysis. I do not examine here the specific causal mechanisms through which political decentralization and regional parties influence these phenomena. These I have already explored in detail in the case studies. I endeavor only to show in this chapter that my argument regarding the effects of decentralization and regional parties apply to democracies more broadly. I also attempt in this chapter to further address the possibility of reciprocal causation using the technique of instrumental variable regression.

In brief, the analysis suggests that decentralization reduces the intensity of ethnic conflict and secessionism when controlling for regional parties, and that regional parties, in contrast, increase the strength of both these phenomena. The analysis also shows that decentralization is less effective in combating intrastate conflict the greater is the electoral strength of regional parties. In demonstrating these results, I first describe in Section 6.1 the data I use and the measurements I employ to test the effect of decentralization and regional parties on both phenomena. Subsequently, in Section 6.2, I show the results for ethnic conflict and secessionism individually, and finally, I present the results of the instrumental variable regression for each form of intrastate conflict.

6.1. Data and measurements

The analysis in this chapter draws on two major datasets. The first is the *Constituency-level Elections* (CLE) dataset (Brancati 2007). The CLE dataset provides election results at the constituency or district level of government, which is the level at which seats are distributed in a country. The dataset includes over 800 elections occurring in fifty democracies around the world between 1944 and 2002 and spans more than 30,000 electoral constituencies.[104] It also incorporates information on national and regional elections for lower and upper house elections. As such, this dataset offers a significant improvement over existing sources of consistency level data.[105] Existing resources are largely confined to specific regions of the world and lack data on regional elections, and in most cases, upper houses as well. Typically, they also lack data on all political parties that participate in an election. Instead, they often impose an inclusion threshold on parties based on the percentage of votes and seats that they win, making it impossible to use them to carefully and systematically study minor parties. I, therefore, compiled the CLE dataset in order to systematically measure the electoral strength of regional parties in the world.

I could not draw on existing scholarly research for this purpose either because most research on regional parties involves case studies of particular regions and/or regional parties (Rokkan and Urwin 1982; de Winter and Türsan 1998). While some of these studies have produced lists of regional parties, these lists are not systematic and do not seem to exist for countries outside of Western Europe. Instead, I have taken a data-driven approach to measuring regional parties. In this approach, I identify parties as regional parties based on the geographic basis of their electoral support, using as my working definition of regional parties the minimal one offered in the introduction of this book, e.g., parties that win votes in one region of a country. While this view of regional parties does not encapsulate information about the specific strategies or goals of regional parties, it lends itself well to cross-national comparison. It is preferable, moreover, to alternatives, such as coding regional parties based on their names or platforms – both of which may be subjective and misleading.

I collected the CLE dataset by identifying every country in the world that held at least two consecutive democratic elections during this period. I consider elections democratic if countries score a 5 or higher on the polity index of democracy (0–10) for that year.[106] Within these countries, I contacted various institutions, including electoral commissions, national statistical offices, ministries of interior, and legislative bodies. To collect data on regional elections, in many cases I contacted regions directly since national institutions usually lacked information on subnational elections. Within each of these regions, I contacted various agencies, as described above. Given this approach, the CLE dataset only includes countries' official election results and does not include secondary resources of any kind.

Generally, I received the election data in paper format, which I subsequently entered manually into a database. I triangulated the data and independently checked the results to ensure accuracy. Often, the data were not in a consistent format across years, including data from the same source. It was not unusual, for example, for the data to be in one language one year and another language the next. It was also very common for the data to indicate the full names of parties in one year and only acronyms in another. Thus, in addition to entering the data manually, I had to ensure that it was consistent across years. In so doing, I checked that the names of constituencies were spelled the same across years and then mapped each constituency to the region in which it belongs. I also identified the full names of parties so that I could associate parties with their appropriate acronyms wherever necessary, and translated the party names into English wherever possible.

Importantly, I have included in the dataset every single party that won seats in an election, whether this party won one vote or millions of votes, and whether it was short-lived or more enduring. The dataset, as a result, includes over 5,000 political parties. This approach is fundamental to this study because many regional parties are small. Imposing an inclusion criterion on parties based on the number of votes or seats that they win, would consequently omit a large number of regional parties. This approach also increases the value of this dataset for other projects that seek to understand issues other than the one at hand here. By including all parties regardless of size, this dataset may be used to study many different phenomena, including legislative fractionalization, the growth of parties over time, and the strength of minority parties as well as independent candidates (Brancati 2008b).

Although these countries are not exhaustive of all democracies in the world, they constitute about two-thirds of the world's democracies and are representative of the larger population. Hailing from every region of the world, these countries include developed as well as emerging economies, heterogeneous as well as homogenous countries, and consolidated as well as inchoate democracies. These countries also exhibit significant variation in the nature of their political systems and decentralization in particular. Approximately two-fifths of the countries in the CLE dataset are decentralized – extending decision-making authority to regional legislatures over at least one issue area. A number of countries have expansive forms of decentralization while others exhibit much more modest forms. Their systems of government also differ with respect to certain features of decentralization, which may influence the electoral strength of regional parties (e.g. number and size of regions and/or regional legislatures and the sequencing of national and regional elections). It is not surprising, therefore, that these countries also demonstrate significant variation in the strength of regional parties both within decentralized systems of government and between centralized and decentralized systems.

The second major dataset that this analysis draws on is the *Minorities at Risk (MAR) Project*, which provides information on conflict on a yearly basis between 1985 and 2000 (CIDCM 2002). The MAR dataset is useful because it provides data on low- and high-intensity conflicts. Many other datasets only provide data on civil wars defined typically as 1,000 battle deaths. The MAR dataset also provides data on two different measures of conflict, namely anti-regime rebellion and intracommunal conflict, which uniquely capture ethnic conflict and secessionism. Not all incidents of conflict are secessionist in nature, which makes distinguishing the two empirically quite valuable. The MAR dataset does not represent nonviolent manifestations of secessionism, however, such as peaceful demonstrations, referendums, public opinion polls, etc. Thus, incidents of secessionism, like those in Czechoslovakia, are not captured in this analysis.

Another potential drawback of the MAR dataset is that it excludes groups that are not considered "at risk" of experiencing intrastate conflict. Consequently, it omits entire countries from the dataset, such as Belgium, Finland, Ireland, etc.[107] I corrected for this bias by measuring the intensity of intercommunal conflict and anti-regime rebellion among excluded groups. I did so by first identifying all groups and countries excluded from MAR using a dataset compiled by James D. Fearon (2003). The Fearon dataset denotes all ethnic groups that comprise at least 1 percent of a country's population. In using this dataset to identify groups excluded from MAR, I merged a number of groups that MAR considers distinct but which the Fearon dataset considers a single group, such as the Jurassians and Francophones in Switzerland. At the same time, I distinguished among other groups, which the MAR dataset considers a single group and the Fearon dataset considers distinct.

I subsequently measured the level of ethnic conflict and secessionism among groups excluded from MAR using two different methods – one involving country experts and the other including primary and secondary research. As part of the first approach, I identified at least two experts on each of the omitted countries. I initially contacted them by postal mail, providing them with the MAR scales for anti-regime rebellion and intercommunal conflict. I sent follow-up reminders by e-mail. In these communications I asked experts to identify the level of anti-regime rebellion and intercommunal conflict in a country per year, as well as the groups involved in each. When solicited, I also provided experts with clarification on the scales, but did not divulge any other type of information.

In the interim, I independently studied the groups and countries excluded from the MAR dataset in order to code the level of conflict in which they were involved. I did so using scholarly articles, newspapers, NGO reports, and so forth. I then compared and contrasted my own codings of conflict with those of the country experts. There were very few discrepancies between the two and most were a result of country experts coding incidents of violence as conflict or rebellion even though they did not involve particular ethnic groups. To resolve discrepancies, I did further research before arriving at a final determination of the level of rebellion and conflict involving the excluded MAR groups. Not surprisingly, the level of violence involving these excluded groups was at the low end of the MAR scale.

6.1.1. Ethnic conflict and secessionism

Anti-regime rebellion, as defined by MAR, encapsulates violent forms of secessionism, while intercommunal conflict captures that of ethnic conflict. Anti-regime rebellion addresses the issue of secessionism since it consists of all forms of conflict between minority groups and states or dominant groups exercising state power. It also encompasses acts of violence that are not necessarily secessionist in nature. However, upon close examination of the data, it appears that all acts of rebellion included in this particular study are secessionist in nature.[108] This may be a consequence of excluding all geographically dispersed groups from this study. I omit these groups because decentralization cannot extend decision-making power to dispersed groups and, thus, is not theorized to have an effect on conflict involving them.[109]

The MAR dataset provides information on anti-regime rebellion on a yearly basis from 1985 to 2000, recording the highest form of anti-regime rebellion experienced by a given group in a country per year. Anti-regime rebellion is divided into eight categories ranging from no rebellion to high levels of rebellion: (0) none reported, (1) political banditry, (2) campaigns of terrorism, (3) local rebellion, (4) small-scale guerilla activity, (5) intermediate guerilla activity, (6) large-scale guerrilla activity, and (7) protracted civil war. For the purpose of this analysis, I aggregate the group-level data to the national level using the maximum level of anti-regime rebellion in a country per year as my dependent variable.[110] The most intense form of anti-regime rebellion in this study occurred in Colombia and India (i.e. large-scale guerilla activity) and Turkey (i.e. protracted civil war). The least intense occurred in the following countries: Argentina, Belgium, Botswana, Canada, Costa Rica, Czechoslovakia, Estonia, Finland, Lithuania, Malaysia, Niger, Norway, Poland, Romania, Slovenia, Sweden, and Venezuela. There were no incidents of anti-regime rebellion in these countries.

Intercommunal conflict represents ethnic conflict well since, by definition, it involves all incidents of conflict among minority groups and between minority and majority groups. The MAR dataset provides data on intercommunal conflict for groups on a yearly basis from 1990 to 2000, recording the highest form of intercommunal conflict experienced by each group in a country per year. Intercommunal conflict is divided into seven categories ranging from no incidents of intercommunal conflict to high levels of conflict: (0) none manifest, (1) acts of harassment, (2) political agitation, (3) sporadic violent attacks, (4) antigroup demonstrations, (5) communal rioting, and (6) communal warfare. For the purpose of this analysis, I aggregate the group-level data to the national level, as I did in the case of rebellion, using the maximum level of intercommunal conflict in a country per year as my dependent variable.[111] The most intense form of intercommunal conflict in this study occurred in India, Indonesia, South Africa, and the United Kingdom. All experienced communal rioting. The least intense occurred in the following countries: Belgium, Bolivia, Botswana, Canada, Costa Rica, Czechoslovakia, Estonia, Finland, Lithuania, Malaysia, Niger, Norway, Poland, Slovenia, Sweden, Switzerland, and Turkey, where there were no incidents of intercommunal conflict.

6.1.2. Political and fiscal decentralization

I measure political decentralization in two basic ways in this study. The first differentiates between systems of government based simply on whether or not countries are decentralized, and does not distinguish between systems that are more or less decentralized. This measure takes on a value of 1 if a country's regional level of government has independent decision-making power over at least one issue area, and 0 otherwise.[112] Based on this measure, I have determined whether or not countries are decentralized according to how their national constitutions divide decision-making power among levels of government. I find no discrepancies between countries that I code as decentralized using this measure and those other scholars consider decentralized using their own measures (Elazar 1994; Gerring et al. 2005). The decentralized countries in this study are: Argentina, Belgium, Bosnia-Herzegovina, Canada, Czechoslovakia, Finland, India, Malaysia, Mexico, South Africa, Spain, Switzerland, the United Kingdom,[113] the United States, and Venezuela.

In reality, decentralization is more extensive in certain countries than in others, which may affect the ability of decentralization to reduce the concerns that drive groups to attack each other and pursue independence in the first place. For this reason, I also constructed an index of decentralization, which measures the depth of regional decision-making authority in countries based primarily on their national constitutions.[114] This index is a five-point ordinal measure of decentralization in which higher values on the index indicate greater degrees of decentralization. I created this measure by assigning countries a point for all of the following items that accurately describe their regional legislatures. That is, that they: (1) are democratically elected, (2) can levy their own taxes, (3) have joint or exclusive control over education, (4) have joint or exclusive control over public order and/or police, and (5) have veto power over the national constitution. Since constitutions are not the only form of legislation that may allocate powers between levels of government, I also incorporated information from additional forms of legislation to create this index, as well as secondary resources on decentralization in particular countries. I also shared the index with country experts to ensure that it accurately reflected decentralization in their countries.

Although I do not incorporate all areas of legislative decision-making into this measure, this index captures significant variation in decentralization across countries. The issues, moreover, that I have incorporated into this index reflect powers central to all governments and address the three major types of issues over which ethnic conflict and secessionism often erupt – economic issues, political/social issues, and security issues. The fifth power noted above is important because it enables regions to protect their autonomy against incursions by the national government. Regional legislatures, however, may use their veto power to frustrate the national constitution, which can undermine state unity. In Czechoslovakia, as you may recall, regional parties used their veto power to thwart bills on the country's new constitution, resulting in the dissolution of Czechoslovakia.

Although regions may have a certain amount of political authority, this authority is toothless unless regions have the funds to carry out their policies. To capture the effect of fiscal decentralization on intrastate conflict, I measure the extent of fiscal decentralization in countries using the International Monetary Fund's *Government Finance Statistics*, available through the World Bank (2005). Regions can accumulate these funds by raising their own revenue or sharing in the national government's revenue. I capture both forms separately, measuring fiscal decentralization in terms of (a) subnational revenue (as a percentage of gross domestic product) and (b) subnational expenditure (as a percentage of total government expenditure and as a percentage of gross domestic product).[115] The expenditure measures do not indicate what percentage of subnational revenue is comprised of national discretionary grants – a large percentage of which may undermine subnational authority.

6.1.3. *Regional party strength*

In order to demonstrate that regional parties mediate the effect of decentralization on ethnic conflict and secessionism, I measure the electoral strength of regional parties in national elections using three different measures.[116] The first is based on the percentage of parties that are regional parties in national elections. The second and third measures are based on the percentage of votes and seats that regional parties win in these elections. The first measure captures the desire of politicians to form regional parties while the latter two reflect the support voters offer these parties. A large discrepancy between the two in favor of the former demonstrates a greater desire of politicians to form regional parties than voters to vote for them.

In order measure regional party strength along these dimensions, I first defined regions as the highest administrative division in a country below the national level of government and identified each region in the dataset using FIPS regional codes.[117] Identifying regions based on FIPS codes provides a standard measure of regions across countries. I define regions in this way because I argue that decentralization increases the electoral strength of regional parties through regional legislatures, which largely coincide with the administrative divisions of countries.[118]

Next, I identified which parties competed in only one region of a country and marked them as regional parties, making sure not to incorrectly code independent candidates as regional parties. Finally, I aggregated the number of votes and seats that regional parties won in each constituency to the regional and national levels of government. The first level of aggregation captures the electoral strength of regional parties in each region of a country while the second reveals their electoral strength in a country as a whole. In this analysis, regional parties win an average of about 5 percent of the vote (range = 0–87 percent) and about 5 percent of the seats (range = 0–89 percent). The percentage of parties that are regional parties in elections is substantially greater. On average, 27 percent of the parties that compete in elections are regional parties in this study (range = 0–83 percent).

While regional parties are more likely to increase ethnic conflict and secessionism than statewide parties, the degree to which statewide parties reduce both phenomena may depend on how equally distributed their support is throughout a country. The less evenly distributed their support, the more statewide parties resemble regional parties and the less likely they are to reduce conflict and secessionism. To capture this effect, I use Pradeep Chhibber and Ken Kollman's measure of denationalization. This measure evaluates how evenly distributed all parties' votes are across constituencies rather than categorizing parties as statewide parties or regional parties. I calculate denationalization by taking the difference between the effective number of electoral parties (ENEP) in a national legislative election and the average effective number of electoral parties (ENEP) in each constituency of a national legislative election (Chhibber and Kollman 1998, 2004). This measure is higher the less evenly distributed all parties' votes are throughout a country. I apply each of the above figures on the electoral strength of regional parties and denationalization to each year of the data in which parties are in office, not just the year in which they won an election.

6.1.4. *Control variables*

In order to ensure that the effects of decentralization and regional parties are not a result of other factors, I include a number of control variables in the analysis. The first set of controls addresses potential alternative explanations for ethnic conflict and secessionism, which suggest that both phenomena are due to the underlying socioeconomic or ethnolinguistic characteristics of countries. Economic underdevelopment is supposed to promote ethnic conflict by making people more vulnerable to extremist ideologies (Lipset 1963), elevating competition for scarce resources (Bates 1983), and intensifying people's grievances against the government (Horowitz 1985). It is also supposed to reduce the opportunity costs of joining conflicts (Collier and Hoeffler 2004) and to undermine the capacity of states to quell rebellion (Fearon and Laitin 2003). Secessionism, meanwhile, may be driven by a region's belief that it would be better off economically as an independent state, which may be motivated by a group's perceptions of its relative development just as much as its actual level of development (Horowitz 1985; Buchanan and Faith 1987; Bookman 1991; Bolton and Roland 1997; Herrera 2005; Hug 2005; Giuliano 2006).[119]

I measure the level of economic development in this study in terms of total GDP (current US dollars), which takes into account the amount of wealth potentially available to governments to suppress rebellion and may be positively associated with cross-regional economic diversity. The second is in terms of GDP per capita (constant 2000 US dollars), which takes into account the size of a country's population and, thus, captures information on small but well-developed countries, as well as large but underdeveloped ones. I base both measures on data from the *World Development Indicators Online* (World Bank 2002).

Equally important in understanding the underlying differences within society is the overall ethnolinguistic heterogeneity of a country. In contrast to economic development, ethnolinguistic heterogeneity is supposed to increase intrastate conflict (Horowitz 1985). Obviously, ethnic conflict cannot occur unless there is more than one ethnic group in a country. Beyond this, however, it is not clear that greater heterogeneity will intensify or mitigate conflict.[120] Whether ethnic heterogeneity has any impact may depend more on the differential treatment of ethnic groups, which measures of overall heterogeneity do not capture. I, nonetheless, control for heterogeneity to address this possibility using the ethnolinguistic fractionalization (ELF) index. This index ranges from 0 to 1, with 0 indicating that every person in a country belongs to the same ethnolinguistic group and 1 signifying that everyone belongs to a different ethnolinguistic group. I have drawn these data from the *Ethno-Linguistic Fractionalization Indices, 1961 and 1985* (Roeder 2001) and applied the 1985 data to the period between 1985 and 2000.[121]

The second set of controls relates to different aspects of countries' political systems, which may affect the outbreak of ethnic conflict and secessionism. Scholars have suggested a number of these institutions as alternatives to decentralization or complements to it, especially in the context of consociationalism (Lijphart 1977). Therefore, it is important to evaluate their effectiveness in reducing intrastate conflict in comparison to decentralization. An important institution in this regard is the extent to which countries enshrine political and civil rights. If national governments enshrine political and civil rights, regional parties may not adopt policies at either the national or subnational level of government that harm regional minorities, as they have done in India. To measure the extent to which countries uphold these rights, I use Freedom House's composite measure of political rights and civil liberties, ranging from 1 (free) to 7 (not free) (Freedom House 2007). For countries in this study, the mean value on this index is 2, and the modal category is 1.

Proportional representation (PR) systems are also supposed to reduce intrastate conflict over plurality and majority systems because they are more inclusive of small parties, which may potentially represent particular ethnic or religious groups in a country (Lipset and Rokkan 1967; Lijphart 1977; Saideman et al. 2002). In enhancing the representation of these groups, PR systems are supposed to reduce intrastate conflict. However, PR systems are more open to regional parties, which may increase conflict and secessionism. I represent the type of electoral system in a country using two indicator variables representing mixed electoral systems and majority/plurality systems. PR systems are the base category. I do not distinguish between majority and plurality systems because of insufficient variation in the data among the two, but I do explore the effect of average district magnitude on conflict and secessionism. However, because I lack information on district magnitude for a number of elections in this analysis, I rely principally on the two indicator variables to identify electoral systems in this study. Three countries have mixed electoral systems in this study – Bolivia, Lithuania, and Mexico, while six countries – Botswana, Canada, India, Malaysia, the United Kingdom, and the United States, have majority or plurality systems.[122]

In general, elections, whether they occur under a PR system or a majoritarian one, may encourage ethnic conflict and secessionism (Brass 1997; Saideman et al. 2002; Wilkinson 2004). Groups may intensify violence during election times to extract concessions from political parties. Prior to an election, some groups may also increase their activity to prevent elections from occurring at all. The effect of elections is not clear-cut, however, since groups may also suspend their activities during election times to prevent parties sympathetic to their views from losing votes to more moderate parties. The likelihood, moreover, of conflict occurring after elections may depend on the extent to which people view these elections as legitimate, as unrest following the 2008 presidential elections in Kenya attests. I measure elections in this study with an indicator variable coded 1 if an election occurs in a given year, and 0 otherwise.

In addition to the potential effects of elections more generally, the first democratic elections in a country are widely believed to increase intrastate conflict since national governments tend to be weak during transitions, making it difficult for governments to prevent conflict and secessionism militarily (Snyder and Mansfield 1995; Snyder 2000). Power vacuums also occur during transitions so that competition among politicians tends to be intense while temptations to resort to ethnic appeals are profound. I measure transitions with three distinct variables that incorporate information about the lengths of these transitions.

The first is an indicator variable representing first elections, coded 1 if the first democratic elections in a country occur in a given year, and 0 otherwise. The second is an indicator variable in which every year that the first democratically elected legislature is in office is coded 1, and 0 otherwise. This approach is consistent with how I have applied the data on regional parties to the analysis. For these two measures, I also assign elections a 1 even if they are not the first ever democratic elections in a country, but instead are the first ones after a prolonged period of nondemocratic rule. Under this coding scheme, I code the first democratic elections held in Eastern Europe after the fall of communism as a 1, even though some countries in this region held democratic elections between World War I and World War II. The third way in which I measure democratic transitions is in terms of the age of democracy. This measure provides a more nuanced measure of transitions. This variable is a continuous variable in which the first democratic elections in a country are coded 0, and all subsequent years are coded 1, 2, 3, etc.

Noted scholars also believe that presidentialism promotes ethnic conflict because presidents are less likely to represent multiple ethnic groups than executives in parliamentary systems of government, where ethnic parties can participate in government through coalition governments (Lijphart 1977; Linz and Valenzuela 1994: 44). The effect of presidentialism on ethnic conflict, I believe, is much more nuanced than this, however. Presidents themselves can belong to more than one ethnic group. They can also appeal to different ethnic groups by wearing clothing or symbols representing these groups, as President Hamid Karzai has done in Afghanistan, and can appoint people of different ethnic groups to their cabinets. In Bosnia-Herzegovina, the presidency itself rotates among three different presidents that de facto represent the three major ethnic groups in the country. Presidents can also embrace multiple ethnic groups through the policies they adopt or, conversely, antagonize certain groups by supporting policies that harm their interests. I measure presidentialism in this study with an indicator variable coded 1 if citizens directly elect the chief executive, and 0 otherwise. The following thirteen countries have presidential systems of government in this study: Argentina, Bolivia, Bosnia-Herzegovina, Colombia, Costa Rica, Lithuania, Mexico, Niger, Poland, Romania, Slovenia, the United States, and Venezuela.

To summarize, I have identified various measures with which to study the effect of decentralization and regional parties. These measures distinguish between ethnic conflict and secessionism and different degrees of decentralization, in addition to regional party strength. I have also developed a number of measures to represent the underlying demographic, economic, and institutional makeup of countries. In order to understand the relationship between these variables and intrastate conflict, I turn to the statistical analysis next.

6.2. Analysis

The following analysis looks at the effect of decentralization on anti-regime rebellion and intercommunal conflict in thirty democracies from 1985 to 2000. These countries are: Argentina, Belgium, Bolivia, Bosnia-Herzegovina, Botswana, Canada, Colombia, Costa Rica, Czechoslovakia, Estonia, Finland, Greece, India, Indonesia, Lithuania, Malaysia, Mexico, Niger, Norway, Poland, Romania, Slovenia, South Africa, Spain, Sweden, Switzerland, Turkey, the United Kingdom, the United States, and Venezuela.[123] I arrived at this set of countries by excluding all countries from the CLE dataset in which I could not measure regional party strength because the constituency level of government traverses more than one region of a country.[124] I also omitted all countries from the CLE dataset that have only widely dispersed ethnic groups since decentralization is not purported to have an effect on conflict involving these groups.[125]

I analyze the effect of decentralization on anti-regime rebellion and intercommunal conflict using ordered logit models with year fixed-effects to control for trends in conflict and rebellion over time.[126] I use ordered logit models because my dependent variables are discrete values of conflict and rebellion ordered from low to high and because countries do not need to experience lower levels of either form of violence to experience higher ones.[127] In order to explore the causal relationship among variables, I use instrumental variable regression, as described at greater length later in this chapter. Alternative models that I discuss in the text but do not present in the tables are available in a supplementary appendix.

6.2.1. Anti-regime rebellion

The ordered logit results for anti-regime rebellion are presented in Tables 6.1–6.3. In Model 1, I test the effect of decentralization on anti-regime rebellion, controlling for different economic, demographic, and political factors, which may affect the intensity of anti-regime rebellion, but not controlling for regional party vote. In this model, as expected, political decentralization reduces the likelihood of anti-regime rebellion and does so substantially, according to an analysis of the marginal effects. Majority and plurality systems and presidentialism also reduce the intensity of anti-regime rebellion according to this model. Interestingly, mixed electoral systems appear to increase rebellion over proportional representation systems. This is in tension with findings on majority and plurality systems, since mixed systems have smaller district magnitudes on average than PR systems, but greater district magnitudes than majority and plurality systems. There is no relationship between average district magnitude and rebellion if I replace the two electoral system variables in Model 1 with average district magnitude. Additionally, if I replace the age of democracy variable, which has a negative but insignificant effect on rebellion, with variables representing the first elections in a country or elections in general, neither variable has a significant effect on anti-regime rebellion.

In contrast, lacking civil and political rights, according Model 1, and having a higher GDP intensifies rebellion. Adding GDP per capita to the model or substituting it for total GDP, reveals that the former diminishes rebellion while the latter elevates it. Model 1 also shows that increasing heterogeneity increases the intensity of rebellion. If I add a squared term for the ELF index to Model 1, I find that both low and high levels of heterogeneity seem to reduce anti-regime rebellion.[128]

In Models 2–4, I introduce regional parties into the analysis. In Model 2, I measure regional parties in terms of the percentage of parties that are regional parties in an election. As expected, decentralization decreases anti-regime rebellion while regional parties increase it.[129] The impact of regional parties is small, though, upon examination of the marginal effects. In Models 3 and 4, I measure regional parties in terms of the percentage of votes and seats that regional parties receive. Likewise, according to these models, as the electoral strength of regional parties increases, the intensity of anti-regime rebellion increases as well, although again the impact is rather small. If I restrict Models 2 and 3 to the same population as Model 4, the effects of decentralization and regional parties are statistically and substantively the same. In alternative models, I substitute denationalization for regional party strength and test its effect on anti-regime rebellion, but do not find a significant

Table 6.1. Anti-regime rebellion: base models

	(1)	(2)	(3)	(4)
Political decentralization	−3.35*** (0.90)	−4.93*** (0.99)	−5.03*** (0.91)	−5.22*** (0.98)
Regional parties[a, b, c]		0.05[a],*** (0.01)	0.11[b],*** (0.03)	0.11[c],*** (0.03)
Freedom House	1.82*** (0.23)	2.28*** (0.30)	2.09*** (0.28)	2.19*** (0.28)
Mixed electoral system	2.75*** (0.74)	4.59*** (1.06)	4.72*** (1.07)	4.26*** (0.99)
Majority and plurality systems	−2.71*** (0.80)	−4.35*** (1.02)	−3.75*** (0.93)	−4.16*** (0.98)
Age of democracy	−0.01 (0.01)	0.002 (0.01)	−0.01 (0.01)	−0.01 (0.01)
Presidentialism	−1.57*** (0.41)	−2.70*** (0.55)	−2.52*** (0.64)	−2.26*** (0.58)
ELF	7.43*** (1.71)	9.13*** (1.89)	10.02*** (1.91)	10.57*** (2.08)
GDP (log)	1.99*** (0.37)	1.98*** (0.30)	2.43*** (0.37)	2.53*** (0.38)
Log pseudolikelihood	−240.422	−224.808	−225.310	−221.031
Observations	306	306	306	303

Year fixed-effects not shown. Robust standard errors in parentheses.
$*p \leq 0.10$, $**p \leq 0.05$, $***p \leq 0.01$.
[a] Number of regional parties (percentage of total parties).
[b] Votes for regional parties (percentage of total votes).
[c] Seats for regional parties (percentage of total seats).

relationship between the two, suggesting that regional parties, in particular, are the real catalysts of rebellion.

In Models 5–7, I examine the effect of regional party vote on anti-regime rebellion in the presence of alternative measures of decentralization. In Model 5, I replace the dichotomous measure of decentralization with the five-point index of decentralization. In this model, regional party vote continues to intensify rebellion while the decentralization index reduces it. Higher degrees of decentralization also reduce the intensity of anti-regime rebellion. The impact, though, of increasing degrees of decentralization among

Table 6.2. Anti-regime rebellion: alternative measures of decentralization

	(5)	(6)	(7)
Political decentralization		−10.49***	−9.30***
		(3.27)	(2.55)
Decentralization index	−4.14***		
	(0.61)		
Fiscal decentralization[a,b]		−0.09[a]	−0.005[b]
		(0.06)	(0.02)
Regional party vote	0.29***	0.11***	0.07***
	(0.04)	(0.03)	(0.03)
Freedom House	3.39***	1.21*	1.67***
	(0.45)	(0.70)	(0.56)
Mixed electoral system	9.09***	5.17***	4.54***
	(1.16)	(1.36)	(1.04)
Majority and plurality systems	−9.09***	1.26	0.05
	(1.59)	(3.11)	(2.33)
Age of democracy	0.02***	−0.09*	−0.07**
	(0.01)	(0.05)	(0.03)
Presidentialism	−2.81***	0.59	−0.04
	(0.50)	(1.76)	(1.10)
ELF	15.06***	18.79***	14.53***
	(2.60)	(6.17)	(3.31)
GDP (log)	4.73***	4.99***	4.21***
	(0.68)	(1.61)	(1.07)
Log pseudolikelihood	−189.094	−107.519	−113.107
Observations	306	214	214

Year fixed-effects not shown. Robust standard errors in parentheses.
*$p \leq 0.10$, **$p \leq 0.05$, ***$p \leq 0.01$.
[a] Subnational expenditure (percent of total expenditure).
[b] Subnational revenue (percent of GDP).

countries that are already decentralized is very small, especially compared to the difference between centralized systems of government and decentralized ones, as demonstrated in Model 1.

In Models 6 and 7, I again measure decentralization as a dichotomous variable rather than an index, which includes subnational tax authority in its calculus, and I add separate measures for fiscal decentralization to the analysis. I restrict these models to the same population as each other to ensure that variations between the two are not due to differences in the population. Due to a lack of data on fiscal decentralization for specific years and countries, the N is notably smaller in these models.[130] In Model 6, I measure fiscal decentralization in terms of subnational expenditure (as a percentage of total expenditure), and in Model 7, I measure it in terms of subnational revenue (as a percentage of GDP). Fiscal decentralization is not significant in either model.[131] Fiscal decentralization is still not significant if I drop political decentralization from the models, restrict the models to decentralized countries, or include alternative measures of regional party strength in them.[132]

In Models 8–10, I explore a number of potential interaction effects between decentralization and regional parties. Interpreting interaction effects is difficult in nonlinear models and conclusions about them should not be based on the size and significance of individual coefficients (Braumoeller 2004; Brambor et al. 2006). Instead, conclusions about statistical significance should be based on the joint significance of the independent variables (Braumoeller 2004; Brambor et al. 2006). Interaction terms introduce collinearity into models and inflate the standard errors of individual coefficients, making them unreliable. Conclusions, moreover, about the substantive importance should be based on the marginal effects, which are presented graphically in this chapter, since interaction effects can vary in size and direction based on different values of the independent variables (Braumoeller 2004; Brambor et al. 2006).

With this in mind, I interact decentralization in Model 8 with the percentage of parties that are regional parties in an election. In Models 9 and 10, I interact decentralization with the percentage of votes and seats that regional parties win. In these models the main effects for decentralization and regional parties, as well as the interaction terms, are jointly significant at the $p \leq 0.01$ level. Substantively, these models reveal that decentralization reduces anti-regime rebellion while regional parties increase it, and that the ability of decentralization to reduce anti-regime rebellion declines as the strength of regional parties grows. I obtain the same results for Models 8 and 9 if I restrict the analysis to the same population

Table 6.3. Anti-regime rebellion: interaction models

	(8)	(9)	(10)
[†]Political decentralization	−5.86***	−5.34***	−5.22***
	(1.13)	(0.95)	(0.98)
[†]Regional parties[a,b,c]	−0.01[a]	−1.24[b]	−0.97[c,*]
	(0.02)	(0.99)	(0.50)
[†]Political decentralization* Regional parties[a,b,c]	0.06[a,**]	1.36[b]	1.08[c,**]
	(0.03)	(1.00)	(0.50)
Freedom House	2.19***	2.10***	2.15***
	(0.30)	(0.28)	(0.29)
Mixed electoral system	5.17***	4.65***	4.37***
	(1.34)	(1.09)	(1.00)
Majority and plurality systems	−3.83***	−3.80***	−4.01***
	(1.07)	(0.96)	(1.02)
Age of democracy	0.004	−0.01	−0.01
	(0.01)	(0.01)	(0.01)
Presidentialism	−3.07***	−2.37***	−2.25***
	(0.61)	(0.62)	(0.57)
ELF	8.46***	10.30***	10.32***
	(1.97)	(1.99)	(2.11)
GDP (log)	1.79***	2.46***	2.48***
	(0.32)	(0.37)	(0.38)
[†]Joint significance χ^2 (p-value)	27.92 0.00	34.46 0.00	43.66 0.00
Log pseudolikelihood	−220.501	−222.202	−220.453
Observations	306	306	303

Year fixed-effects not shown. Robust standard errors in parentheses.
*$p \leq 0.10$, **$p \leq 0.05$, ***$p \leq 0.01$.
[a] Number of regional parties (percentage of total parties).
[b] Votes for regional parties (percentage of total votes).
[c] Seats for regional parties (percentage of total seats).

as Model 10. I also get the same results if I measure decentralization as an index rather than as a dichotomous variable.

The graph in Figure 6.1 illustrates these results. The graph indicates the predicted probability that anti-regime rebellion does not occur in a country with a decentralized system of government. The dashed line represents the change in the predicted probability of no rebellion for a decentralized system of government as the percentage of parties that are regional parties in an election varies between 0 and 100 percent. The solid line represents the change in the probability of no rebellion for a decentralized system of government when the vote for regional parties varies between 0 and 100 percent, and the dotted line represents it when the percentage of seats that regional parties win are within this range.

This graph makes it starkly apparent that as the percentage of votes and seats that regional parties win in an election increases, the probability of no rebellion drops dramatically for a decentralized system of government. The extent to which regional parties win votes and seats has a much greater effect on rebellion than the percentage of parties that are regional parties in an election. In additional models with different combinations of predictors, the latter measure of regional parties has a larger effect on rebellion. The effect is still much smaller, though, than for the percentage of votes and seats that regional parties win in an election, all of which suggests

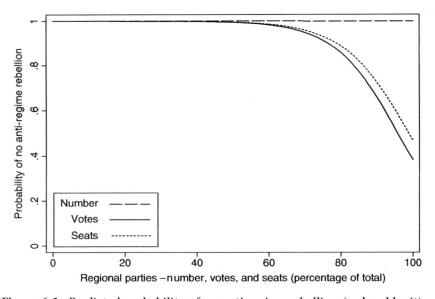

Figure 6.1. Predicted probability of no anti-regime rebellion (ordered logit)

Note: In the above graph, decentralization, Freedom House, majority/plurality systems and presidentialism are set to 1, mixed electoral systems and age are set to 0, and the ELF index and GDP (log) are set at their means.

that regional parties in government, not those outside of it, are the real drivers of conflict. Regional parties also reduce the effectiveness of decentralization in minimizing rebellion if I measure decentralization as a five-point index instead of a dichotomous variable.

To summarize, the previous analyses demonstrate that political decentralization substantially reduces anti-regime rebellion (i.e. violent forms of secessionism), while regional parties intensify it. More importantly, it shows that regional parties diminish the ability of decentralization to reduce anti-regime rebellion. The analysis also shows that the percentage of votes and seats that regional parties win have a greater impact on rebellion than the percentage of parties that are regional parties in an election. It further reveals that more extensive forms of political decentralization reduce anti-regime rebellion over less extensive ones, although the effect is modest. Fiscal decentralization, in contrast, does not seem to have a robust effect on anti-regime rebellion, although better data is needed to confirm these results. Finally, the analysis shows that ethnic heterogeneity, GDP, political and civil rights, presidentialism, and electoral systems affect the likelihood of rebellion, but that the effects of decentralization and regional parties on anti-regime rebellion are still robust when these factors are controlled for in the analysis.

6.2.2. Intercommunal conflict

The ordered logit results for intercommunal conflict are presented in Tables 6.4–6.6. In Model 11, I test the effect of decentralization on intercommunal conflict controlling for different economic, demographic, and political factors that may affect conflict, but not for regional party vote. In this model, political decentralization reduces intercommunal conflict, but its effect is not significant. Poorly protected political and civil rights, higher total GDPs, and greater degrees of ethnic heterogeneity intensify conflict, as in the case of anti-regime rebellion. If I include a squared term for the ELF index in the model, I find that for all values of the ELF index (0–1), heterogeneity increases conflict.

Presidentialism also increases the intensity of conflict according to Model 1 in contrast to the findings regarding anti-regime rebellion. The conflict results do not appear to be driven by particular countries or world regions, although a number of presidential systems, which have experienced conflict in this study, are in Latin America. Differences between the conflict and rebellion models do not appear to be driven by differences in population either, since restricting the conflict and rebellion models to the same population leads to the same conclusions. These results may be symptomatic, rather of the contingent role that presidents play in managing intrastate conflict, as previously mentioned. According to Model 11, the type of electoral system and the age of democracy have no effect on the outbreak of intercommunal conflict. If I substitute

Table 6.4. Intercommunal conflict: base models

	(11)	(12)	(13)	(14)
Political decentralization	−1.31* (0.74)	−1.75** (0.74)	−2.96*** (0.93)	−2.48*** (0.89)
Regional parties[a,b,c]		0.02[a] (0.01)	0.08[b],*** (0.02)	0.06[c],*** (0.02)
Freedom House	0.33** (0.17)	0.37** (0.16)	0.32** (0.15)	0.36** (0.16)
Mixed electoral system	−0.90 (0.56)	−0.36 (0.66)	0.08 (0.73)	−0.18 (0.68)
Majority and plurality systems	1.56** (0.68)	1.41** (0.66)	1.92** (0.76)	1.52** (0.72)
Age of democracy	−0.02*** (0.01)	−0.02*** (0.01)	−0.02*** (0.01)	−0.02*** (0.01)
Presidentialism	1.42*** (0.41)	1.12** (0.48)	1.07** (0.46)	1.19** (0.47)
ELF	3.94*** (1.10)	4.12*** (1.16)	5.16*** (1.30)	4.89*** (1.38)
GDP (log)	0.98*** (0.23)	0.95*** (0.21)	1.26*** (0.23)	1.16*** (0.23)
Log pseudolikelihood	−183.770	−181.844	−174.704	−173.363
Observations	230	230	230	227

Year fixed-effects not shown. Robust standard errors in parentheses.
*$p \leq 0.10$, **$p \leq 0.05$, ***$p \leq 0.01$.
[a] Number of regional parties (percentage of total parties).
[b] Votes for regional parties (percentage of total votes).
[c] Seats for regional parties (percentage of total seats).

first elections or elections in general for the age of democracy, these variables increase the intensity of conflict, but only the variable representing the first democratically elected legislature is significant.

In Models 12–14, I introduce regional parties into the analysis. In these models, decentralization continues to significantly reduce intercommunal conflict, while regional parties increase it. According to Models 13 and 14, the percentage of votes and seats that regional parties win in an election significantly intensifies intercommunal

Table 6.5. Intercommunal conflict: alternative measures of decentralization

	(15)	(16)	(17)
Political decentralization			−9.39***
			(3.00)
Decentralization index	−1.68***	−10.40***	
	(0.49)	(3.46)	
Fiscal decentralization[a,b]		0.03[a]	−0.04[b]
		(0.07)	(0.03)
Regional party vote	0.13***	0.10**	0.13***
	(0.04)	(0.04)	(0.04)
Freedom House	0.43**	1.64*	1.17*
	(0.18)	(0.84)	(0.60)
Mixed electoral system	0.69	0.97	1.31
	(0.94)	(1.03)	(1.04)
Majority and plurality systems	1.07	1.05	1.83
	(0.76)	(1.31)	(1.52)
Age of democracy	−0.02***	−0.06***	−0.06***
	(0.01)	(0.02)	(0.02)
Presidentialism	1.62***	1.13	1.58**
	(0.43)	(0.77)	(0.77)
ELF	4.94***	13.27***	13.21***
	(1.23)	(4.68)	(4.80)
GDP (log)	1.77***	3.98***	3.78***
	(0.30)	(1.18)	(1.09)
Log pseudolikelihood	−168.117	−94.882	−94.360
Observations	230	160	160

Year fixed-effects not shown. Robust standard errors in parentheses.
*$p \leq 0.10$, **$p \leq 0.05$, ***$p \leq 0.01$.
[a] Subnational expenditure (percent of total expenditure).
[b] Subnational revenue (percentage of GDP).

conflict. The percentage of parties that are regional parties in an election does not have a significant effect on conflict according to Model 12, although the effect is positive. Restricting Models 12 and 13 to the same population as Model 14 yields the same results. In alternative models, I explore the effect on denationalization on intercommunal. As in the case of anti-regime rebellion, denationalization does not have a significant effect on intercommunal conflict.

In Models 15–17, I explore the effect of alternative measures of decentralization on intercommunal conflict. In Model 15, I replace the dichotomous measure of decentralization with the five-point index of decentralization. According to this model, more extensive forms of decentralization significantly reduce conflict over less extensive forms. For countries that are already decentralized, however, increasing degrees of decentralization has a moderate effect on the likelihood of conflict. In Models 16 and 17, I return to my original dichotomous measure of decentralization, since the index includes fiscal decentralization in its calculus, and add separate measures for fiscal decentralization to the analysis. I restrict these models to the same population to ensure that the results are not driven by differences in population.

According to these models, political decentralization reduces the intensity of intercommunal conflict while the effect of fiscal decentralization is more ambiguous. Fiscal decentralization, measured in terms of subnational expenditure (percentage of total expenditure) has a positive, but insignificant, effect on intercommunal conflict according to Model 16. Measured in terms of subnational revenue (percentage of GDP), fiscal decentralization has a negative, but likewise insignificant, effect on intercommunal conflict according to Model 17.[133] The effect of subnational expenditure in Model 16 is still insignificant if I drop political decentralization from the model. However, the effect of subnational revenue is negative and significant in Model 17 if I drop political decentralization from the model. If I restrict the models to only decentralized systems of government, neither measure of fiscal decentralization has a significant effect on conflict. Since the number of observations in all of these models is rather small, and the models themselves are very sensitive to specification, one should be very cautious about drawing conclusions from them about the effect of fiscal decentralization.

In Models 18–20, I explore several potential interaction effects between decentralization (measured as a dichotomous variable) and regional parties. Once again conclusions about the substantive and statistical significance of the interaction effects are based on the marginal effects and joint significance of the main effects and the

Table 6.6. Intercommunal conflict: interaction models

	(18)	(19)	(20)
[†]Political decentralization	−1.54*	−3.12***	−2.49***
	(0.82)	(0.97)	(0.89)
[†]Regional parties[a,b,c]	0.02[a]	−0.12[b]	0.02[c]
	(0.02)	(0.17)	(0.24)
[†]Decentralization* Regional parties[a,b,c]	−0.01[a]	0.20[b]	0.05[c]
	(0.02)	(0.17)	(0.24)
Freedom House	0.39**	0.30**	0.36**
	(0.17)	(0.15)	(0.17)
Mixed electoral system	−0.42	0.20	−0.14
	(0.65)	(0.76)	(0.76)
Majority and plurality systems	1.31*	1.96**	1.54**
	(0.70)	(0.76)	(0.75)
Age of democracy	−0.02***	−0.02***	−0.02***
	(0.01)	(0.01)	(0.01)
Presidentialism	1.11**	1.15**	1.19**
	(0.48)	(0.48)	(0.46)
ELF	4.21***	5.24***	4.85***
	(1.20)	(1.31)	(1.39)
GDP (log)	0.97***	1.26***	1.15***
	(0.21)	(0.23)	(0.24)
[†]Joint significance χ^2	6.64	11.59	9.83
(p-value)	0.08	0.01	0.02
Log pseudolikelihood	−181.679	−174.326	−173.350
Observations	230	230	227

Year fixed-effects not shown. Robust standard errors in parentheses.
*$p \leq 0.10$, **$p \leq 0.05$, ***$p \leq 0.01$.
[a] Number of regional parties (percentage of total parties).
[b] Votes for regional parties (percentage of total votes).
[c] Seats for regional parties (percentage of total seats).

interaction term. In Models 19 and 20, the main effects for decentralization and regional parties and the interaction term are jointly significant ($p \leq 0.01$). They are marginally significant in Model 18 ($p \leq 0.10$), where I measure regional parties in terms of the percentage of parties that are regional parties in an election, which is perhaps not surprising in light of the insignificant results in Model 12.

According to Models 18–20, the ability of decentralization to reduce intercommunal conflict is diminished as the electoral strength of regional parties increases. The graph in Figure 6.2 illustrates the results of these models. The dashed line represents the change in the predicted probability of no intercommunal conflict for a decentralized system of government as the percentage of parties that compete in elections ranges between 0 and 100 percent. The solid line represents the change in the predicted probability of no intercommunal conflict for a decentralized system of government as regional party vote ranges between 0 and 100 percent. The dotted line represents the change in the predicted probability of no intercommunal conflict for a decentralized system of government as the number of regional party seats ranges between 0 and 100 percent. As this graph illustrates, the likelihood of no conflict occurring decreases as the strength of regional parties increases. Regional parties also reduce the effectiveness of decentralization in diminishing conflict if I measure decentralization as a five-point index instead of a dichotomous variable.

To summarize, the results of this analysis suggest that decentralization reduces intercommunal (i.e. ethnic conflict) while regional parties, measured in terms of the percentage of votes and seats that regional parties receive, increase it. It also reveals that the effect of decentralization depends on the electoral strength of regional parties. That is, as regional parties participate in elections more often and win more votes and seats, the effectiveness of decentralization in reducing intercommunal conflict diminishes. Furthermore, a more expansive form of political decentralization seems to reduce intercommunal conflict over a more limited one, although the effect is moderate for systems of government that are already decentralized. Again, as in the analysis of anti-regime rebellion, this analysis shows that the underlying demographic and economic makeup of

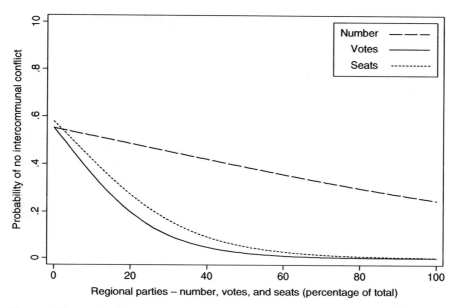

Figure 6.2. Predicted probability of no intercommunal conflict (ordered logit)

Note: In the above graph, decentralization, Freedom House, majority/plurality systems and presidentialism are set to 1, mixed electoral systems and age are set to 0, and the ELF index and GDP (log) are set at their means.

countries, and the institutional milieu in which decentralization is embedded, affects the likelihood of intercommunal conflict, but that the effect of decentralization and regional parties on conflict is still significant when controlling for these factors.

6.2.3. *Instrumental variable regression*

At this point, the statistical analysis has not yet addressed the possibility that intercommunal conflict and anti-regime rebellion may affect decentralization and regional parties, not vice versa. To address this issue, I employ instrumental variable (IV) regression analysis.[134] IV regression yields consistent, albeit biased, estimates when a covariate is correlated with the error term. It does so by using a proxy or instrument for the suspect variable. A strong instrument is correlated with the suspect variable but is uncorrelated with the error term. In other words, a good instrument has no direct effect on the dependent variable, but only an indirect effect by means of the instrumented variable.

In the first stage of the IV regression, the suspect variable is regressed on the instrument and all other exogenous variables in the model. A high partial R-squared and/or F-test for the excluded instruments suggests that the instrument is strongly correlated with the instrumented variable (Bound et al. 1995). In the second stage the dependent variable is regressed on the predicted values from the first stage equation. I present the results of my second stage models for anti-regime rebellion and intercommunal conflict in Table 6.6. To determine if the instrumented variable is endogenous, I compare OLS models of a given specification with IV models of the same specification. Under the null hypothesis of the Hausman test, the OLS models are consistent and efficient, while the IV models are consistent but inefficient. Rejecting the null indicates that the variable in question is endogenous and that only the IV model is consistent.

In general, the effectiveness of IV regressions depends on the relevance of the instrument, that is, on how closely it is correlated with the instrumented variable (Bartels 1991; Bound et al. 1995; Stock 2002). Estimates relying on weak instruments are biased toward the OLS estimates and are especially problematic in the presence of multiple weak instruments. The utility of IV regressions also depends on instruments being uncorrelated with the dependent variable. One cannot test for exogeneity directly but one can test for it indirectly using tests of overidentifying restrictions, as long as each suspect variable is proxied by more than one instrument. Through these tests (e.g. Sargan Test and Hansen's J Test), one can compare the estimates of a just-identified model (i.e. a model with one instrument per instrumented variable) with a model that is overidentified. Under the null hypothesis, all instruments are valid (i.e. uncorrelated with the residual in the original model) and both estimates are consistent. Rejecting the null indicates that the additional instruments in the overidentified model are not valid.

In this chapter, I conduct two separate sets of IV regressions. The first examines the effect of political decentralization on intercommunal conflict and anti-regime rebellion using instruments for political decentralization. For these analyses, I use UK colonial heritage, the physical size of a country, and the contiguity of its land, as instruments for decentralization. I use whether or not a country is a former colony of the United Kingdom as an instrument for decentralization, since many countries are decentralized today because they were once colonies of the United Kingdom. The United Kingdom used decentralization as part of a system of divide-and-rule to extract taxes from the populace and maintain control over its colonies more generally, while other colonial powers, like France and Spain, did not (Young 1994; Herbst 2000). With few exceptions, UK colonies continued to use decentralization as a means of government once they gained independence after World War II. Countries that were once colonies of the United Kingdom in this dataset, even if only part of their territory was under UK rule, include: Botswana, Canada, India, Malaysia, South Africa, and the United States.

Whether a country was a colony of the United Kingdom is not directly related to the presence of ethnic conflict and secessionism in the period studied in this analysis between 1985 and 2000. Most of the UK colonies gained independence thirty or more years prior to this period. The United Kingdom, moreover, did not use decentralization to control its colonies because they were more likely to experience ethnic conflict and secessionism than those of other colonial powers. France and Spain's colonies also had fissiparous tendencies because they were very heterogeneous (in terms of ethnicity, languages, tribe, and religion, etc.) and underdeveloped economically, but neither France nor Spain used decentralization for this purpose. Furthermore, in terms of the data, the correlations between UK colonial heritage and anti-regime rebellion or intercommunal conflict, are weak and insignificant ($r = 0.03$ and $r = 0.12$, respectively). UK colonial heritage is coded 1 if a country is a former colony of the United Kingdom, and 0 otherwise.

I use the physical size of a country as an instrument for decentralization since large countries often adopt decentralized systems of government because they cannot easily manage their affairs through a single central government located far away from most of its constituents (Treisman 2002). All of the large democracies in the world today are decentralized, including Canada, India, Russia, and the United States. In terms of the data, countries that are decentralized are more than six times larger that countries that are not decentralized. Country size, moreover, is not directly related to ethnic conflict and secessionism. The correlations between country size and anti-regime rebellion ($r = -0.03$) and intercommunal conflict ($r = 0.05$) are weak and insignificant. I measure the physical size of a country in terms of square kilometers using data from the *World Development Indicators*.

Population may be related to decentralization since populous countries, like large countries, may be difficult to manage by means of a single national government. Nonetheless, I do not use population, which is only weakly related to physical size, as a proxy for decentralization because some scholars have suggested that populous countries are more prone to civil war (Fearon and Laitin 2003; Collier and Hoeffler 2004). These empirical findings may be spurious, however. That is, they may be an artifact of the definition of civil wars as 1,000 battle deaths. MAR does not define conflict in these terms.

Nevertheless, I do use territorial contiguity as an instrument for decentralization because noncontiguity is positively related to decentralization. Countries with noncontiguous lands tend to be decentralized because it is very difficult for countries to govern areas that are not adjacent by means of one central government. Many countries with noncontiguous territories, including Spain and the United States, are decentralized. Noncontiguity, in turn, should not affect intercommunal conflict and anti-regime rebellion directly. After all, the process by which noncontiguous lands are incorporated into countries is not necessarily different from the process by which contiguous lands are integrated. Specifically, both contiguous and noncontiguous lands have been peacefully, as well as forcibly, incorporated into countries.

Fearon and Laitin (2003) have suggested, though, that contiguity should reduce civil wars because it is easier for governments to repress rebels when land is contiguous. They do not find strong evidence for this effect, however, in their statistical analysis.

Noncontiguity is significant in only one of their models of civil war, which includes wars between colonial powers and colonies. One can reasonably argue that these wars are international wars, and are not included in this analysis. The correlations, furthermore, between contiguity and anti-regime rebellion ($r = 0.04$) and contiguity and intercommunal conflict ($r = 0.22$) are weak and insignificant in the case of rebellion. I measure noncontiguity with a simple indicator variable coded 1 if a country's land is not contiguous, and 0 otherwise. Examples of countries in the dataset with noncontiguous lands include: Canada, Finland, Greece, Indonesia, Malaysia, Spain, and the United States.

The second set of IV regressions estimates the relationship between regional parties and intercommunal conflict and anti-regime rebellion, using the concurrency of executive and legislative elections and cross-regional voting laws as instruments for regional parties. I measure the concurrency of these elections with two indicator variables – one for presidential systems of government with concurrent executive and legislative elections and one for presidential systems of government without concurrent elections. Parliamentary systems of government, which always have concurrent executive and legislative elections, are the base category.

While concurrency and regional party strength are directly related (see the next chapter for a discussion of this relationship and statistical evidence to this effect), the concurrency of executive and legislative elections is not directly related to conflict or rebellion. Countries with presidential systems of government hold elections nonconcurrently for various reasons unrelated to the strength of regional parties. Sometimes, elections are not held concurrently because presidents and legislatures have terms of office that are of different lengths, or because presidents do not complete their terms of office having either resigned, been impeached or died in office. They can also hold elections at different times because legislatures have staggered legislative terms (whereby representatives are elected for the same period of time but not all at the same time). Furthermore, in terms of the data, the correlations between the two concurrency variables and intercommunal conflict and anti-regime rebellion are weak. The Pearson's r is less than 0.16 for both concurrency variables and their relationships to intercommunal conflict and anti-regime rebellion, and is insignificant in the case of intercommunal conflict.

I also use cross-regional voting laws, which require parties to compete in a certain number of regions, if not every region of a country, in order to participate in elections. Cross-regional voting laws are strongly related to the electoral strength of regional parties. In this analysis every country that has these laws in place (i.e. Indonesia, Mexico, and Turkey) lacks regional parties. Cross-regional voting laws are strongly related to anti-regime rebellion, however, which makes them a potentially much less valuable instrument for regional parties in the rebellion models. The correlation between cross-regional voting laws and rebellion is 0.78, but it is driven primarily by Turkey ($p \leq 0.01$). The correlation between these laws and intercommunal conflict is only 0.03 and is insignificant.

In Table 6.7, I present the second stage results of my regression analysis. I conducted many different regression models to test for endogeneity, using different combinations of my instruments and different model specifications. In this table, I present only the results of my baseline models, which examine the effect of decentralization (measured as a dichotomous variable) and regional party vote on anti-regime rebellion and intercommunal conflict. For these models, I present the combination of instruments, which maximizes the fit of my first stage regression models and passes the requisite tests of overidentifying restrictions.

In Model 21, I test the effect of decentralization on anti-regime rebellion, instrumenting for decentralization with UK colonial status and physical size. Shea's partial R-squared for the first stage model is 0.08, indicating that the instruments used in this model are relevant. Both UK colonial status and physical size have significant effects on decentralization in this model. Albeit strong, the fit is even better if I measure decentralization as an index and instrument for it with the same two instruments used here. (Shea's partial R for the first stage model in this analysis is 0.17.) The instruments in Model 21 also appear exogenous, passing Sargan's tests

Table 6.7. Instrumental variable regression

	(21)	(22)	(23)	(24)
	Rebellion	**Rebellion**	Conflict	Conflict
Political decentralization	−3.40*** (1.01)	11.50* (6.21)	−6.09*** (2.22)	−1.10*** (0.37)
Regional party vote	0.05*** (0.02)	−1.09* (0.56)	0.12*** (0.03)	0.05*** (0.02)
Freedom House	0.84*** (0.10)	1.72*** (0.62)	0.09 (0.14)	0.15** (0.07)
Age of democracy	−0.001 (0.002)	−0.03 (0.02)	−0.01*** (0.004)	−0.004*** (0.001)
Mixed electoral system	0.67** (0.30)	−4.27* (2.44)	−0.01 (0.59)	−0.10 (0.17)
Majority and plurality systems	−1.63*** (0.42)	1.27 (1.70)	−0.37 (0.47)	0.27 (0.22)
Presidentialism	−0.95*** (0.16)	3.81 (2.68)	0.11 (0.30)	
ELF	4.31*** (1.33)	−8.51 (5.32)	7.69*** (2.72)	1.75*** (0.54)
GDP (log)	0.91*** (0.21)	−0.89 (0.67)	1.25*** (0.41)	0.34*** (0.08)
Constant	−23.75*** (5.52)	22.56 (17.03)	−31.86*** (10.43)	−8.73*** (2.06)
Centered R-squared	0.380	−25.64	−1.34	0.320
Observations	306	306	230	230

Robust standard errors in parentheses.
*$p \leq 0.10$, **$p \leq 0.05$, ***$p \leq 0.01$.
Instrumented Variables: Model 21 and Model 23 (Decentralization) and Model 22 and Model 24 (Regional party vote). *Instrumental Variables*: Model 21 (UK colony and Physical size), Model 22 (Cross-regional voting laws), Model 23 (UK colony and Non-contiguity) and Model 24 (Cross-regional voting laws and Concurrency).

of overidentifying restrictions and the model itself is identified based on an Anderson cannon correlations likelihood ratio test.[135] According to Model 21, decentralization reduces anti-regime rebellion while regional parties increase it. Comparing this model with an OLS model of the same specification with a Hausman test, I find that the differences between the two are not systematic. The relationship between decentralization and anti-regime rebellion appears, therefore, to be exogenous.

In Model 22, I instrument for regional party vote rather than decentralization. Shea's partial R-squared is much smaller than desirable at 0.01. In light of the high correlation between cross-regional voting laws and regional party vote, this may not be surprising. Cross-regional voting laws, however, are significantly related to regional party vote in the first stage model. The fit of the first stage is also higher if I use alternative measures of regional party strength. According to the second-stage results in Model 22, the effect of decentralization and regional parties is in the opposite direction than hypothesized. A Hausman test, though, comparing Model 22 with a straightforward OLS model suggests that differences in the two models are not systematic.

In Model 23, I turn to intercommunal conflict. In this model I use intercommunal conflict as my dependent variable and instrument for decentralization using UK colonial status and noncontiguity. The fit of the first stage regression model is again rather weak. Shea's partial R-squared for the first stage model is 0.03. If I measure decentralization as an index, however, the fit is much higher (Shea's partial R-squared is 0.18). This model, like Model 23, passes Sargan's test of overidentifying restrictions, suggesting indirectly that the instruments are exogenous. According to both models, decentralization significantly reduces conflict. Differences, moreover, between these models and OLS models of the same specification, are not systematic.

Finally, in Model 24, instead of instrumenting for decentralization, I instrument for regional party vote using cross-regional voting laws and the concurrency of presidential and legislative elections. Shea's partial R-squared for this model is 0.13. The fit is slightly lower if I measure regional party strength in terms of the percentage of seats that regional parties win, but much higher if I measure it in terms of the percentage of parties that are regional parties in an election. According to Model 24, regional party vote increases the strength of intercommunal conflict. Finally, differences between this model and an OLS model of the same specification are not systematic, indicating that the OLS model is the preferred model. While the technique of instrumental variable regression is never wholly satisfactory because of the difficulty of finding perfect instruments, given the tools available for observational studies, the confirmatory results in this chapter, as well as the process-tracing utilized in the case studies, suggest that decentralization and regional parties have a strong, independent effect on ethnic conflict and secessionism, not vice versa.

6.3. Conclusion

The statistical analysis presented in this chapter shows that decentralization does not intensify ethnic conflict and secessionism, as some scholars have suggested, and, in fact, seems to diminish it. The analysis also shows that the ability of decentralization to reduce these phenomena hinges on the electoral strength of regional parties. According to the analysis, as regional parties win more votes, the likelihood of decentralization reducing both ethnic conflict and secessionism diminishes. This runs counter to some scholars' claims that regional parties minimize intrastate conflict by representing groups whose interests are otherwise overlooked by the government (Rokkan and Urwin 1982; de Winter and Türsan 1998; Birnir 2007). The effects of decentralization and regional parties on both these phenomena are significant even when controlling for other characteristics of countries. This analysis may also even understate the effect of regional parties on intrastate conflict since it focuses on national elections, where regional parties have much weaker positions than they do in regional elections.

More extensive forms of political decentralization also seem to reduce ethnic conflict and secessionism over less extensive forms, but all forms of political decentralization are less effective in reducing conflict and secession as regional parties win more votes. These findings also challenge the engrained view that offering groups some autonomy will whet their appetite for more and more autonomy until they demand full independence (Nordlinger 1972; Gleason 1990; Kymlicka 1998; Hechter 2000). They also cast doubt on notions that decentralization heightens conflict and secessionism by providing more resources for groups to engage in these activities (Roeder 1991; Kymlicka 1998; Bunce 1999; Leff 1999; Snyder 2000). According to this analysis, these resources are only important when regional parties control them.

Fiscal decentralization does not seem to have a robust effect on intrastate conflict. There may be theoretical, as well as empirical, reasons for this null effect. The first is that fiscal decentralization may reduce conflict among economically advanced regions, and may increase it in disadvantaged regions, something this national-level analysis does not capture. Fiscal decentralization may only reduce conflict, moreover, among advanced regions if funds resulting from it are effectively invested in the regions. Empirically, fiscal decentralization may not have a robust effect on conflict because this analysis does not distinguish among the different ways in which countries may be fiscally decentralized. Finally, the time period and countries for which data on fiscal decentralization are available are limited. Only richer more nuanced data will help us resolve this issue. Building on the findings for political decentralization and regional parties in this chapter, I analyze the relationship between the two in the subsequent chapter.

7

Regional Parties

Having established in the previous chapter that regional parties reduce the effectiveness of decentralization in managing intrastate conflict, in this chapter I examine the effect of decentralization on regional parties by means of quantitative analysis. In order to highlight differences among decentralized systems of government, I also explore the effect of particular features of decentralization on regional parties, such as the number and size of regions and the sequencing of national and regional elections. I also examine in this chapter the possibility of reciprocal causation between decentralization and regional parties using instrumental variable regression.

In brief, the analysis indicates that overall political decentralization strengthens regional parties electorally, not vice versa, and that more extensive forms of political decentralization strengthen them more than less extensive forms. The analysis also reveals that having large regions bolsters regional parties in certain respects. It further demonstrates that regions with autonomy have stronger regional parties than those without it, as do regions with nonconcurrent regional and national elections. In presenting these results, I first describe in Section 7.1 the data I use and the measures I employ to test the impact of decentralization on regional parties. In Sections 7.2–7.4, I analyze the effect of decentralization on regional parties in legislative elections at both the national and regional levels of government, and in Section 7.5, I describe the results of the instrumental variable regression. In the last section,

I discuss the implications of these findings for my argument more generally.

7.1. Data and measurements

The analysis in this section draws on many of the same datasets that I introduced in the previous chapter (e.g. the CLE dataset, MAR dataset, and *World Development Indicators*) and a number of the same variables. I will not, therefore, discuss them again here in detail. Instead, I will focus on the theories that I test using these resources. I will also describe in this chapter the new datasets that I use and measures that I employ in this analysis.

7.1.1. *Regional party strength*

Regional parties, I define and evaluate their strength as I did in the previous chapter in terms of the percentage of parties that are regional parties in an election, as well as the percentage of votes and seats that they win. For national elections I measure the electoral strength of regional parties in a country as a whole, as well as in each region of a country.[136] For regional elections I only calculate the latter.[137] For national elections, I also analyze the party system in terms of Chhibber and Kollman's measure of denationalization (denat), which does not categorize parties as either statewide or regional parties, but takes into account the distribution of their votes throughout a country, and is moderately correlated with regional party strength.

In order to explore preliminarily the disparate strength of regional parties in centralized and decentralized systems of government, I have graphed the electoral strength of regional parties under the two systems of government. The results are based on national election results (1944–2002) for the thirty-nine countries included in this study. These countries are: Argentina, Australia, Belgium, Bermuda, Bolivia, Bosnia-Herzegovina, Botswana, Canada, Colombia, Costa Rica, Czechoslovakia, Estonia, Finland, Germany, Greece,

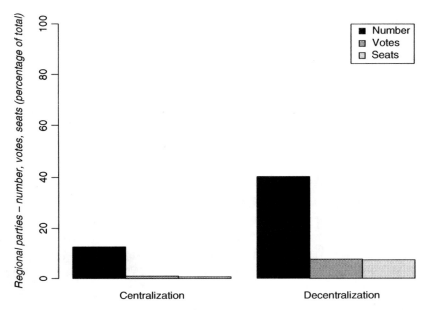

Figure 7.1. Electoral strength of regional parties in centralized versus decentralized systems of government (national lower and upper house elections, 1944–2002)

Hungary, Iceland, India, Indonesia, Ireland, Italy, Latvia, Lithuania, Malaysia, Mauritius, Mexico, Niger, Norway, Poland, Romania, Slovenia, South Africa, Spain, Sweden, Switzerland, Turkey, the United Kingdom, United States, and Venezuela.

As Figure 7.1 makes starkly apparent, the electoral strength of regional parties is far weaker in centralized systems of government than in decentralized ones. Not surprisingly, the mean differences between centralized and decentralized systems for each of these variables are statistically significant ($p \leq 0.01$ level).

7.1.2. Political and fiscal decentralization

I also define and measure political decentralization as I did in the previous chapter, both in terms of a simple dichotomous variable and a five-point index. The former differentiates between systems

197

of government that extend decision-making authority to the regional level of government (in at least one issue area) and those that do not. The latter distinguishes among systems of government in terms of degrees of decentralization. As detailed in the previous chapter, I created this index by assigning countries a point for all of the following items that accurately describe their regional legislatures. That is, they: (1) are democratically elected, (2) can levy their own taxes, (3) have joint or exclusive control over education, (4) have joint or exclusive control over public order and/or police, and (5) have veto power over the national constitution.

According to the dichotomous measure of decentralization, seventeen of the thirty-nine countries included in this analysis are decentralized, although not necessarily for the entire period of observation. These countries are: Argentina, Australia, Belgium, Bosnia-Herzegovina, Canada, Finland, Germany, India, Italy, Malaysia, Mexico, South Africa, Spain, Switzerland, United Kingdom, United States, and Venezuela. All of these countries score a 2 or above on the decentralization index. Incidentally, 2 is the modal category for all countries on this index.

In addition to these two basic measures of political decentralization, I identified several structural features of decentralization that may strengthen regional parties. In particular, I examine the effect of the number and size of regions in a country, as well as the concurrency of national and regional elections. I do not analyze the procedures by which upper houses of government are elected in this study because the dataset exhibits insufficient variation in these procedures.[138] However, as you may recall, the case studies of India and Spain strongly suggest that having upper houses directly elected by regional legislatures significantly increases the electoral strength of regional parties at the national level of government.

I identify the number of regions in a country, meanwhile, with a simple continuous variable. In national elections, this variable may be inversely related to a region's share of national legislative seats. That is, the more regions there are in a country, the fewer seats each region has within the legislature. Regional parties, however, are less likely to govern at the national level if they compete in small regions than in large ones. Politicians may have fewer incentives, therefore, to form regional parties in countries divided into a large number of small regions. Voters may also have fewer incentives to vote for them for this reason. However, the more small regions there are in a country, the less likely parties are to compete in every single region of a country. Thus, having many, small regions may result in parties competing in a large number of regions, but not necessarily all of them.

I measure regional size in terms of the percentage of seats that a region has within a national legislature. I do not measure it in terms of population or surface area but in terms of seat share, since seat share affects the ability of parties to govern. Nevertheless, there may be a close correlation between the population of a region and national legislative seat share – with large regions having more seats than small regions. Small regions are sometimes overrepresented, though, in upper houses of government to enhance their influence in the national arena (Patterson and Mughan 1999; Stepan 1999).

I also measure the concurrency of national and regional elections since concurrent legislative elections may weaken the electoral strength of regional parties in regional elections. National legislatures are usually more powerful than regional ones, and elections to them generally capture more public attention as well. As a result, parties that win a lot of votes at the national level tend to win the same at the regional level, but only when elections to the two occur simultaneously. Since statewide parties tend to dominate national elections, concurrent national and regional elections should favor statewide parties in regional elections.

I capture information about the concurrency of national and regional legislative elections in two different ways. In the first, I measure the concurrency of national and regional legislative elections with a single indicator variable coded 1 if national and regional elections are concurrent, and coded 0 if they are not.[139] In the second, I distinguish among presidential and parliamentary systems. I do so by creating three indicator variables representing nonconcurrent elections that occur in presidential systems, nonconcurrent elections that occur in parliamentary systems, and concurrent elections that occur in presidential systems of government. Concurrent elections in parliamentary systems of government are the base category.

Finally, I measure decentralization in terms of the extent of fiscal decentralization in a country. Emphasizing the degree of decentralization over the structure of decentralization, Chhibber and Kollman (1998, 2004) hypothesize that political and fiscal decentralization discourage parties from competing throughout a country by giving them fewer incentives to merge with other parties to control decisions made at the national level. The effect of fiscal decentralization may also depend, though, on whether fiscal decentralization is a result of subsidies from the national government or the ability of regions to raise their own taxes.[140] If it is due to the former, regional politicians may affiliate with statewide parties that have strong positions at the national level in order to secure funding and patronage from this level of government (Krause and Bowman 2005). Regional politicians do not face the same incentives if fiscal decentralization is a result of their regions' own tax-raising abilities. The latter obviously favors regional parties over the former. For this reason, I measure fiscal decentralization using the same IMF measures I used in the previous chapter in terms of subnational revenue and expenditure (measured as either a percentage of total government revenue/expenditure and/or GDP).[141]

7.1.3. Control variables

In order to address potential alternative explanations for the effect of decentralization on regional parties, I also include a number of control variables in the analysis. The first set of controls represents the underlying ethnolinguistic heterogeneity of countries. These controls try to capture conventional views of regional parties, which suggest that regional parties are a function of underlying societal differences and not decentralization.[142] I capture ethnolinguistic heterogeneity with two variables. The first is the ethnolinguistic fractionalization (ELF) index, which I have defined in the previous chapter. It measures the overall heterogeneity of countries. The source I use for this index provides data for two time periods, 1961 and 1985 (Roeder 2001). Making maximum use of these data, I apply the 1961 data to the period between 1945 and 1974, and apply the 1985 data to the period between 1975 and 2002.[143]

This second measure takes into account the extent to which ethnolinguistic groups are regionally concentrated. Unlike in the previous chapter, where I was only interested in the ability of decentralization to reduce conflict among territorially concentrated groups, I do not restrict this analysis to groups that are territorially concentrated. Instead, I include a measure of geographic dispersion in the analysis. I have derived this measure from the regional base variable in the *Minorities at Risk Project* (MAR), according to which, ethnic groups have a regional base if 25 percent or more of the group resides in a region that is spatially contiguous and larger than an urban area (CIDCM 2002). This group must also be the predominant ethnic group in that region. Using population figures from the Fearon (2003) dataset on ethnic groups, I determined what proportion of a country's population each of these groups constituted (Fearon 2003).

MAR does not provide data on all ethnic groups living in the thirty-nine countries included in this analysis because it does not contain groups that are not "at-risk." To rectify this problem, I used the Fearon dataset (2003) to identify which groups are not included in the dataset and what percentage of the population they constitute. I then used census data and other secondary resources to determine whether groups excluded from MAR had a regional base. Finally, I measured the proportion of a total country's population that has a regional base.[144] Countries like Costa Rica, Iceland, and Sweden have low scores on this index, while countries like Belgium and Bosnia-Herzegovina have high scores on this index.

The second set of control variables included in this analysis represents additional political institutions that may affect the strength of regional parties, such as electoral proportionality, cross-regional voting laws, first elections, and presidentialism. Proportional representation (PR) systems are supposed to strengthen regional parties over majority and plurality systems because they impose a lower threshold on parties in order to win seats and are more open, therefore, to small parties (Duverger 1969; Cox 1997). Sartori's work (1997) suggests, however, that majority and plurality systems may benefit regional parties when ethnolinguistic groups are concentrated in regions. In these cases, groups can pass the high vote threshold that majority and plurality systems impose on parties in order to win seats within particular districts, so long as they make up a large proportion of the electorate in these districts.

I measure the proportionality of an electoral system as I did in the previous chapter with two indicator variables – one representing majority/plurality systems and one representing mixed electoral systems – with PR systems as the base category. I do not distinguish between majority and plurality systems because this study contains insufficient variation in the two.[145] Given the even higher threshold that majority systems impose on parties to win seats, one may suspect that plurality systems favor regional parties over majority ones. I also measure proportionality in terms of average district magnitude, which captures variation within and across different electoral systems. However, since I lack data on district magnitude for a number of countries, I do not use this variable in my primary analyses. To address the potential interaction between electoral systems and ethnic group dispersion, I also interact the type of electoral system in a country with the regional base variable.

Cross-regional voting laws, in contrast, weaken regional parties, or eliminate them entirely, because they oblige parties to compete in a certain number of regions of a country in order to be elected. I represent cross-regional voting laws with an indicator variable coded 1 if cross-regional voting laws are in place for a particular legislative election, and 0 otherwise. Cross-regional voting laws exist for legislative elections in Hungary, Indonesia, Mexico, and Turkey in this study. To be elected in Hungary, parties that compete in multimember districts (MMD) must compete in one-fourth of the constituencies within these districts, and must compete in at least two MMD districts. To win compensatory seats, they must compete in at least seven MMD districts.

In Indonesia, parties must have branches in all nine provinces of the country and half of the districts in each of these provinces. In Mexico, parties must compete in at least 200 of the country's uninominal districts in order to win seats in the PR aspect of Mexico's electoral system, and in Turkey, a candidate may only be elected if the party s/he represents: (1) is fully organized in at least half of the country's provinces and one-third of the districts within these provinces, and (2) has nominated two candidates for each parliamentary seat in at least half of the country's provinces. Of these four countries, only Mexico has a decentralized system of government.

Whether or not elections are the first democratic elections in a country may also affect regional party strength. First elections may increase it because of the failure of politicians and voters to coordinate during these elections (Cox 1997). Politicians, for their part, may form regional parties during the first elections in a country because they have not yet identified parties with similar views in other areas of a country with which to merge and form larger parties. Voters, for their part, may fail to coordinate with each other and vote for regional parties because they are not certain which parties are likely to win the first elections in a country and survive until the next election.

For national elections, I code the first national democratic election in a country 1, and all remaining elections 0. For regional elections, I code the first regional democratic election in each region 1, and all other regional elections 0. In only two countries, Spain and the United Kingdom, were the first regional elections held at different times than the first national elections. In Spain, the first national elections occurred in 1977 while the country's first regional elections did not occur until 1980. In this year, the Basque Country and Catalonia held their first elections. In the United Kingdom, the first regional elections in Northern Ireland occurred in 1921, while those in Scotland and Wales did not occur until 1998 and 1999 – more than 150 years after the country's first democratic elections.[146]

In keeping with the practice established in the previous chapter, I code elections as the first ones in a country even if they are not the first ever elections in a country, but are the first elections after a prolonged period of nondemocratic rule. I follow this practice for both national and regional elections. For this reason, I have coded the 1998 elections held in Northern Ireland a 1. In order to have a more nuanced evaluation of democratic transitions, I also measure the age of democracy. Accordingly, I code the first elections in a country a 0, and all subsequent elections by the number of years that have transpired since this election. As in the previous chapter, if there is a break in democracy, I restart the age variable at 0 beginning with the next democratic election in a country.

In addition to the electoral system, the type of executive system in a country may also influence the electoral strength of regional parties. Parliamentary systems of government may strengthen regional parties because they are open to coalition governments. Regional parties tend to be small and thus have a better chance of participating in government through coalitions than on their own. Some presidential systems also have explicit requirements that candidates compete and/or win votes in a certain number of regions of a country in order to be elected. The Electoral College system in the United States has this effect in practice. To test these hypotheses, I measure presidential systems of government with a single indicator variable coded 1 if the populace directly elects the chief executive in a country, and 0 otherwise.

The concurrency of national executive and legislative elections may also affect the strength of regional parties. According to Gary Cox (1997), parties coordinate across districts when these elections occur at the same time because large parties are more likely to win executive posts than small ones. Prime ministerial elections are always concurrent, but presidential elections are not. When presidential and legislative elections are concurrent, the party that wins the presidency tends to win a majority in the national legislature, with the president's popularity carrying over to his or her party in the legislature (Shugart and Carey 1992). Since statewide parties tend to be larger than regional parties and, therefore, more likely than regional parties to win presidential posts, concurrent elections should favor statewide parties in national legislative elections.

I measure the concurrency of national executive and national legislative elections in this study with two indicator variables. The first represents national legislative elections in which presidential elections occur at the same time as legislative elections, and the second represents those in which they do not. The base category represents national legislative elections under parliamentary systems of government, which are always concurrent with national executive elections. While there is significant variation in this study in terms of presidential and national legislative concurrency, all presidential elections that are concurrent with regional elections are also concurrent with national legislative elections.

7.2. National legislative elections (national level results)

In the first set of analyses I test the effect of political decentralization on the electoral strength of regional parties in thirty-nine countries with national elections (lower and upper houses) as the unit of analysis. The analysis contains fewer countries than the CLE dataset because I exclude countries in which the constituency-level of government traverses more than one region of a country. When constituencies include more than one region, as they do in countries with single nation-wide districts, I cannot calculate measures of regional party strength. There are 300 national elections included in this study, which I analyze using ordinary least squares regression with robust standard errors to correct for heteroskedasticity and decade fixed-effects to control for trends over time.[147] The results of models discussed in the text but not presented in the tables are available in a supplementary appendix.

In Model 1, I examine the effect of ethnolinguistic heterogeneity and regional dispersion on the electoral strength of regional parties in order to test conventional views of regional parties as products simply of the underlying heterogeneity of countries. According to this model, more heterogeneous countries, as measured by the

ELF index, and countries in which more of the population has a regional base, significantly increase the strength of regional parties, as predicted. I find the same positive relationship between heterogeneity and regional parties if I measure the latter in terms of the percentage of parties that are regional parties in an election or the percentage of seats that they win. Including a squared term for the ELF index in Model 1 suggests that regional parties win a smaller percentage of the vote in very homogenous countries and very heterogeneous ones.

In Model 2, I introduce decentralization into the model. According to this model, decentralization increases the percentage of votes that regional parties win in an election by about 6 percentage points. The ELF index is insignificant in this model as well as all subsequent models. For this reason, as well as the index's weak theoretical linkage to regional parties, I exclude it from these models. I continue to include the regional base variable in these models, however, since it is strongly linked theoretically and empirically to regional parties. Including the ELF index, though, does not change the substantive or statistical significance for decentralization. The relationship observed between decentralization and regional parties in Model 2 also extends to other measures of regional parties based on the percentage of parties that are regional parties in an election, as well as the percentage of seats that they win.

While the regional base variable is a much better predictor of regional party strength than overall heterogeneity, this variable's effect may depend on the type of electoral system in a country. As Model 3 indicates, majority and plurality systems favor regional parties over proportional representation systems when even a small proportion of the population has a regional base. According to Model 3, when none of the population has a regional base, though, majority and plurality systems decrease the percentage of votes that regional parties receive. Mixed electoral systems decrease the electoral strength of regional parties regardless. The main effects for majority and plurality systems and the regional base variable are jointly significant with their interaction term at

Table 7.1. National elections: base models (national level results)

	(1)	(2)	(3)
	Votes	Votes	Votes
Political decentralization		6.14***	6.71***
		(1.43)	(1.85)
ELF	4.06***	−2.17	
	(1.21)	(1.51)	
Ethnic groups with regional base	0.40***	0.39***	0.36***
	(0.06)	(0.06)	(0.07)
Mixed electoral system			−5.43***
			(2.11)
Majority and plurality systems			−5.46***
			(1.93)
Regional base*Mixed systems			3.14
			(5.77)
Regional base*Majority/plurality systems			7.17***
			(2.00)
Constant	−1.14**	−2.33**	−2.34**
	(0.53)	(1.06)	(1.10)
R-squared	0.160	0.212	0.237
Observations	300	300	300

Decade fixed-effects not shown. Robust standard errors in parentheses.
*$p \leq 0.10$, **$p \leq 0.05$, ***$p \leq 0.01$.

the $p \leq 0.01$ level, as are the main effects and interaction terms for mixed electoral systems.

In Models 4–7, I add controls for different political institutions that may affect the electoral strength of regional parties. In Model 4, political decentralization increases the percentage of parties that are regional parties in an election by nearly 20 percentage points. In Models 5 and 6, political decentralization increases the percentage of votes and seats that regional parties win by between 6 and 7 percentage points. This is an interesting effect given the average size of these variables in the dataset and their impact on anti-regime rebellion and intercommunal conflict. Finally, in Model 7, decentralization increases the extent to which the party system is denationalized, although, if you

Table 7.2. National elections: full models (national level results)

	(4)	(5)	(6)	(7)
	Number	**Votes**	**Seats**	**Denat**
Political decentralization	21.29*** (3.12)	7.65*** (1.79)	8.03*** (1.95)	1.11*** (0.20)
Ethnic groups with regional base	0.36*** (0.06)	0.34*** (0.07)	0.25*** (0.09)	−0.002 (0.003)
Concurrent presidential and legislative elections	0.53 (3.02)	−1.15 (1.12)	−1.62 (1.23)	−0.54*** (0.14)
Nonconcurrent presidential and legislative elections	9.52*** (2.86)	1.53 (1.41)	0.96 (1.52)	0.24 (0.24)
Mixed electoral system	−10.95** (4.38)	−6.32*** (2.03)	−5.96** (2.39)	−0.14 (0.41)
Majority and plurality systems	19.39*** (3.23)	−1.26 (1.50)	−2.09 (1.70)	−0.33 (0.27)
Age of democracy	−0.07*** (0.03)	−0.06*** (0.01)	−0.05*** (0.01)	−0.01*** (0.002)
Number of regions	0.03 (0.06)	−0.01 (0.02)	−0.02 (0.03)	0.0001 (0.003)
Cross-regional voting laws	−15.37*** (3.66)	−3.57*** (1.30)	−3.05** (1.40)	−0.61*** (0.23)
Constant	2.26 (3.47)	−0.83 (1.23)	−0.71 (1.29)	1.40*** (0.36)
R-squared	0.494	0.309	0.269	0.295
Observations	300	300	287	287

Decade fixed-effects not shown. Robust standard errors in parentheses.
$*p \leq 0.10$, $**p \leq 0.05$, $***p \leq 0.01$.
Concurrent and nonconcurrent presidential and legislative elections are jointly significant at the $p \leq 0.01$ level in Models 4 and 7 according to Wald tests.

recall in the previous chapter, denationalization does not have a significant effect on anti-regime rebellion or intercommunal conflict. Restricting Models 4 and 5 to the same population as Models 6 and 7, yields the same results.

According to the models in Table 7.2, other institutions also affect the electoral strength of regional parties, although the effect of decentralization is still robust when these variables are controlled for in the analysis. Older electoral systems, for example, decrease the strength of regional parties although the effect is very small. A ten-year increase in the age of an electoral system, according to these models, decreases the percentage of parties that are regional parties in an election, as well as the percentage of votes and seats that they win, by less than 1 percentage point. A ten-year increase in the age of democracy decreases denationalization by a trivial 0.06 points. If I replace the age of democracy with first elections, first elections increase the strength of regional parties, but only have a marginally significant effect on the percentage of parties that are regional parties in an election.

Mixed electoral systems seem to decrease the strength of regional parties, as do majority and plurality systems for the most part. Replacing mixed electoral systems, as well as majority and plurality systems, with a single continuous variable measuring average district magnitude does not have a significant effect on any measure of regional party strength, except the percentage of parties that are regional parties in an election, which it decreases. The effect of district magnitude, however, works in consonance with the underlying differences within society. Consistent with the findings of Model 3, I find that increasing district magnitude reduces the extent to which the regional base variable strengthens regional parties according to all four measures of my dependent variable that are analyzed in Table 7.2.[148]

Not surprisingly, cross-regional voting requirements decrease the electoral strength of regional parties. The effect is quite large, with cross-regional voting requirements decreasing the percentage of parties that are regional parties in an election by 15 percentage points according to Model 4, and the percentage of votes and seats that regional parties win by about 3–4 percentage points, according to Models 5 and 6. Having more regions does not have a significant effect on regional parties according to these models, putting aside concerns that countries with more regions simply have more regional parties.

However, nonconcurrent presidential and legislative elections seem to favor regional parties over concurrent ones. The coefficient for nonconcurrent elections is significant on its own in Model 4, and jointly significant with concurrent elections in Models 4 and 7. Excluding Bosnia-Herzegovina (BiH) makes little difference to the concurrency models. Omitting BiH from the analysis is reasonable since BiH has a unique presidential system that should not reduce the strength of regional parties. In BiH, the presidency rotates among three directly elected presidents that de facto represent the three major ethnic groups in the country. Given this unique system, all presidential and legislative elections are nonconcurrent in BiH in this study. The results are also the same if I discard countries with weak, albeit directly elected presidents, such as Iceland and Ireland.

If I include a variable for presidentialism in the model (omitting the variable distinguishing between concurrent and nonconcurrent presidential elections), I find that presidentialism marginally increases the percentage of parties that are regional parties in an election. If I discard BiH from this analysis, the results are the same. The results for presidential systems are not significant in any model if I exclude Iceland and Ireland from the analysis.

In Table 7.3, I explore the effect of alternative measures of decentralization on the electoral strength of regional parties. In Model 8, I replace the dichotomous measure of political decentralization with the five-point ordinal one. Going from the lowest to the highest value on this index, results in a 19 percentage point increase in regional party vote. No country in this dataset has undergone a five-point change in decentralization, although Spain has undergone a four-point change. In additional models, I also find a significant relationship between decentralization, measured as an index, and the electoral strength of regional parties, measured in terms of the percentage of parties that are regional parties in an election and the percentage of seats that they win in an election.

In Models 9 and 10, I explore the effect of fiscal decentralization on the percentage of votes that regional parties win in an election. These models are restricted to the same population as each other for the purposes of comparison. In these models, the effect of political decentralization on regional party vote is significant and about the same size as it was in previous models, although the

Table 7.3. National elections: alternative measures of decentralization (national level results)

	(8)	(9)	(10)	(11)	(12)
	Votes	Votes	Votes	Denat	Denat
Political decentralization		8.64*** (1.83)	8.05*** (1.61)	0.95*** (0.30)	0.77*** (0.28)
Decentralization index	3.75*** (0.87)				
Fiscal decentralization[a,b]		0.02[a] (0.04)	0.10[b] (0.06)	−0.01[a] (0.01)	0.01[b] (0.01)
Ethnic groups with regional base	0.33*** (0.07)	−4.77** (1.87)	−4.08** (1.57)	2.58*** (0.41)	2.88*** (0.37)
Nonconcurrent presidential and legislative elections	−0.49 (1.37)	3.42* (2.02)	3.48* (1.89)	0.60* (0.34)	0.68** (0.31)
Concurrent presidential and legislative elections	−2.32** (1.16)	−0.24 (1.14)	−0.27 (1.09)	−0.49*** (0.17)	−0.41** (0.16)
Mixed electoral system	−5.06** (2.06)	−2.53** (1.22)	−2.49** (1.11)	0.72* (0.38)	0.71* (0.36)
Majority and plurality systems	−0.85 (1.41)	1.30 (1.44)	1.08 (1.48)	0.08 (0.35)	0.13 (0.34)
Age of democracy	−0.08*** (0.01)	−0.07*** (0.02)	−0.08*** (0.02)	−0.01*** (0.003)	−0.01*** (0.003)
Number of regions	−0.01 (0.02)	0.06* (0.03)	0.07* (0.04)	0.01 (0.01)	0.01 (0.01)
Cross-regional voting laws	−6.00*** (1.53)	−12.68*** (3.07)	−13.13*** (3.21)	−2.79*** (0.58)	−2.73*** (0.58)
Constant	−4.86*** (1.52)	2.40 (2.21)	1.49 (2.04)	0.78** (0.35)	0.43 (0.31)
R-squared	0.346	0.404	0.423	0.582	0.579
Observations	300	157	157	149	149

Decade fixed-effects not shown. Robust standard errors in parentheses.
*$p \leq 0.10$, **$p \leq 0.05$, ***$p \leq 0.01$.
[a] Subnational expenditure (percentage of total expenditure).
[b] Subnational revenue (percentage of total GDP).

number of elections analyzed in these models is nearly half that of the previous models. At the same time, these models reveal that fiscal decentralization does not have a significant effect on regional party vote. In part, these results may be a function of the sparse data available on fiscal decentralization and the number of variables in the analysis. Stripping the models down to only political and fiscal decentralization, however, or only fiscal decentralization, does not reveal a robust relationship between fiscal decentralization and the electoral strength of regional parties.

In Models 11 and 12, I analyze the effect of fiscal decentralization on the Chhibber and Kollman measure of denationalization. These models are again restricted to the same population. As in the previous models, fiscal decentralization does not have a significant effect on denationalization. These results are also sensitive to specification. A number of models of only fiscal decentralization, and only political and fiscal decentralization, show a statistically significant negative relationship between fiscal decentralization and denationalization, in contrast to expectations.

These results may be different from those of Chhibber and Kollman for at least three different reasons. First, fiscal decentralization does not correspond very well to the degree of political decentralization in a country such that any relationship observed between fiscal decentralization and regional party vote may be due to political, not fiscal decentralization.[149] Second, these analyses include more countries than Chhibber and Kollman's analyses and include control variables for different political institutions, as well as ethnicity.[150]

Third, as suggested in the theoretical discussion of fiscal decentralization, fiscal decentralization may lash regional politicians to national level politics if fiscal decentralization is derived primarily from national transfers and grants. Politicians, that is, at the regional level of government may not be able to secure transfers from the national government without belonging to the party that dominates this level of government – a party likely to be a statewide party. Thus, a high degree of fiscal decentralization may diminish the strength of regional parties in countries. Better data are needed to explore these possibilities, which are more differentiated and include more countries.

To summarize the results presented thus far, having a politically decentralized system of government substantively and significantly increases the electoral strength of regional parties. Having a population in which ethnic groups are segmented into regions, rather than dispersed throughout a country, also adds to the electoral strength of regional parties. Importantly, however, the effect of political decentralization on regional parties is still strong when controlling for geographic dispersion. These models also reveal that more extensive forms of political decentralization increase the electoral strength of regional parties over less extensive forms. Greater fiscal decentralization, though, does not increase regional party vote or denationalization, as Chhibber and Kollman (1998, 2004) suggest, and actually decreases it in some models. Finally, other aspects of political systems, such as cross-regional voting laws and the age of democracy, affect the strength of regional parties. Particular features of decentralization, besides the extent of decentralization, may also influence the electoral strength of regional parties. I explore these characteristics, which vary by region, in the next set of analyses.

7.3. National legislative elections (regional level results)

In the second set of analyses, I study the strength of regional parties in national (lower and upper house) elections as I did in the previous analyses, but in these analyses, I disaggregate the election results by region. Thus, the dependent variable in these models is the electoral strength of regional parties in national elections within each region of a country. This allows me to explore directly how certain characteristics of regions, including autonomy and seat share in the national legislature, influence the strength of regional parties.[151] The analysis includes the same thirty-nine countries studied in the previous analysis.[152] There are nearly 1,000 different regions in this analysis.

Unless otherwise noted, I use ordinary least squares regression with robust standard errors to correct for heteroskedasticity, as well decade fixed-effects to control for trends in regional parties over time. In these models, unlike the previous ones, I also use fixed-effects for countries because there is significant variation in my main variables of interest (i.e. autonomy and regional size) within countries across regions.[153] The results of these analyses are presented in Table 7.4. The results of analyses discussed in the text but not reported in the table are available from the author.

In Models 13–15, I analyze the relationship between regional autonomy, measured dichotomously, and the electoral strength of regional parties. In these models, I control for the same variables that I did in the previous set of analyses, as well as the percentage of seats that individual regions have in the national legislature. According to Model 13, the percentage of parties that are regional parties in an election is about 5 percentage points greater in regions that have autonomy than those that do not. Regional parties also win about 2–3 percentage points more votes and seats in these regions as well, according to Models 14 and 15. These results do not change if I exclude India from the analysis. India is the one country in the study that has significantly changed its regional boundaries over time and the one country for which regional parties have successfully agitated for their own regions.

In alternative models, I explore whether regional parties have stronger positions in regions that have gained autonomy between 1945 and 2002 than in regions that have not. I do so by adding an indicator variable, which is coded 1 if a region has gained autonomy in this period (and only for the years in which it has autonomy) and 0 otherwise. The variable is positive, but only marginally significant in the case of regional party vote. I also explore whether regions that have conversely lost autonomy have fewer votes than they did previously. In this study, only one region, Northern Ireland, has ever lost its autonomy.

According to these models, a greater percentage of the parties that competed in Northern Ireland after it lost autonomy were regional parties than before. They also won a greater percentage

Table 7.4. National elections: full models (regional level results)

	(13)	(14)	(15)	(16)	(17)	(18)
	Number	Votes	Seats	Number	Votes	Seats
Autonomy	5.18***	2.62**	2.57**			
	(1.34)	(1.18)	(1.28)			
Autonomy index				1.55***	1.03**	1.48***
				(0.39)	(0.45)	(0.57)
Ethnic groups with regional base	0.17**	0.30**	0.29*	0.20***	0.32**	0.32**
	(0.07)	(0.14)	(0.16)	(0.07)	(0.14)	(0.16)
Regional size	0.45***	−0.06*	−0.06	0.44***	−0.06*	−0.06
	(0.04)	(0.04)	(0.04)	(0.04)	(0.04)	(0.04)
Nonconcurrent presidential and legislative elections	1.54	1.10***	1.48***	0.52	0.40	0.45
	(1.02)	(0.33)	(0.39)	(1.10)	(0.51)	(0.63)
Concurrent presidential and legislative elections	−2.52*	−3.62***	−3.24***	−3.57**	−4.33***	−4.29***
	(1.46)	(0.91)	(1.00)	(1.52)	(0.99)	(1.12)
Mixed systems	−1.31	−1.07***	−1.24***	−3.63***	−2.61***	−3.47***
	(0.92)	(0.30)	(0.35)	(1.13)	(0.78)	(0.99)
Majority and plurality systems	7.97***	5.95***	4.25***	7.92***	5.91***	4.19***
	(1.00)	(1.10)	(1.49)	(0.99)	(1.09)	(1.48)
Age of democracy	0.02	0.01	0.004	0.03**	0.02	0.02
	(0.01)	(0.02)	(0.02)	(0.02)	(0.02)	(0.02)
Number of regions	0.03	0.02	−0.02	0.07**	0.06*	0.04
	(0.03)	(0.02)	(0.03)	(0.03)	(0.03)	(0.04)
Cross-regional voting laws	−27.47***	−27.89***	−26.11***	−23.82***	−25.50***	−22.71***
	(1.62)	(1.85)	(2.15)	(1.89)	(2.16)	(2.58)
Constant	19.50***	23.75***	22.07***	17.43***	21.54***	17.67***
	(2.20)	(2.26)	(2.61)	(2.59)	(2.91)	(3.55)
R-squared	0.424	0.367	0.265	0.423	0.367	0.266
Observations	6622	6622	6622	6622	6622	6622

Country and decade fixed-effects not shown. Robust standard errors in parentheses.
*$p \leq 0.10$, **$p \leq 0.05$, ***$p \leq 0.01$.

of votes and seats as well. One can imagine that voters offer more support to regional parties after losing autonomy than before in order to regain this autonomy. Regional parties, for their part, may not respond to the disincentive that a lack of autonomy entails since they already have a foothold in the electorate. In this way, regional parties may have a stronger position in regions that lose autonomy than in regions that never had it. More data is needed, however, to see if this trend emerges in other regions.

Model 13 also indicates that regional parties participate in elections more frequently in large regions, but Models 14 and 15 suggest that they do not win more votes or seats in these regions. According to Model 13, for every 10 percentage point increase in the percentage of seats that a region has in the national legislature, the percentage of parties that are regional parties in an election grows by nearly 5 percentage points. In Models 14 and 15 an equivalent increase in the size of regions results in regional parties winning a smaller percentage of votes and seats. The effects are only marginally significant in the case of votes. They are positive, moreover, but insignificant if I cluster the standard errors by country or region instead of using country fixed-effects. These results suggest that politicians are more responsive to the opportunities large regions offer them in terms of controlling the government than voters are in electing them.

In Models 16–18, I substitute the five-point ordinal measure of autonomy for the dichotomous one.[154] According to this model, going from the lowest value on this index to the highest, increases the percentage of votes and seats that regional parties win by 5 and 7 percentage points, respectively. An equivalent change in this index increases the percentage of parties that are regional parties in an election by a slightly greater amount. No region in this study has gone from 0 to 5 on this index, but a number of regions in Spain (e.g. Basque Country, Catalonia, Galicia, and Valencia) have gone from 0 to 4. The remaining regions in Spain increased their level of autonomy from 0 to 3. The size of regions has the same effect in these models as in the previous ones. If I cluster the standard errors in Models 16–18 by country or region, the results for the autonomy index are the same. The results for regional size are also the same in Model 16.

They are not the same, though, in Models 17 and 18. Regional size has a positive effect in these models, which is consistent with expectations, but the effect is insignificant.

To summarize, the results of the previous analysis indicate that the electoral strength of regional parties in national elections is stronger in regions that have autonomy than in those that do not, and that the electoral strength of regional parties is greater in regions with more extensive decision-making authority than in regions with less substantial decision-making authority. Increasing degrees of decentralization, however, do not have as much of an effect on regional parties as does decentralization alone. The analysis also reveals that regional parties compete more frequently in regions with a larger percentage of national legislative seats. This result suggests that the ability to govern is an important factor in the decisions of politicians to form regional parties. In the subsequent section, I explore the features of decentralization that may affect the electoral strength of regional parties at the subnational level.

7.4. Regional legislative elections

In the third set of analyses, I examine the electoral strength of regional parties in regional elections and the effect, in particular, of electoral sequencing. The unit of analysis is the regional election.[155] There are almost 400 regional elections in this analysis occurring between 1977 and 1999 drawn from ten different countries around the world. The analysis includes only a subset of countries in the CLE dataset that have regional elections for which I was able to collect election data. These countries are: Argentina, Belgium, Bosnia-Herzegovina, Czechoslovakia, India, Indonesia, Malaysia, South Africa, Spain, and the United Kingdom. The sequencing of national and regional elections varies in this analysis across countries, within countries, and within regions of the same countries. The analysis is conducted using ordinary least squares regression with robust standard errors and decade fixed-effects.[156] The results of the analysis are presented in Table 7.5.

Table 7.5. Regional elections

	(19)	(20)	(21)	(22)	(23)
	Votes	**Votes**	**Votes**	**Votes**	**Votes**
Majority and plurality systems	−8.57** (3.93)	−9.54*** (3.05)	−8.68** (4.16)	−8.30** (4.15)	−8.68** (3.93
Concurrent with national legislative elections (presidential systems)	0.32 (5.86)		0.53 (6.24)	1.40 (6.32)	1.29 (6.03)
Nonconcurrent with national legislative elections (parlimentary systems)	17.48*** (3.70)		17.36*** (3.82)	16.19*** (3.76)	16.48*** (3.95)
Nonconcurrent with national legislative elections (presidential systems)	20.08*** (5.65)		19.91*** (5.87)	20.17*** (5.82)	19.01*** (5.82)
Number of regional elections	−0.94*** (0.30)	−0.91*** (0.29)	−0.93*** (0.32)	−0.82*** (0.32)	−0.92*** (0.31)
Concurrent with executive elections		−17.99*** (2.74)			
Cross-regional voting laws	−5.34 (6.18)	−6.09 (5.14)	−4.95 (6.94)	−6.36 (6.81)	−3.45 (6.42)
First national elections			−0.63 (5.97)	−10.09 (10.59)	
First regional elections				9.38 (8.56)	
First national and regional elections concurrent					−3.24 (4.15)
Constant	29.95*** (7.93)	47.84*** (7.61)	30.04*** (7.86)	27.99*** (8.07)	30.62*** (7.95)
R-squared	0.204	0.203	0.204	0.209	0.205
Observations	398	398	398	398	398

Decade fixed-effects not shown. Robust standard errors in parentheses.
*$p \leq 0.10$, **$p \leq 0.05$, ***$p \leq 0.01$.

In Model 12, I study the effect of concurrency on the vote for regional parties in regional elections, controlling for the type of electoral system in a country as well as cross-regional laws, among other things. According to Model 12, when regional elections are not concurrent with national legislative elections, regional parties win a greater percentage of the vote than when they are concurrent. In presidential systems with nonconcurrent legislative elections, regional parties win a slightly greater percentage of the vote than in parliamentary systems with nonconcurrent elections. If I do not distinguish between types of executive systems based on concurrency, and simply analyze the effect of different types of executive systems (i.e. presidential versus parliamentary), I do not find a significant effect for executive systems.

In Model 13, I do not distinguish between types of executive systems. Instead, I analyze the effect of current national and regional elections regardless of whether they occur under a presidential or parliamentary system. According to Model 13, concurrent national and regional elections decrease the percentage of votes that regional parties win in regional elections by 18 percentage points. While these effects suggest that the sequencing of national and regional legislative elections affects the electoral strength of regional parties, it is not possible to disentangle this effect from the concurrency of national executive and regional legislative elections. That is, where national legislative and regional legislative elections are concurrent, national executive and regional legislative elections are also concurrent. The election of a national chief executive may have an impact on regional legislative elections, although the effect may depend on the strength of the chief executive (Samuels 2000). The results, nevertheless, show that dynamics at the national level of government (either in the executive or legislative branch) influence electoral outcomes at the regional level when elections to the two are concurrent.

According to every model in Table 7.5, majority and plurality systems decrease the percentage of votes that regional parties win in regional elections over proportional representation systems.[157] They do so by 8 to 10 percentage points. Cross-regional voting laws, as expected, also have a negative effect on regional parties. However, only one country, Indonesia, has cross-regional voting laws in this analysis. Not surprisingly, the effect is not significant. The more regions there are in a country also decreases, as expected, the percentage of votes that regional parties win.

In Models 21–23, I explore the effect of democratic transitions on the electoral strength of regional parties in regional elections. In neither model do transitions affect the strength of regional parties. According to Model 21, having regional elections that occur in the same year as the first national elections in a country does not have a statistically significant effect on the electoral strength of regional parties. Including a variable in the model for the age of democracy instead does not change these results. In Model 22, I add a variable for the first regional elections in a country. These elections do not occur at the same time as the first national elections in two countries – Spain and the United Kingdom. This variable, while positive, is not significant. Dropping the variable for the first national elections in a country does not change this result.

Finally, in Model 23, I analyze if having the first national elections in a country precede the first regional elections has an effect on the electoral strength of regional parties in the first regional elections. Juan Linz and Alfred Stepan (1992) have suggested that holding national elections before regional elections limits the nationalistic dialog present during democratic transitions. In this analysis, I do not find a significant effect for the sequencing of the first national and regional elections on regional parties. However, there are only three countries in this analysis. Belgium, Spain and the United Kingdom, in which the first regional elections are not concurrent with the first national ones, and no cases where the first regional elections are observed and precede the first national ones. Thus, more data are needed to fully test this argument.

7.5. Instrumental variable regression

Thus far, the statistical analysis has not addressed the potential endogeneity between decentralization and regional parties. In order to explore this possibility, I use instrumental variable regression analysis. In this analysis, I study the effect of political decentralization on regional parties in national elections, where the national election year is the unit of analysis. I offer a more detailed discussion of the utility of this estimation technique, and its associated tests of instrument relevance and exogeneity, in the previous chapter. I also describe in the previous chapter the rationale for using the following four variables as instruments for decentralization: physical size, population, territorial noncontiguity, and former UK colony.[158]

While these variables are theoretically linked to decentralization, they do not appear to be related theoretically or empirically to the strength of regional parties other than through their effect on decentralization. In terms of the data, the correlation between regional party vote and the physical size of a country in this analysis is −0.03 and is not significant. The correlation between regional party vote and the remaining three instruments namely, former UK colony, population, and territorial contiguity, are −0.06, 0.04, and −0.03, respectively. None of these relationships are significant. The correlations between these instruments and alternative measures of regional party strength, including denationalization, are similarly low.[159]

I present the second-stage regression results of this analysis in Table 7.6. I do not show the first-stage results but describe them further below. I present models in this table for three different types of analyses. They include: (1) baseline models controlling for ethnolinguistic heterogeneity and dispersion, (2) full models controlling for dispersion as well as alternative institutions that may affect regional party strength, and (3) full models with alternative measures of decentralization as well as regional party strength. For each of these different models, I have explored different combinations of instruments. Ultimately, I have presented in Table 7.6

Table 7.6. Instrumental variable regression

	(24)	(25)	(26)	(27)
	Vote	Vote	Vote	Denat
Political decentralization	−5.03 (4.54)	6.73 (4.20)		
Decentralization index			2.36 (1.59)	
Fiscal decentralization[a]				0.20*** (0.06)
Ethnic groups with regional base	0.44*** (0.09)	0.38*** (0.08)	0.38*** (0.08)	2.35 (1.91)
ELF	9.33* (5.36)			
Concurrent presidential and legislative elections		−1.78 (1.84)	−2.93* (1.61)	1.04 (1.40)
Nonconcurrent presidential and legislative elections		1.34 (2.08)	−0.67 (1.77)	4.76*** (1.54)
Number of regions		−0.03 (0.05)	−0.05 (0.04)	0.02 (0.03)
Age of democracy		−0.05*** (0.02)	−0.06*** (0.02)	−0.07*** (0.01)
Mixed electoral system		−3.75 (3.11)	−3.39 (3.08)	−2.26 (2.54)
Majority and plurality systems		−0.19 (2.29)	0.75 (1.94)	2.59** (1.32)
Cross-regional voting law		−2.86 (3.34)	−4.00 (3.49)	−5.23 (5.19)
Constant	2.56* (1.44)	5.25** (2.56)	3.57 (3.76)	−0.97 (2.20)
Uncentered R-squared	0.108	0.354	0.381	0.382
Observations	262	262	262	160

Decade fixed-effects not shown. Standard errors in parentheses.
*$p \leq 0.10$, **$p \leq 0.05$, ***$p \leq 0.01$.
[a] Subnational expenditure (percentage of total expenditure).
Instrumented Variables: Decentralization. *Instrumental Variables*: Models 24 (Population, Non-contiguity, Physical size, and UK colony), Models 25, 26 and 27 (Population and size).

those models for which the fit of the first-stage regression models is greatest and the instruments are exogenous, according to Sargan's tests of overidentifying restrictions. All the models presented in Table 7.6 not only pass the requisite tests of overidentifying restrictions, but they are also identified according to Anderson cannon correlations likelihood ratio tests. The fits of the first-stage models are also reasonably strong. Shea's partial R-squared for Models 24–27 are 0.15, 0.13, 0.13, and 0.35, respectively.

In all but one of the second-stage regression models presented in Table 7.6, decentralization increases the electoral strength of regional parties. Decentralization's effect, though, is only significant in the case of denationalization. For all of the models presented in this table, Hausman tests indicate that the differences between the IV regressions and OLS models are not systemic. The null hypothesis of the Hausman test is that the OLS models yield consistent estimates. In no case can I reject this null hypothesis. Therefore, I conclude that the OLS models are preferable over the IV models and that decentralization affects regional party vote, rather than vice versa. While instrumental variable regression is never fully satisfying because of the difficulty of finding perfect instruments, the analyses presented in this chapter, as well as the process-tracing of the case studies, suggest that decentralization has an independent effect on regional parties, and is not simply a product of them.

7.6. Conclusion

To summarize, I find that political decentralization increases the electoral strength of regional parties, not vice versa. I also find that more extensive forms of decentralization strengthen regional parties over less extensive ones, although simply having a decentralized system of government seems to have the greatest effect. This is consistent with my argument that decentralization affects regional parties primarily through its institutional structure. The analysis also reveals that certain characteristics of decentralization, such as the number and size of regions and the sequencing of national and regional elections, influence the strength of regional parties. According to the analysis, having large regions and nonconcurrent national and regional elections strengthens regional parties. Fiscal decentralization, however, does not have a robust effect on decentralization, and if anything, has a negative one. In part, this negative relationship may be due to the particular form that fiscal decentralization assumes.

The effect of political decentralization is robust, however, to the inclusion of a number of controls, regarding the institutional context in which decentralization operates and the underlying ethno-linguistic heterogeneity. Accordingly, nonconcurrent presidential elections increase the vote for regional parties over parliamentary systems, while cross-regional voting laws reduce it. Having ethno-linguistic groups segmented into regions also increases the electoral strength of regional parties, although having countries that are heterogeneous overall does not. The type of electoral system in a county does not seem to affect the strength of regional parties. Its effect, however, may depend on the distribution of groups throughout a country and the way in which electoral boundaries are drawn.

Together, the statistical analyses in this chapter, as well as the one in the previous chapter, substantiate my argument that, in general, the ability of decentralization to reduce ethnic conflict and secessionism hinges on the electoral strength of regional parties, and that decentralization itself affects the strength of regional parties depending on particular features of decentralization. Integrating the findings from the two analyses helps in mapping out a plan to construct decentralization successfully. At its core, this plan must focus on establishing parties that compete fairly equally throughout a country. However, the institutions used to create this party system should not themselves have negative effects on ethnic conflict and secessionism. In the conclusion of this book, I further discuss the advantages and disadvantages of different features of decentralization and how to design decentralization effectively in order to build peace within countries.

8
Conclusion

Thus far, the debate surrounding decentralization has focused on whether or not decentralization is an effective tool in mitigating intrastate conflict. This study has tried to shift the focus of this debate, however, from a discussion of whether or not decentralization is effective, to when it is and under what conditions. Decentralization, as this study demonstrates, can reduce intrastate conflict in democracies, but its effectiveness hinges on the shape of the party system, and the balance it strikes between statewide and regional parties. Advancing this debate further, this analysis also identifies the conditions under which parties are more or less likely to alleviate intrastate conflict, and the ways in which political systems may be designed to foster a salutary party system.

Decentralization, I argue, is most successful in reducing intrastate conflict when statewide parties dominate the political landscape and effectively integrate regional interests into their agendas. It is least successful when regional parties are in control. Regional parties create regional identities and are not simply a product of them, fostering identities based on which cleavages yield them the greatest electoral advantage under a given political system. Regional parties also advocate legislation harmful to other regions and regional minorities, and mobilize groups to engage in intrastate conflict while also supporting extremist organizations dedicated toward these ends.

Regional parties, though, are more likely to promote intrastate conflict in certain contexts than in others – a number of which this analysis highlights. Regional parties pose a considerable threat to countries during democratic transitions, as both the cases of Spain and Czechoslovakia demonstrate. Political identities are inchoate in these periods, party competition intense, and political systems subject to major redesign. Party leadership is also important in this regard. The different strategies of regional parties in Spain and India – some violent, others not – all aimed at the same separatist goals makes this apparent. Ethnic composition is likewise relevant. This analysis has focused on conflict involving groups with a regional base because they are the only groups for which decentralization is purported to have an effect. All of these regions are not necessarily homogeneous, however, and regional parties do not necessarily instigate conflict in the two types of regions in the same way. In heterogeneous regions comprised of a single dominant group, regional parties, for example, may build support among regional majorities by neglecting or, still worse, betraying regional minorities, as they have consistently done in India. Regional parties are unlikely, though, to instigate conflict in this manner in completely heterogeneous or completely homogenous regions.

Generally, statewide parties have a more salutary effect on intrastate conflict than regional parties. In competing throughout a country, statewide parties tend to foster identities that transcend regions. They also tend to advocate legislation, which balances the interests of different regions against each other, and at the same time, they never appear to support secession. Often, statewide parties instill more moderate behavior in regional parties as well – inducing regional parties to relinquish demands for independence or support for extremist groups through coalition governments or other bargaining arrangements.

Failing to integrate regional interests into their agendas, statewide parties can have deleterious effects on conflict, as the case of India demonstrates. Like regional ones, though, statewide parties are more likely to reduce intrastate conflict in certain contexts than in others. Statewide parties, for example, are more apt to address the interests of particular regions or groups if their electoral support is pivotal to a party's success. Many factors, in turn, may influence the degree to which either is pivotal, such as legislative seat share, the dispersion of groups throughout a country, and the availability of alternative means of maintaining power. As with regional parties, leadership can play a role in determining the effectiveness of statewide parties in reducing intrastate conflict. The Congress Party, for example, was much less effective in incorporating regional interests into its agenda and quelling conflict, under Indira Gandhi, who had a very centralized leadership style, than under other Congress leaders.

Extending this debate still further, this study suggests a number of ways in which decentralization may be designed to bolster statewide parties and encourage them to integrate regional interests into their agendas. The fact that certain features of decentralization promote regional parties more than others is essential to explaining why decentralization does not reduce intrastate conflict equally in all countries. Electorally, regional parties tend to be strongest in countries that have large regions with their own regional legislatures, and national upper houses of government elected by regional legislatures, as well as nonconcurrent national and regional elections. Thus, in trying to reduce the strength of regional parties, countries may seek to avoid these institutions or seek alternative means by which to limit regional parties, such as cross-regional voting laws.

Ultimately, the influence of regional parties depends not only on the electoral strength of regional parties, but also on the political power of the legislatures in which these parties dominate, as the analysis of Czechoslovakia demonstrates. Therefore, institutions must be designed not only to reduce the electoral strength of regional parties, but also to prevent regional parties from overwhelming the political arena. One way to do this is by denying individual regions a veto power over the national constitution (or any associated legislation), as regions had in Czechoslovakia. Another way is to prevent regional parties from violating the political and civil rights of regional minorities at the subnational level by reifying these rights at the national level. Constitutional courts, which in decentralized systems of government seek to ensure that legislation passed at different levels of government does not violate the national constitution, can play a vital role in this respect.

227

Identifying the conditions under which decentralization is most likely to reduce intrastate conflict, and the institutions most favorable to them, is essential for constructing decentralization in a way that effectively manages intrastate conflict. For these systems to have a real impact on peace, though, these recommendations must also be feasible to implement in practice. Fortunately, decentralization, as outlined in this study, is feasible both logistically as well as politically. It would be naïve to say that this system of government is easy to implement. It is never easy to change any country's political system no matter the arrangement. However, political systems do change and in this case, political incentives are aligned to bring about this change.

Furthermore, logistically, decentralization is more practicable than other apparent solutions to intrastate conflict, such as partition. To decentralize, countries must create subnational legislatures, host free elections, and decide how to distribute authority among different levels of government. Undeniably, these are expensive undertakings and deciding how to allocate authorities among levels of government is complicated. However, subnational legislatures already exist in many centralized countries, even though they do not have decision-making powers as they do in decentralized systems of government. Moreover, a number of international bodies, such as the World Bank, may aid in this process, offering countries advice on decentralization at a minimum. Furthermore, decisions about how to allocate authorities are never absolute, but rather are always recast to incorporate new issues and demands.

Partition, in contrast, typically entails large population transfers, which along with nondivisible resources make partition difficult, if not impossible, while partition itself can create fragile rump states that are vulnerable to attack (Byman 1997; Sambanis 2000). Likewise, consociationalism (Lijphart 1977, 1996), of which decentralization is only one component, is not necessarily conducive to peace. In fact, certain elements of consociationalism, including minority veto powers, are counterproductive to decentralization for reasons already described. Consociationalism can also foster and empower parties that form along regional and ethnic lines, thereby, freezing identities along these lines and immobilizing legislatures. A sundry of empirical research questions the utility of consociationalism in this regard (Wilkinson 2004; Norris 2008).

Certain features of decentralization, moreover, which limit the influence of regional parties, are also feasible to implement logistically. Of course, some features are easier to put into practice than others, such as changes in regional boundaries. Large regions are more conducive to regional parties while very small regions reduce the incentives for statewide parties to incorporate regional interests into their agenda. Ideally, regions would thus be moderately and equally sized. Regional boundaries rarely change, however. Exceptional cases include India and Nigeria, the latter having changed its boundaries several times over the course of history.

Other features of decentralization are easier to manipulate than regional boundaries, however, including the procedure by which countries elect upper houses. Changing an existing system in which regional legislatures elect upper houses to one in which they do not, requires little more than a change in electoral law. Admittedly, direct elections to upper houses are likely to be more costly than indirect ones, since the former entails large public campaigns while the latter does not. Yet, this seems like a small price to pay to potentially reduce intrastate conflict, a cost most countries with two chambers already shoulder. Nevertheless, to reduce the costs of these campaigns while curtailing regional parties, countries may link upper house elections to lower house ones.

The sequencing of national and regional elections is also rather easy to manipulate. The two are easiest to coordinate in systems where chief executives have fixed terms. In these systems, synchronizing national and regional elections again requires little more than a change in electoral law. In parliamentary systems, though, where legislatures frequently throw chief executives out of office before their terms end, elections are harder to synchronize. Even if elections initially occur in these systems at the same time, they may be delinked if national or regional legislatures prematurely throw their government out of office. In order to resynchronize them, the government still standing would have to abbreviate its term of office.

Features orthogonal to decentralization, such as the electoral system, may also help regulate the strength of regional parties. Cross-regional voting laws are valuable in this regard, and many countries already have them in place (e.g. Hungary, Mexico, Russia, Turkey, and the United States by means of the Electoral College). These laws oblige parties to compete in a certain number of regions in order to win seats, and can even require parties to compete in a certain number of districts within these regions in order to win seats. The former compels parties to incorporate the interests of multiple regions into their agendas, while the latter obliges them to incorporate the interests of various groups within these regions. Whether or not parties ultimately undertake these measures depends on the number of districts in which parties must compete and the distribution of groups within these regions. If groups are segmented into districts within regions, requiring parties to compete in a certain number of districts will compel parties to incorporate multiple groups into their agendas. If they are dispersed throughout districts, this dictate will not have the same effect.

The institutions countries use to shape their party systems should not themselves have negative effects on ethnic conflict and secessionism. Cross-regional voting laws exemplify institutions, which reduce the strength of regional parties without seeming to affect intrastate conflict adversely. Election concurrency is another avenue through which countries can reduce the electoral strength of regional parties without seemingly harmful side effects on intrastate conflict. Holding executive and legislative elections concurrently at the national level can reduce regional parties and does not seem to have an independent effect on intrastate conflict. In parliamentary systems, these elections are always concurrent. In presidential systems, they must be intentionally coordinated, which may have the added benefit of increasing voter turnout in legislative elections (Franklin and Hirczy 1998).

The system of government outlined in this study is not only feasible logistically, but also politically as well. The support of statewide parties is key in this regard since statewide parties generally dominate politics in centralized systems of government. Fortunately, statewide parties often support decentralization and, in fact, were major proponents of decentralization in all three cases analyzed in this study. Statewide parties are most likely to support decentralization if they believe they can maintain or expand their own power through decentralization. The system of government identified here is consistent with these objectives.

Garnering public support for decentralization in situations where statewide parties do not dominate politics, as in Czechoslovakia, is more challenging. In these cases, international involvement and pressure is critical. Pressure or guidance from international bodies may help entice domestic actors to support decentralization and the variant of decentralization proposed here. Fortunately, as I already indicated, international organizations and major powers, like the United States, are often supportive of decentralization. The United States played this role in the reconstruction of Iraq, advocating decentralization as a means to end protracted conflict in this country and offering Iraqis advice on how to decentralize. The World Bank also offers financial inducements to countries to decentralize fiscally, as well as guidance on how to do so successfully.

Building institutions to foster peace is a complex and challenging process for which the ideas presented in this book I hope have offered a strong foundation. Still, though, the factors that I have isolated here, while important, are not necessarily the only factors helpful for harnessing the positive effects of decentralization. In other words, there may be other features of decentralization that this study has not explored or that it has touched on only lightly, which may impinge on the ability of decentralization to ameliorate intrastate conflict, including constitutional courts and local governments. Similarly, the factors that I identify here as favoring a salutary party system, while likewise important, are not necessarily the only factors that influence the types of parties that arise in countries and their political behavior within countries. International factors, including regional integration schemes, are an interesting but underexplored area in this regard. Undoubtedly, much work remains to be done in this area, although this study I hope has opened the door to a new and exciting debate about how to design peace through decentralization.

References

Abadie, A. and Gardeazabal, J. (2003). The Economic Costs of Conflict: A Case Study of the Basque Country. *American Economic Review* 93 (1): 113–32.

Achen, C. H. (1986). *The Statistical Analysis of Quasi-Experiments*. Berkeley: University of California Press.

——(2000). *Why Lagged Dependent Variables Can Suppress the Explanatory Power of Other Independent Variables*. Unpublished Manuscript.

Agarwal, U. C. (1997). National Dilemma: Regionalization of Politics and Power. In *Coalition Government and Politics in India*, edited by Subhash C. Kashyap, 27–40. New Delhi: Uppal Publishing House.

Agranoff, R. and Ramos Gallarín, J. A. (1998). La Evolución Hacia una Democracia Federal en España: Un Examen del Sistema de Relaciones Intergubernamentales. In *El Estado de las Autonomías ¿Hacia un Nuevo Federalismo?*, edited by Robert Agranoff and Rafael Bañón i Martínez, 55–103. Bilbao, España: Instituto Vasco de Administración Pública.

Aja Fernández, E. (1991). Los Parlamentos de las Comunidades Autónomas. In *El Futuro de las Autonomías Territoriales: Comunidades Autónomas, Balance y Perspectivas*, edited by Luis Martín Rebollo, 109–29. Santander, España: Universidad de Cantabria.

Alberti Rovira, E. (1991). La Colaboración entre el Estado y las Comunidades Autónomas. In *El Futuro de las Autonomías Territoriales: Comunidades Autónomas, Balance y Perspectivas*, edited by Luis Martín Rebollo, 201–26. Santander, España: Universidad de Cantabria.

Alcántara Sáez, M. and Martínez Rodríguez, A., eds. (1998). *Las elecciones Autonómicas en España, 1980–97*. Madrid: Centro de Investigaciones Sociológicas.

Alesina, A. and Spolare, E. (1997). On the Number and Size of Nations. *The Quarterly Journal of Economics* 112 (4): 1027–56.

Armet, L. et al. (1988). *Federalismo y Estado de las Autonomías*. Barcelona: Planeta.

Arora, B. (2002). The Political Parties and the Party System: The Emergence of New Coalitions. In *Parties and Party Politics in India*, edited by Zoya Hasan, 504–32. New Delhi, India: Oxford University Press.

Aznar Grasa, A. and López Laborda, J. (1994). *Una Metodología para la Determinación de las Necesidades de Gasto de las Comunidades Autónomas.* Madrid: Instituto de Estudios Fiscales.

Bakke, K. M. and Wibbels, E. (2006). Diversity, Disparity and Civil Conflict in Federal States. *World Politics* 59 (October): 1–50.

Banerjee, K. (1984). *Regional Political Parties in India.* New Delhi, India: B.R. Publishing Corporation.

Bañón i Martínez, R. and Tamayo, M. (1998). Las Relaciones Intergubernamentales en España: El Nuevo Papel de la Administración Central en el Modelo de Relaciones Intergubernamentales. In *El Estado de las Autonomías ¿Hacia un Nuevo Federalismo?*, edited by Robert Agranoff and Rafael Bañón i Martínez, 105–59. Bilbao, España: Instituto Vasco de Administración Pública.

Bartels, L. M. (1991). Instrumental and "Quasi-Instrumental" Variables. *American Journal of Political Science* 35 (3): 777–800.

Bates, R. H. (1983). Modernization, Ethnic Competition and the Rationality of Politics in Contemporary Africa. In *State versus Ethnic Claims: African Policy Dilemmas*, edited by Donald S. Rothchild and Victor A. Olorunsola, 152–71. Boulder, CO: Westview Press.

Beramendi, J. G. (1995). Identity, Ethnicity and State in Spain: 19th and 20th Centuries. *Nationalism and Ethnic Politics* 5 (3/4): 79–100.

Beramendi, P. and Máiz, R. (2004). Spain: Unfulfilled Federalism (1978–1996). In *Federalism and Territorial Cleavages*, edited by Ugo M. Amoretti and Nancy Bermeo, 123–54. Baltimore, MD: The Johns Hopkins University Press.

Bermeo, N. (2002). The Import of Institutions. *Journal of Democracy* 13 (2): 96–110.

Bertrand, M., Duflo, E., and Mullainathan, S. (2004). How Much Should We Trust Difference in Differences Estimates? *Quarterly Journal of Economics* 119 (1): 249–75.

Bhargava, P. K. (1984). Transfers from the Center to the States in India. *Asian Survey* 24.6 (June): 665–87.

Bhatnagar, S. and Kumar, P., eds. (1988a). *Regional Political Parties in India.* New Delhi, India: Ess Ess Publications.

——(1988b). Preface. In *Regional Political Parties in India*, edited by Satyavan Bhatnagar and Pradeep Kumar, vii–xi. New Delhi, India: Ess Ess Publications.

Birnir, J. K. (2007). Divergence in Diversity? The Dissimilar Effects of Cleavages on Electoral Politics in New Democracies. *American Journal of Political Science* 51 (3): 602–19.

Biswas, G. (1992). Emergence of the United Minorities Front in Assam. In *Regional Political Parties in North East India*, edited by L. S. Gassah, 47–76. New Delhi, India: Omsons Publications.

Blumi, I. (2001). Kosovo: From the Brink – and Back Again. *Current History* 100 (649): 369–74.

Bolton, P. and Roland, G. (1997). The Breakup of Nations: A Political Economy Analysis. *The Quarterly Journal of Economics* CXII (November): 1057–90.

Bombwall, K. R. (1967). *The Foundations of Indian Federalism*. New York: Asia Publishing House.

Bookman, M. Z. (1991). *The Political Economy of Discontinuous Development: Regional Disparities and Inter-regional Conflict*. New York: Praeger.

Bound, J., Jaeger, D. A., and Baker, R. M. (1995). Problems with Instrumental Variable Estimation when Correlation between the Instruments and the Endogenous Explanatory Variable is Weak. *Journal of the American Statistical Association* 90 (430): 443–50.

Brady, H. E. and Collier, D., eds. (2004). *Rethinking Social Inquiry: Diverse Tools, Shared Standards*. Berkeley, CA: Rowman & Littlefield, Inc.

Brambor, T., Clark, W. R., and Golder, M. (2006). Understanding Interaction Models: Improving Empirical Analyses. *Political Analysis* 14 (1): 63–82.

Brancati, D. (2003). *Design over Conflict: Managing Ethnic Conflict and Secessionism through Decentralization*. PhD Thesis, Columbia University.

——(2005). Pawns Take Queen: The Destabilizing Effects of Regional Parties in Europe. Special Issue, *Constitutional Political Economy* 16 (2): 143–59.

——(2006). Decentralization: Fueling the Fire or Dampening the Flames of Ethnic Conflict and Secessionism. *International Organization* 60 (July): 651–85.

——(2007). *Constituency-level Elections (CLE) dataset*. New York: New York. http://cle.wustl.edu

——(2008a). The Origins and Strengths of Regional Parties. *British Journal of Political Science* 38 (1): 135–59.

——(2008b). Winning Alone: The Fate of Independent Candidates Worldwide, *Journal of Politics*, 3 (July): 648–662.

Braña, F. J. and Serna de los Mozos, V. M. (1997). *La Descentralización de Competencias de Gasto Público: Teoría y Aplicación a España.* Madrid: Editorial Civitas, SA

Brass, P. R. (1974). *Language, Religion and Politics in North India.* Cambridge: Cambridge University Press.

——(1997). *Theft of an Idol.* Princeton, NJ: Princeton University Press.

Brassloff, A. (1989). Spain: The State of the Autonomies. In *Federalism and Nationalism,* edited by Murray Forsyth, 24–50. Leicester: Leicester University Press.

Braumoeller, B. F. (2004). Hypothesis Testing and Multiplicative Interaction Terms. *International Organization* 58 (4): 807–20.

Brubaker, R. (1996). *Nationalism Reframed: Nationhood and the National Question in the New Europe.* Cambridge: Cambridge University Press.

Brzinski, J. B. (1999). The Changing Forms of Federalism and Party Electoral Strategies: Belgium and the European Union. *Publius: The Journal of Federalism* 29 (1): 45–70.

Buchanan, J. M. and Faith, R. L. (1987). Secession and the Limits of Taxation: Toward a Theory of Internal Exit. *The American Economic Review* LXXVII: 1023–31.

Bunce, V. (1999). *Subversive Institutions: The Design and the Destruction of Socialism and the State.* Cambridge: Cambridge University Press.

Burgess, M. (1993). Federalism as Political Ideology: Interests, Benefits and Beneficiaries in Federalism and Federation. In *Comparative Federalism and Federation: Competing Traditions and Future Directions,* edited by Michael Burgess and Alain-G. Gagnon, 102–14. Toronto: University of Toronto Press.

Buse, M. (1984). *La Nueva Democracia Española: Sistema de Partidos y Orientación del Voto 1976–1983.* Madrid: Unión Editorial, SA.

Byman, D. (1997). Divided They Stand: Lessons about Partition from Iraq and Lebanon. *Security Studies* 7 (1): 1–29.

Campbell, T. (1997). Innovations and Risk Taking: The Engine of Reform in Local Government in Latin America and the Caribbean. *World Bank Discussion Papers, No. 357.* Washington, DC: World Bank.

Candland, C. (1997). Congress Decline and Party Pluralism in India. *Journal of International Affairs* 51.1 (summer): 19–35.

Caramani, D. (2000). *Elections in Western Europe since 1815: Election Results by Constituencies.* London: Macmillan Reference.

Carey, J., and Shugart, M. S. (1995). Incentives to Cultivate a Personal Vote: A Rank Ordering of Electoral Formulas. *Electoral Studies* 14 (4): 417–39.

References

Cederman, Lars-Erik and Girardin, L. (2007). Beyond Fractionalization: Mapping Ethnicity onto Nationalist Insurgencies. *American Political Science Review* 101 (1): 173–85.

Center for International Development and Conflict Management (CIDCM). (2002). *Minorities at Risk Project*. College Park, MD: University of Maryland Press. http://www.cidcm.umd.edu/mar/. Accessed December 1, 2007.

Centro de Investigaciones Sociológicas (CIS). (1996). *Identidad Regional y Nacionalismo en el Estado de las Autonomías, CIS 2228*. Madrid: Centro de Investigaciones Sociológicas.

——(1998). *Instituciones y Autonomías, CIS 2286*. Madrid: Centro de Investigaciones Sociológicas.

——(2001). *Situación Social y Política del País Vasco, XIII, CIS 2407*. Madrid: Centro de Investigaciones Sociológicas.

——(2003). *Instituciones y Autonomías, CIS 2455*. Madrid: Centro de Investigaciones Sociológicas.

Chandler, W. M. (1987). *Federalism and Political Parties*. In *Federalism and the Role of the State*, edited by Herman Bakvis and William M. Chandler, 149–70. Toronto: University of Toronto Press.

Chandra, K. (2004). *Why Ethnic Parties Succeed: Patronage and Ethnic Headcounts in India*. Cambridge: Cambridge University Press.

——(2005). Ethnic Parties and Democratic Stability. *Perspectives on Politics* 3 (2): 235–52.

Chhibber, P. K. (1995). Political Parties, Electoral Competition, Government Expenditures and Economic Reform in India. *Journal of Development Studies* 32.1 (October): 74–96.

——(1999). *Democracy Without Associations: Transformation of the Party System and Social Cleavages in India*. Ann Arbor, MI: University of Michigan Press.

——and Kollman, K. (1998). Party Aggregation and the Number of Parties in India and the United States. *American Political Science Review* 92 (2): 329–42.

————(2004). *The Formation of National Party Systems: Federalism and Party Competition in Great Britain, Canada, India and the United States*. Princeton, NJ: Princeton University Press.

——and Petrocik, J. R. (1989). The Puzzle of Indian Politics: Social Cleavages and the Indian Party System. *British Journal of Political Science* 19.2 (April): 191–210.

Chong, D. and Druckman, J. N. (2007). Framing Public Opinion in Competitive Democracies. *American Political Science Review* 101 (4): 637–55.

Christiansen, T. (1998). *Plaid Cymru*: Dilemmas and Ambiguities of Welsh Regional Nationalism. In *Regionalist Parties in Western Europe*, edited by Lieven de Winter and Huri Türsan, 125–43. New York: Routledge.

Christin, T. and Hug, S. (2006). Federalism and the Geographic Location of Groups and Conflict. *Paper Presented at the Annual Meeting of the American Political Science Association*, Philadelphia, Pennsylvania.

Chueca Rodríguez, R. L. and Montero, J. R., eds. (1995). *Elecciones Autonómicas en Aragón*. Madrid: Editorial Tecnos.

Collier, P. and Hoeffler, A. (2004). Greed and Grievance in Civil War. *Oxford Economic Papers* 56 (4): 563–96.

Cotarelo, R. G. (1992). Los Partidos Políticos. In *Transición Política y Consolidación Democrática en España (1975–1986)*, edited by Ramón García Cotarelo, 299–325. Madrid: Centro de Investigaciones Sociológicas.

Cox, G. W. (1997). *Making Votes Count: Strategic Coordination in the World's Electoral System*. Cambridge: Cambridge University Press.

Cox, R. H. and Frankland, E. G. (1995). The Federal State and the Breakup of Czechoslovakia: An Institutional Analysis. *Publius: The Journal of Federalism* 25 (1): 71–88.

de Burgos, J. (1983). *España: por un Estado Federal*. Barcelona: Editorial Argos Vergara, S.A.

Dědek, O. (1997). *Ekonomické Aspekty Zániku Československa: Příklad Kulturního Rozchodu Národů*. Praha, Česká Republika: Nakladatelství Fortuna.

de Esteban, J. and López Guerra, L. M. (1982). *Los Partidos Políticos en la España Actual*. Barcelona: Editorial Planeta.

Desposato, S. W. (2004). The Impact of Federalism on National Political Party Cohesion in Brazil. *Legislative Studies Quarterly* XXIX (2): 259–85.

de Winter, L. and Türsan, H., eds. (1998). *Regionalist Parties in Western Europe*. New York: Routledge.

Diamond, L. and Tsalik, S. (1999). Size of Democracy: The Case for Decentralization. In *Developing Democracy: Toward Consolidation*, edited by Larry Diamond, 117–60. Baltimore, MD: The Johns Hopkins University Press.

Dikshit, R. D. (1975). *The Political Geography of Federalism: An Inquiry into the Origins and Stability*. Delhi, India: Macmillan Company of India.

Dorff, R. H. (1994). Federalism in Eastern Europe: Part of the Solution or Part of Problem? *Publius: The Journal of Federalism* 24.2 (spring): 99–114.

Dua, B. D. (1985). Federalism or Patrimonialism: The Making and Unmaking of Chief Ministers in India. *Asian Survey* 25.8 (August): 793–804.

Duchacek, I. D. (1987). *Comparative Federalism: The Territorial Dimension of Politics*. Lanham, MD: University Press of America.

——(1988). Dyadic Federations and Confederations. *Publius: The Journal of Federalism* 18.2 (spring): 5–31.

Dutta, A. (1998). *Growth and Development of a Regional Political Party: The Asom Gana Parishad*. In *Regional Political Parties in India*, edited by Satyavan Bhatnagar and Pradeep Kumar, 29–49. New Delhi, India: Ess Ess Publications.

Dutta, N. (1992). Regional Political Parties of Assam. In *Regional Political Parties in North East India*, edited by L. S. Gassah, 11–7. New Delhi, India: Omsons Publications.

Duverger, M. (1969). *Political Parties: Their Organization and Activity in the Modern State*. London: Metheun.

Dvořáková,V. and Kunc, J. (1996). Zrod Českeho Straniského Systému. In *Krystalizace Struktury Politických Stran v České Republice po Roce 1989*, edited by Vladimíra Dvořáková and Aleš Gerloch, 55–63. Praha, Česká Republika: Česká Společnost pro Politické Vědy.

Eaton, K. (2004). *Politics Beyond the Capital: The Design of Subnational Institutions in South America*. Stanford, CA: Stanford University Press.

Elazar, D. J. (1987). *Exploring Federalism*. Tuscaloossa, AL: University of Alabama Press.

——, ed. (1994). *Federal Systems of the World: A Handbook of Federal, Confederal, and Autonomy Arrangements*. Harlow, UK: Longman Current Affairs.

Election Commission of India. (1991). *Statistical Report on the General Elections, 1991 to the Tenth Lok Sabha*. New Delhi, India: Election Commission of India.

——(1996). *Statistical Report on the General Elections, 1996 to the Eleventh Lok Sabha*. New Delhi, India: Election Commission of India.

——(1998). *Statistical Report on the General Elections, 1998 to the Twelfth Lok Sabha*. New Delhi, India: Election Commission of India.

——(1999). *Statistical Report on the General Elections, 1999 to the Thirteenth Lok Sabha*. New Delhi, India: Election Commission of India.

Elkins, Z. and Sides, J. (2007). Can Institutions Build Unity in Multiethnic States? *American Political Science Review* 101 (4): 693–708.

Elster, J. (1995). Consenting Adults or the Sorcerer's Apprentice? Explaining the Breakup of the Czechoslovak Federation. *East European Constitutional Review* (winter): 36–41.

Erkizia, T., Garitano, M., Baigorri, E., Cereceda, J. L., Egido, J. A., and de la Cueva, J. (1988). *Euskadi, la Renuncia del PSOE*. Bilbao, España: Txalaparta Argitaletxea, S. L.

Escobar-Lemmon, M. (2003). Political Support for Decentralization: An Analysis of the Colombian and Venezuelan Legislatures. *American Journal of Political Science* 47 (4): 683–97.

Falleti, T. G. (2005). A Sequential Theory of Decentralization: Latin American Cases in Comparative Perspective. *American Political Science Review* 99 (3): 327–46.

Fearon, J. D. (2003). Ethnic and Cultural Diversity by Country. *Journal of Economic Growth* 8 (2): 195–222.

Fearon, J. D. and Laitin, D. D. (1996). Explaining Interethnic Cooperation. *American Political Science Review* 90 (4): 715–35.

————(2003). Ethnicity, Insurgency and Civil War. *American Political Science Review* 97 (1): 75–90.

Fearon, J. D., Kasara, K., and Laitin, D. D. (2007). Ethnic Minority Rule and Civil War Onset. *American Political Science Review* 101 (1): 187–93.

Fearon, J. D. and van Houten, P. (2002). The Politicization of Cultural and Economic Difference: A Return to the Theory of Regional Autonomy Movements. *Paper Presented at the Fifth Meeting of the Laboratory in Comparative Ethnic Processes (LiCEP)*, May 10–11, 2002.

Federal Statistical Office. (1991). *Preliminary Results of the Population and Housing Census: Czech and Slovak Federal Republics, March 3, 1991*. Prague, Czechoslovakia: Federal Statistical Office.

Filippov, M., Ordeshook, P. C., and Shvetsova, O. (2004). *Designing Federalism: A Theory of Self-sustainable Federal Institutions*. Cambridge: Cambridge University Press.

Fossas, E. (1999). Asimetría y Plurinacionalidad en el Estado Autonómico. In *Asimetría Federal y Estado Plurinacional: El Debate Sobre la Acomodación de la Diversidad en Canada, Bèlica y España*, edited by Enric Fossas and Ferrán Requejo, 275–301. Madrid: Editorial Trotta, S.A.

Foster, E. M. (1997). Instrumental Variables for Logistic Regression: An Illustration. *Social Science Research* 26 (4): 487–584.

Franklin, M. N. and Hirczy, W. P. (1998). Separated Powers, Divided Government and Turnout in U.S. Presidential Elections. *American Journal of Political Science* 41 (1): 316–26.

References

Freedom House. (2007). *Freedom in the World* 1972–2007. Washington, DC: Freedom House.

Fusi Aizpurua, J. P. (2000). *España: La Evolución de la Identidad Nacional.* Madrid: Ediciones Temas de Hoy.

Gagnon Jr., V. P. (1994/1995). Ethnic Nationalism and International Conflict. *International Security* 19 (3): 130–66.

Ganguly, S. (1996). Explaining the Kashmir Insurgency: Political Mobilization and Institutional Decay. *International Security* 21.2 (autumn): 76–107.

García Ferrando, M. (1982). Regionalismo y Autonomias en España 1976–1979. Madrid: Centro de Investigaciones Sociológicas.

—— López Aranguren, E. M. and Beltrán, M. (1994). *La Conciencia Nacional y Regional en la España de las Autonomías.* Madrid: Centro de Investigaciones Sociológicas.

Garmendia Martínez, J. A., Parraluna, F., and Pérez-Agote, A. (1982). *Abertzales y Vascos: Identificación Vasquista y Nacionalista en el País Vasco.* Madrid: Akal Editor.

Gassah, L. S., ed. (1992). Regional *Political Parties in North East India.* New Delhi, India: Omsons Publications.

Gavela, D. (1980). "El Federalista Daniel Elazar, en el Congreso de Citep 'El Sistema Autonómico Español Tiende al Separatismo.'" *El País*, 30 Noviembre 1980, 18.

Geddes, B. (1990). How the Cases You Choose Affect the Answers You Get: Selection Bias in Comparative Politics. *Political Analysis* 2 (1): 131–50.

Gerring, J., Thacker, S. C., and Moreno, C. (2005). Centripetal Democratic Governance: A Theory and Global Inquiry. *American Political Science Review* 99:4 (November) 567–81.

Ghobarah, H. A., Huth, P., and Russett, B. (2003). Civil Wars Kill and Maim People – Long After the Shooting Stops. *American Political Science Review* 97 (2): 189–202.

Gibson, J. L. and Gouws, A. (2000). Social Identities and Political Intolerance: Linkages within the South African Mass Public. *American Journal of Political Science* 44 (2): 278–92.

Giuliano, E. (2000). Who Determines the Self in the Politics of Self-Determination? Identity and Preference Formation in Tatarstan's Mobilization. *Comparative Politics* 32 (3): 295–316.

—— (2006). Secessionism from the Bottom Up: Democratization, Nationalism and Local Accountability in the Russian Transition. *World Politics* 58 (2): 276–310.

Gleason, G. (1990). *Federalism and Nationalism: The Struggle for Republican Rights in the USSR.* Boulder, CO: Westview Press.

Grau Creus, M. (2000). *The Effects of Institutions and Political Parties upon Federalism: The Channeling and Integration of the Autonomous Communities within the Central-Level Policy Process in Spain (1983–1996).* PhD Thesis. European University Institute, Florence.

Gregor, M. and Caha, L. (1993). Volby a Okresy. *Sociologický Časopis* XXIX (4): 493–515.

Grzymala-Busse, A. M. (2002). *Redeeming the Communist Past: The Regeneration of the Communist Successor Parties in East Central Europe.* Cambridge: Cambridge University Press.

Guerrero Salom, E. (2000). *Crisis y Cambios en las Relaciones Parlamento-Gobierno 1993–1996.* Madrid: Editorial Tecnos, SA.

Gunther, R., Sani, G. and Shabad, G. (1986). *Spain After Franco: The Making of a Competitive Party System.* Berkeley, CA: University of California Press.

Gurr, T. R. (2000). *Peoples versus States: Minorities at Risk in the New Century.* Washington, DC: United States Institute of Peace Press.

Habyarimana, J., Humphreys, M., Posner, D. N., and Weinstein, J. M. (2007). Why Does Ethnic Diversity Undermine Public Goods Provision. *American Political Science Review* 101 (4): 709–25.

Hale, H. E. (2004). Divided We Stand: Institutional Sources of Ethnofederal State Survival and Collapse. *World Politics* 56 (2): 165–93.

Hamann, K. (1999). Federalist Institutions, Voting Behavior and Party Systems in Spain. *Publius: The Journal of Federalism* 29 (1): 111–37.

Hamilton, A., Madison, J. and Jay, J. (1987). *The Federalist Papers,* edited by Isaac Kramnick. Harmondsworth: Penguin Classics.

Hampl, S. (1991). *Informace.* 18/4. Praha, Československo: Institut pro Výzkum Veřejného Mínění.

—— (1992). *Názory Čs. Veřejnosti na Státoprávní Uspořádání a na Referendum.* 2/17. Praha, Československo: Institut pro Výzkum Veřejného Mínění.

Hardgrave Jr., R. L. (1994). India: The Dilemmas of Diversity. In *Nationalism, Ethnic Conflict and Democracy,* edited by Larry Diamond and Marc F. Plattner, 71–85. Baltimore, MD: The John Hopkins University Press.

Hardin, R. (1997). *One for All: The Logic of Group Conflict.* Princeton, NJ: Princeton University Press.

Hart, H. C. (1988). Political Leadership in India: Dimensions and Limits. In *India's Democracy: An Analysis of Changing State-Society Relations,* edited by Atul Kohli, 18–61. Princeton, NJ: Princeton University Press.

References

Hartzell, C. and Hoddie, M. (2003). Institutionalizing Peace: Power Sharing and Post-Civil War Conflict Management. *American Journal of Political Science* 47 (2): 318–32.

Hasan, Z. (2002). Introduction: Conflict Pluralism and the Competitive Party System in India. In *Parties and Party Politics in India*, edited by Zoya Hasan, 1–36. New Delhi, India: Oxford University Press.

Havel, M. (1991). Nové Zákony o Rozpočtových Pravidlech. *Finance a Úvěr* 41 (4): 143–51.

Hearl, D. J., Budge, I., and Pearson, B. (1996). Distinctiveness of Regional Voting: A Comparative Analysis across the European Community Countries (1979–93). *Electoral Studies* 15 (2): 167–82.

Heath, A. and Yadav, Y. (2002). The United Colours of Congress: Social Profile of Congress Voters, 1996–1998. In *Parties and Party Politics in India*, edited by Zoya Hasan, 107–49. New Delhi, India: Oxford University Press.

Hechter, M. (1992). The Dynamics of Secession. *Acta Sociologica* 35 (4): 267–83.

——(2000). *Containing Nationalism*. New York: Oxford University Press.

Henderson, K. (1995). Czechoslovakia: The Failure of Consensus Politics and the Breakup of the Federation. *Regional and Federal Studies* 5 (2): 111–33.

Herbst, J. (2000). *States and Power in Africa: Comparative Lessons in Authority and Control*. Princeton, NJ: Princeton University Press.

Herrera, Y. M. (2005). *Imagined Communities: The Sources of Russian Regionalism*. Cambridge: Cambridge University Press.

Hewitt, J. J., Wilkenfeld, J., and Gurr, T. R. (2008). *Peace and Conflict 2008*. College Park, MD: Center for International Development and Conflict Management (CIDCM).

Holzer, A. and Schwegler, B. (1998). The *Südtiroler Volkspartei*: A Hegemonic Ethnoregionalist Party. In *Regionalist Parties in Western Europe*, edited by Lieven de Winter and Huri Türsan, 158–73. New York: Routledge.

Honajzer, J. (1996). *Občanské Fórum: Vznik, Vývoj a Rozpad*. Praha, Česká Republika: Orbis.

Horowitz, D. L. (1985). *Ethnic Groups in Conflict*. Berkeley, CA: University of California Press.

——(1991). *A Democratic South Africa? Constitutional Engineering in a Divided Society*. Berkeley, CA: University of California Press.

Hug, S. (2003). Selection Bias in Comparative Research: The Case of Incomplete Data Sets. *Political Analysis* 11 (3): 255–74.

——(2005). Federal Stability in Unequal Societies. Special Issue, *Constitutional Political Economy* 16 (3): 113–24.

——(2007). *Institutions and Conflict Resolution: Dealing with Endogeneity*, University of Zurich, Unpublished Manuscript.

Innes, A. (1997). The Breakup of Czechoslovakia: The Impact of Party Development on the Separation of the State. *East European Politics and Societies* 11 (3): 393–435.

International Monetary Fund (IMF). (2001). *Government Finance Statistics*. Washington, DC: International Monetary Fund.

Iyengar, S. (1991). *Is Anyone Responsible: How Television Frames Issues?* Chicago: University of Chicago Press.

——and Valentino, N. A. (2000). Who Says What? Source Credibility as a Mediator of Campaign Advertising. In *Elements of Reason: Cognition, Choice and the Bounds of Rationality*, edited by Arthur Lupia, Matthew D. McCubbins and Samuel L. Popkin, 108–29. Cambridge: Cambridge University Press.

Iyer, V. R. K. (1999). The Alarum Rings – The Constitution's Soul Must Be Saved. In *Reconstructing the Republic*, edited by Upendra Baxi, Alice Jacob, and Tarlok Singh, 49–68. New Delhi, India: Har-Anand Publications Pvt. Ltd.

Janda, K. (1980). *Political Parties: A Cross-national Survey*. New York: Free Press.

Jensen, N. M. and Young, D. J. (2008). Investment Risk: What Makes the Developing World Countries Seem Prone to Violence? *Journal of Conflict Resolution*, 52 (4): 527–547.

Jozífková, B. (1990). *Veřejné Mínění o Ekonomické Reformě*. 21/5. Praha, Česká Republika: Institut pro Výzkum Veřejného Mínění.

Kahneman, D. and Tversky, A. (1979). Prospect Theory: An Analysis of Decision under Risk. *Econometrica* 47: 263–91.

Kalyvas, S. N. (1996). *The Rise of Christian Democracy in Europe*. Ithaca, NY: Cornell University Press.

Kaufmann, C. (1996). Possible and Impossible Solutions to Ethnic Civil Wars. *International Security* 20 (4): 136–75.

Keating, M. (1998). *The New Regionalism in Western Europe: Territorial Restructing and Political Change*. Northampton, MA: Edward Elgar.

Keele, L. and Kelly, N. J. (2005). Dynamic Models for Dynamic Theories: The Ins and Outs of Lagged Dependent Variables. *Political Analysis* 14 (2): 186–205.

References

Khanna, H. R. (1999). Use and Misuse of Article 356. In *Reconstructing the Republic*, edited by Upendra Baxi, Alice Jacob, and Tarlok Singh, 154–60. Delhi, India: Har-Anand Publications Pvt. Ltd.

King, G., Keohane, R. O., and Verba, S. (1994). *Designing Social Inquiry: Scientific Inference in Qualitative Research*. Princeton, NJ: Princeton University Press.

Kohli, A. (1998). Enduring Another Election. *Journal of Democracy* 9 (3): 7–20.

Kopecký, P. (2000). From "Velvet Revolution" to "Velvet Split": Consociational Institutions and the Disintegration of Czechoslovakia. In *Irreconcilable Differences? Explaining Czechoslovakia's Dissolution*, edited and translated by Michael Kraus and Allison Stanger, 69–86. New York: Rowman and Littlefield Publishers, Inc.

Kostelecký, T. (1994). Economic, Social and Historical Determinants of Voting Patterns: In the 1990 and 1992 Parliamentary Elections in the Czech Republic. *Czech Sociological Review* 2 (2): 209–28.

Kothari, R. (2002). The Congress 'System' in India. In *Parties and Party Politics in India*, edited by Zoya Hasan, 39–55. New Delhi, India: Oxford University Press.

Krause, G. A. and Bowman, A. O'M. (2005). Adverse Selection, Political Parties, and Policy Delegation in the American Federal System. *Journal of Law, Economics, and Organization* 21 (2): 359–87.

Krejčí, O. (1994). *Kniha o Volbách*. Praha, Česká Republika: Victoria.

——(2000). A Comment on Čarnogurský and Pithart. In *Irreconcilable Differences? Explaining Czechoslovakia's Dissolution*, edited and translated by Michael Kraus and Allison Stanger, 235–40. Lanham, MD: Rowman and Littlefield Publishers, Inc.

Kroupa, A. and Kostelecký, T. (1996). Party Organization and Structure at National and Local Level in the Czech Republic since 1989. In *Party Structure and Organization in East-Central Europe*, edited by Paul G. Lewis, 89–115. Cheltenham, UK Edward Elgar.

Kroupa, D. (1996). *Daniel Kroupa: Svoboda a Řád (Sváteční Rozhovory)*. By Jan Šícha. Praha, Česká Republika: Éós.

Kučera, M. and Pavlík, Z. (1995). Czech and Slovak Demography. In *The End of Czechoslovakia*, edited by Jiří Musil, 15–39. New York: Central European University Press.

Kumar, G. G. (1986). *Regional Political Parties and State Politics*. New Delhi, India: Deep and Deep Publications.

Kumar, P. (1988). Akali Dal in Punjab. In *Regional Political Parties in India*, edited by Satyavan Bhatnagar and Pradeep Kumar, 107–29. New Delhi, India: Ess Ess Publications.

Kusý, M. (1995). Slovak Exceptionalism. In *The End of Czechoslovakia*, edited Jir̆í Musil, 139–58. New York: Central European University Press.

Kymlicka, W. (1998). Is Federalism a Viable Alternative to Secessionism? *Theories of Secession*, edited by Percy B. Lehning, 111–50. New York: Routledge Press.

L., A. (1994). Nacionalismus a Masmédia. *Mezinárodní Politika* 18 (8): 15.

Lagares Díez, N. (1999). Génesis y Desarollo del Partido Popular de Galicia. Madrid: Editorial Tecnos, S.A.

Laitin, D. D. (1985). Hegemony and Religious Conflict: British and Imperial Control and Political Cleavages in Yorubaland. In *Bringing the State Back In*, edited by Peter B. Evans, Dietrich Rueschemeyer, and Theda Skocpol, 285–316. Cambridge: Cambridge University Press.

Leff, C. S. (1999). Democratization and Disintegration in Multinational States: The Breakup of the Communist Federations. *World Politics* 51 (2): 205–35.

——(2000). Inevitability, Probability, Possibility: The Legacies of the Czech-Slovak Relationship, 1918–1989, and the Disintegration of the State. In *Irreconcilable Differences? Explaining Czechoslovakia's Dissolution*, edited and translated by Michael Kraus and Allison Stanger, 29–48. New York: Rowman and Littlefield Publishers, Inc.

Levi, M. and Hechter, M. (1985). A Rational Choice Approach to the Rise and Decline of Ethnoregional Parties. In *New Nationalisms of the Developed West: Toward Explanation*, edited by Ronald Rogowski and Edward A. Tiryakian, 128–46. Winchester: Allen and Unwin.

Lieberman, E. S. (2005). Nested Analysis as a Mixed-Method Strategy for Comparative Research. *American Political Science Review* 99 (3): 435–52.

Lijphart, A. (1977). *Democracy in Plural Societies: A Comparative Exploration*. New Haven, CT: Yale University Press.

——(1996). Puzzle of Indian Democracy: A Consociational Interpretation. *American Political Science Review* 90 (June): 258–68.

Lijphart, A., Rogowski, R., and Weaver, R. K. (1993). Separation of Powers and Cleavage Management. In *Do Institutions Matter? Government Capabilities in the United States and Abroad*, edited by R. Kent Weaver and Bert A. Rockman, 302–44. Washington, DC: Brookings Institution Press.

References

Linz, J. J., and Montero, J. R. (1999). *The Party System of Spain: Old Cleavages and New Challenges*. Madrid, Spain: Centro de Estudios Avanzados en Ciencias Sociales.

Linz, J. J. and Stepan, A. (1992). Political Identities and Electoral Sequences: Spain, the Soviet Union and Yugoslavia. *Daedalus* 121 (spring): 123–39.

Linz, Juan J. and Arturo Valenzuela. 1994. *The Failure of Presidential Democracy*. Baltimore: The John Hopkins University Press.

Lipset, S. M. (1963). *Political Man: The Social Bases of Politics*. Garden City, NY: Anchor Books.

——and Rokkan, S. (1967). Cleavage Structures, Party Systems and Voter Alignments: An Introduction. In *Party Systems and Voter Alignments: Cross-national Perspectives*, edited by Seymour Martin Lipset and Stein Rokkan, 1–64. New York: Free Press.

Llera Ramo, F. J. (1984). El Sistema de Partidos Vascos: Distancia, Ideológica y Legitimación Política. *Revista Española de Investigaciones Sociológicas* 28: 171–201.

——(1993). *The Construction of the Basque Polarized Pluralism*. Barcelona, Spain: Institut de Ciències Polítiques i Socials.

——(1995). Basque Polarization: Between Autonomy and Independence. *Nationalism and Ethnic Politics* 5 (3/4): 101–20.

Lundell, K. (2004). Determinants of Candidate Selection: The Degree of Centralization in Perspective. *Party Politics* 10 (1): 25–47.

Lustik, I. S., Miodownik, D., and Eidelson, R. J. (2004). Secessionism in Multicultural States: Does Sharing Power Prevent or Encourage It? *American Political Science Review* 98 (2): 209–229.

Macek, M. (2000). Fragments from the Dividing of Czechoslovakia. In *Irreconcilable Differences? Explaining Czechoslovakia's Dissolution*, edited and translated by Michael Kraus and Allison Stanger, 241–46. Lanham, MD Rowman and Littlefield Publishers, Inc.

Malcolm, N. (1996). *Bosnia: A Short History*. New York: New York University Press.

Manor, J. (1998). Making Federalism Work. *Journal of Democracy* 9 (3): 21–35.

Marcet, J. and Argelaguet, J. (1998). Nationalist Parties in Catalonia: *Convergència Democràtica de Catalunya* and *Esquerra Republicana* In *Regionalist Parties in Western Europe*, edited by Lieven de Winter and Huri Türsan, 70–86. New York: Routledge.

Martínez, R. (1995). Procesos Políticos y Electorales. In *Elecciones Autonómicas en Aragón*, edited by Ricardo Luis Chueca Rodríguez and José Ramón Montero, 109–34. Madrid: Editorial Tecnos.

McGraw, K. M. and Hubbard, C. (1996). Some of the People Some of the Time: Individual Differences in Acceptance of Political Accounts. In *Political Persuasion and Attitude Change*, edited by Diana C. Mutz, Richard A. Brody, and Paul M. Sniderman, 145–70. Ann Arbor, MI: University of Michigan Press.

Meadwell, H. (1993). Transition to Independence and Ethnic Nationalist Mobilization. In *Politics and Rationality*, edited by William James Booth, Patrick James and Hudson Meadwell, 191–216. Cambridge: Cambridge University Press.

Meguid, B. M. (2002). *Competition between Unequals: The Role of Mainstream Party Strategy in Rising Party Success in Western Europe*. PhD Dissertation. Harvard University.

Miguel, E., Satyanath, S., and Sargenti, E. (2004). Economic Shocks and Civil Conflict: An Instrumental Variables Approach. *Journal of Political Economy* 112 (4): 725–53.

Ministerio del Interior. (2000). *Procesos Electorales de Ámbito Estatal, 1976–1999*. Madrid: Ministerio del Interior.

——(2001). *Elecciones a Cortes Generales 2000: Aplicación de Consulta*. Madrid: Ministerio del Interior.

Ministerio para las Administraciones Públicas (MAP). (1992). *Los Acuerdos Autonómicos de 28 de febrero de 1992*. Madrid: MAP.

——(1994). *Informe Económico-Financiero de las Administraciones Territoriales en 1993*. Madrid: Ministerio para las Adminstraciones Publicas.

Ministry of Finance (1998–2000) *Indian Public Finance Statistics, 1998–2000*. New Delhi, India: Ministry of Finance. Economic Division.

——2006–7. *Indian Public Finance Statistics, 2006–7*. New Delhi, India: Ministry of Finance, Economic Division, 12–3.

Ministerio de Hacienda. (1997–2008). *Presupuestos Generales del Estado*. Madrid: Ministerio de Hacienda.

Mišovič, J. (1990). *Informace*. 18/2. Praha, Československo: Institut pro Výzkum Veřejného Mínění.

Montero, J. R., Llera Ramo, F. J., Pallarés Posta, F. (1998). Los Partidos de Ámbito No Estatal en España: Notas Actitudinales sobre Nacionalismos y Regionalismos. In *El Estado de las Autonomías ¿Hacia un Nuevo Federalismo?*, edited by Robert Agranoff and Rafael Bañón i Martínez, 205–44. Bilbao, España: Instituto Vasco de Administración Pública.

Montero, J. R., Pallarés Posta, F. and Õnate Rubalcaba, P. (1995). El Subsistema de Partidos. In *Elecciones Autonómicas en Aragón*. edited by

Ricardo Luis Chueca Rodríguez and José Ramón Montero, 193–236. Madrid: Editorial Tecnos.

Moreno, L. (1997). Federalization and Ethnoterritorial Concurrence in Spain. *Publius: The Journal of Federalism* 27 (4): 65–84.

Mueller, J. (2000). The Banality of "Ethnic War." *International Security* 25 (1): 42–70.

Murdoch, J. C. and Sandler, T. (2002). Economic Growth, Civil Wars, and Spatial Spillovers. *Journal of Conflict Resolution* 46 (1): 91–110.

Musil, J. (1995). Czech and Slovak Society. In *The End of Czechoslovakia*, edited Jiří Musil, 77–96. New York: Central European University Press.

Narang, A. S. (1995). *Ethnic Identities and Federalism*. Shimla, India: Indian Institute of Advanced Study.

Narula, R. S. (1999). Restructuring the Political System. In *Reconstructing the Republic*, edited by Upendra Baxi, Alice Jacob, and Tarlok Singh, 69–85. New Delhi, India: Har-Anand Publications Pvt. Ltd.

Nayar, V. K. S. (1986). Foreword. In *Regional Political Parties and State Politics*, edited by G. Gopa Kumar, 8–10. New Delhi, India: Deep and Deep Publications.

Newell, J. L. (1998). The Scottish Nationalist Party: Development and Change. In *Regionalist Parties in Western Europe*, edited by Lieven de Winter and Huri Türsan, 105–24. New York: Routledge.

Nordlinger, E. A. (1972). *Conflict Regulation in Divided Societies*. Cambridge, MA: Center for International Affairs, Harvard University.

Norris, P. (2008). *Driving Democracy: Do Power-sharing Regimes Work?* New York: Cambridge University Press.

Núñez, X-M. (1999). Autonomist Regionalism within the Spanish State of the Autonomous Communities: An Interpretation. *Nationalism and Ethnic Politics* 5 (3/4): 121–41.

Občanské Fórum. (1990). *První Návrh Nové Ústavy*. Praha, Česká Republika: Občanské Fórum.

Obrman, J. and Mates, P. (1994). Subdividing the Czech Republic: The Controversy Continues. *RFE/RL Research Report* 3 (9): 27–32.

Office of the Registrar General. (2001). *Census of India*. New Delhi, India: Office of the Registrar General.

O'Leary, B. and McGarry, J. (1995). Regulating Nations and Ethnic Communities. In *Nationalism and Rationality*, edited by Albert Breton, Gianluigi Galeotti, Pierre Salmon, Ronald Wintrobe, 245–89. Cambridge: Cambridge University Press.

Olson, D. (1993). The Dissolution of the State: Political Parties and the 1992 Election in Czechoslovakia. *Communist and Post-communist Studies* 26 (3): 301–14.

——(1994). The New Parliaments of New Democracies: The Experience of the Federal Assembly of the Czech and Slovak Federal Republic. In *The Emergence of East Central European Parliaments: The First Steps*, edited by Attila Ágh, 35–47. Budapest, Hungary: Hungarian Centre for Democracy Studies.

Olson, M. (1971). *The Logic of Collective Action: Public Goods and the Theory or Groups*. Cambridge, MA: Harvard University Press.

O'Neill, K. (2003). Decentralization as an Electoral Strategy. *Comparative Political Studies* 36 (9): 1068–91.

Ornstein, N. and Coursen, K. (1992). As the World Turns Democratic, Federalism Finds Favor. *The American Enterprise* (January/February): 20–4.

Padró-Solanet, A. and Colomer, J. M. (1992). Espacio Político-Ideológico y Temas de Campaña: El Ejemplo de las Elecciones Autonómicas de Cataluña de 1992. *Revista de Estudios Políticos* 78 (Octubre/Diciembre): 131–60.

Pai, S. (1998). The Indian Party System under Transformation: Lok Sabha Elections 1998. *Asian Survey* XXXVII (9): 836–52.

Pal, C. (1984). *State Autonomy in Indian Federation: Emerging Trends*. New Delhi, India: Deep and Deep Publications.

Panizza, U. (1999). On the Determinants of Fiscal Centralization: Theory and Evidence. *Journal of Economics* 74 (1): 97–139.

Patterson, S. C. and Mughan, A., eds. (1999). *Senate: Bicameralism in the Contemporary World*. Columbus, OH: Ohio State University Press.

Pehe, J. (1993). Czechoslovakia: Toward Dissolution. *RFE/RL Research Report* 2 (1): 84–8.

Penn, E. M. (2007a). Citizenship versus Ethnicity: The Role of Institutions in Shaping Identity Choice. Unpublished Manuscript, Harvard University.

——(2007b). From Many, One: State Representation and the Construction of an American National Identity, Unpublished Manuscript, Harvard University.

Pérez Vilariño, J. (1987). Las Primeras Elecciones al Parlamento Gallego. In *Comportamiento Electoral y Nacionalismo en Cataluña, Galicia y País Vasco*, edited by José Pérez Vilariño, 57–90. Santiago de Compostela, España: Universidad de Santiago de Compostela.

References

Pérez-Nievas, S. and Fraile, M. (2000). *Is the Nationalist Vote Really Nationalist: Dual Voting in Catalonia (1980–1999)*. Estudio/Working Paper 2000/147. Madrid: Instituto Juan March de Estudios e Investigaciones.

Perulles Romero, J. M. (1991). La Financiación de las Comunidades Autónomas. In *El Futuro de las Autonomías Territoriales: Comunidades Autónomas, Balance y Perspectivas*, edited by Luis Martín Rebollo, 227–60. Santander, España: Universidad de Cantabria.

Pithart, P. (1995). The Division of Czechoslovakia: A Preliminary Balance Sheet for the End of a Respectable Country. *Canadian Slavonic Papers/ Revue Canadienne des Slavistes* XXXVII (3/4): 321–36.

Popkin, S. L. (1994). *The Reasoning Voter: Communication and Persuasion in Presidential Campaigns*. Chicago: University of Chicago Press.

Posner, D. N. (2004). The Political Salience of Cultural Difference: Why Chewas and Tumbukas Are Allies in Zambia and Adversaries in Malawi. *American Political Science Review* 98 (4): 529–45.

Příhoda, P. (1995). Mutual Perceptions in Czech-Slovak Relationships. In *The End of Czechoslovakia*, edited by Jiří Musil, 128–38. New York: Central European University Press.

Průcha, V. (1995). Economic Development and Relations, 1918–1989. In *The End of Czechoslovakia*, edited by Jiří Musil, 40–77. New York: Central European University Press.

Rabushka, A. and Shepsle, K. A. (1972). *Politics in Plural Societies: A Theory of Democratic Instability*. Columbus, OH: Merrill.

Rao, M. G. (1998). India: Intergovernmental Fiscal Relations in a Planned Economy: The Case of India. In *Fiscal Decentralization in Developing Countries*, edited by Richard M. Bird and François Vaillancourt, 78–114. Cambridge: Cambridge University Press.

Řeháková, B. (1999). Social Stratification and Voting Behavior. In *Ten Years of Rebuilding Capitalism: Czech Society after 1989*, edited by Jiří Večerník and Petr Matějů, 228–50. Praha, Česká Republika: Academia.

Requejo, F. (1999). La Acomodación Federal de la Plurinacionalidad. Democracia Liberal y Federalismo Plural. In *Asimetría Federal y Estado Plurinacional: El Debate Sobre la Acomodación de la Diversidad en Canadá, Bèlica y España*, edited by Enric Fossas and Ferrán Requejo, 303–44. Madrid: Editorial Trotta, S.A.

Reventós, J. (1979). Las Razones del 'Sí' Socialista. *El País*, 16 de Octubre, 13.

Riker, W. H. (1964). *Federalism: Origin, Operation, Significance*. Boston: Little, Brown and Company.

Rocca, F. X. (1999). Out of their League: How Did a Champion of Decentralized Government and Regional Pride End Up Betraying Both Causes? With Opportunism, Overreaching and Crude Charisma. *The American Spectator* (March): 34–9:

Rodden, J. (2004). Comparative Federalism and Decentralization: On Meaning and Measurement. *Comparative Politics* 36 (4): 481–500.

Roeder, P. G. (1991). Soviet Federalism and Ethnic Mobilization. *World Politics* 43 (2): 196–232.

—— (2001). *Ethno-Linguistic Fractionalization Indices, 1961 and 1985*. http://weber.ucsd.edu/~proeder/elf.htm. Accessed December 3, 2007.

Rokkan, S. and Urwin, D. W., eds. (1982). *The Politics of Territorial Identity: Studies in European Regionalism*. London: Sage Publications.

Ross, M. L. (2004). How Do Natural Resources Influence Civil War? Evidence from Thirteen Cases. *International Organization* 58 (winter): 35–67.

Rothschild, J. (1974). *East Central Europe Between the Two World Wars*. Seattle: University of Washington Press.

Rousseau, D. L. and García-Retamero, R. (2007). Identity, Power, and Threat Perception: A Cross-National Experimental Study. *Journal of Conflict Resolution* 51 (5): 744–71.

Rychlík, J. (1995). National Consciousness and the Common State (A Historical-Ethnological Analysis). In *The End of Czechoslovakia*, edited by Jiří Musil, 97–105. New York: Central European University Press.

Saideman, S. M., Lanoue, D., Campenni, M., and Stanton, S. (2002). Democratization, Political Institutions, and Ethnic Conflict: A Pooled, Cross-Sectional Time Series Analysis from 1985–1998. *Comparative Political Studies* 35 (1): 103–29.

Sambanis, N. (2000). Partition as a Solution to Ethnic War: An Empirical Critique of the Theoretical Literature. *World Politics* 52 (July): 437–83.

—— (2001). Do Ethnic and Non-ethnic Civil Wars Have the Same Causes? A Theoretical and Empirical Inquiry (Part I). *Journal of Conflict Resolution* 45 (3): 259–82.

Samuels, D. (2000). The Gubernatorial Coattails Effect: Federalism and Congressional Elections in Brazil. *The Journal of Politics* 62 (1): 240–53.

Sartori, G. (1997). *Comparative Constitutional Engineering: An Inquiry into Structures, Incentives and Outcomes*. New York: New York University Press.

References

Sen, S. R. (1999). India's Political System: What Is to Be Done? In *Reconstructing the Republic*, edited by Upendra Baxi, Alice Jacob, and Tarlok Singh, 86–110. New Delhi, India: Har-Anand Publications Pvt. Ltd.

Sengupta, A. (1992). Regional Political Parties in Assam: An Observation on Asom Gana Parishad. In *Regional Political Parties in North East India*, edited by L. S. Gassah, 42–46. New Delhi, India: Omsons Publications.

Seshia, S. (1998). Divide and Rule in Indian Party Politics: The Rise of the Bharatiya Janata Party. *Asian Survey* 38 (11): 1036–50.

Shabad, G. (1986). Las elecciones de 1982 y las Autonomías. In *Crisis y Cambio: Electores y Partidos en la España de los Años Ochentas*, edited by Juan José Linz and José Ramón Montero, 525–85. Madrid: Centro de Estudios Constitucionales.

Shugart, M. S., and Carey, J. M. (1992). *Presidents and Assemblies: Constitutional Design and Electoral Dynamics*. Cambridge: Cambridge University Press.

Singh, G. (2000). *Ethnic Conflict in India: A Case Study of Punjab*. New York: St. Martin's Press.

Singh, K. (1997). Our Democratic Polity: Minority and Coalition Governments. In *Coalition Government and Politics in India*, edited by Subhash C. Kashyap, 1–6. New Delhi, India: Uppal Publishing House.

Singh, S. D. (1998). *The Fragmental Party System: A Study of the Viability of Indian Political Parties*. Ranchi, India: Catholic Press.

Singh, V. B. and Bose, S. (1986). *Elections in India: Data Handbook on Lok Sabha Elections*. 2nd ed., vols.1–2. New Delhi, India: Sage Publications.

Slavíková, J. (1990). *Kdy Začít s Hospodářskými Reformami?* 21/4. Praha, Československo: Institut pro Výzkum Veřejného Mínění.

——(1992). *V České Republice Názory Kritické, ve Slovenské Republice Ještě Kritičtější. 21/19*. Praha, Československo: Institut pro Výzkum Veřejného Mínění.

Snyder, J. L. (2000). *From Voting to Violence: Democratization and Nationalist Conflict*. New York: W.W. Norton and Company.

Snyder, J. L. and Ballentine, K. (1996). Nationalism and the Marketplace of Ideas. *International Security* 21 (2): 5–40.

Snyder, J. L. and Mansfield, E. D. (1995). Democratization and the Danger of War. *International Security* 20 (1): 5–38.

Sridharan, E. (2002). The Fragmentation of the Indian Party System, 1952–1999: Seven Competing Explanations. In *Parties and Party Politics in India*, edited by Zoya Hasan, 475–503. New Delhi, India: Oxford University Press.

Stanger, A. (2000). The Price of Velvet: Constitutional Politics and the Demise of the Czechoslovak Federation. In *Irreconcilable Differences? Explaining Czechoslovakia's Dissolution*, edited and translated by Michael Kraus and Allison Stanger, 137–62. Lanham, MD: Rowman and Littlefield Publishers, Inc.

Stein, E. (2000). *Czecho/Slovakia: Ethnic Conflict, Constitutional Fissure and Negotiated Breakup*. Ann Arbor, MI: University of Michigan Press.

Stepan, A. C. (1999). Federalism and Democracy: Beyond the US Model. *Journal of Democracy* 10 (4):19–34.

Stock, J. H. (2002). Instrumental Variables in Economics and Statistics. *International Encyclopedia of the Social and Behavioral Sciences*, vol. 20, edited by Neil J. Smelser and Paul B. Baltes, 7577–82. Amsterdam, Netherlands: Elsevier.

Suberu, R. T. (1994). The Travails of Federalism in Nigeria. In *Nationalism, Ethnic Conflict and Democracy*, edited by Larry Diamond and Marc F. Plattner, 56–70. Baltimore, MD: The John Hopkins University Press.

Subirats i Humet, J. (1998). El Papel de las Comunidades Autónomas en el Sistema Español de Relaciones Intergubernamentales: Quince Años de Comunidades Autónomas en España. Luces y Sombras de una Realidad Aún en Discusión. In *El Estado de las Autonomías ¿Hacia un Nuevo Federalismo*, edited by Robert Agranoff and Rafael Bañón i Martínez, 161–80. Bilbao, España: Instituto Vasco de Administración Pública.

Suresh, K. (2000). Identity Articulation and Emerging Political Formation in India. In *Coalition Politics and Power Sharing*, edited by Akhtar Majeed, 36–68. New Delhi, India: Manak Publications Pvt. Ltd.

Svejnar, J. (2000). Explaining Czechoslovakia's Dissolution: Assessing Economic Performance Before and After the Breakup. In *Irreconcilable Differences? Explaining Czechoslovakia's Dissolution*, edited and translated by Michael Kraus and Allison Stanger, 183–99. Lanham, MD: Rowman and Littlefield Publishers, Inc.

Svitek, I. (1992). The 1992 State Budgets in Czechoslovakia. *RFE/RL Research Report* (February): 34–7.

Tajfel, H. and Turner, J. C. (1979). An Integrative Theory of Intergroup Conflict. In *The Social Psychology of Intergroup Relations*, edited by William G. Austin and Stephen Worchel, 38–43. Monterey, CA: Brooks-Cole.

Tarchi, M. (1998). The Lega Nord. In *Regionalist Parties in Western Europe*, edited by Lieven de Winter and Huri Türsan, 143–58. New York: Routledge.

Thandavan, R. (1998). AIADMK in Tamil Nadu: Its Emergence and Unprecedented Growth. In *Regional Political Parties in India*, edited by Satyavan Bhatnagar and Pradeep Kumar, 131–65. New Delhi, India: Ess Ess Publications.

Tomek, I. and Forst, V. (1990). Czechoslovak Citizens' Attitudes Towards Federation (September/October 1990). Prague, Czech Republic: Public Opinion Research Institute.

Tornos Más, J. (1991). La Distribución de Competencias entre el Estado y las Comunidades Autónomas: Problemas de Articulación. In *El Futuro de las Autonomías Territoriales: Comunidades Autónomas, Balance y Perspectivas*, edited by Luis Martín Rebollo, 45–77. Santander, España: Universidad de Cantabria.

Treisman, D. (2002). Defining and Measuring Decentralization: A Global Perspective. Unpublished Manuscript, University of California, Los Angeles.

——(2007). *Architecture of Government: Rethinking Political Decentralization*. Cambridge: Cambridge University Press.

Tremblay, R. C. (1996). Nation, Identity and the Intervening Role of the State: A Study of the Secessionist Movement in Kashmir. *Pacific Affairs* 69 (4): 471–97.

Trudeau, P. E. (1968). *Federalism and the French Canadians*. Toronto: Macmillan of Canada.

Truman, D. B. (1955). Federalism and the Party System. In *Federalism: Mature and Emergent*, edited by Arthur W. MacMahon, 115–36. Garden City, NY: Double Day and Company.

Tsebelis, G. (1990). Elite Interaction and Constitution Building in Consociational Societies. *Journal of Theoretical Politics* 2 (1): 5–29.

Tummala, K. K. (1992). India's Federalism Under Stress. *Asian Survey* 32 (6): 538–53.

Ugarte, B. A. and Pérez-Nievas, S. (1998). Moderate Nationalist Parties in the Basque Country: Partido Nacionalista Vasco and Eusko Alkartasuna. In *Regionalist Parties in Western Europe*, edited by Lieven de Winter and Huri Türsan, 87–104. New York: Routledge.

Unión de Pueblo Navarro (UPN). (2000). *20 Años al Servicio de Navarra del Siglo XX al Siglo XXI*. Pamplona, España: Unión del Pueblo Navarro.

Vachudová, M. A. (1993). Divisions in the Czech Communist Party. *RFE/RL Research Report* 2 (37): 28–33.

Vadas, M. (2000). Notes on the Role of Television in Czechoslovakia's Dissolution. In *Irreconcilable Differences? Explaining Czechoslovakia's Dis-*

solution, edited and translated by Michael Kraus and Allison Stanger, 269–86. Lanham, MD: Rowman and Littlefield Publishers, Inc.

Valko, E., Zelenay, R., and Kovář, J. (1992). Interviews by Jakub Císař and Stanislav Benda. *Rozvod po Československu: Úvahy o Rozpadu Státu*. Praha, Česká Republika: Jakub Císař and Stanislav Benda.

Van Houten, P. J. (2008). Regionalist Challenges to European States: A Quantitative Assessment. *Ethnopolitics* 6 (4): 545–68.

Varshney, A. (1998). Why Democracy Survives. *Journal of Democracy* 9 (3): 36–50.

——(2001). Ethnic Conflict and Civil Society: India and Beyond. *World Politics* 53 (3): 362–98.

Vodička, K. (1996). Vývojové Fáze Stranického Systému v České Republice v Mezinárodním Kontextu. In *Krystalizace Struktury Politických Stran v České Republice po Roce 1989*, edited by Vladimíra Dvořáková and Aleš Gerloch, 77–83. Praha, Česká Republika: Česká Společnost pro Politické Vědy.

Walter, B. F. (2002). *Committing to Peace: The Successful Settlement of Civil Wars*. Princeton, NJ: Princeton University Press.

——(2006). Building Reputation: Why Governments Fights Some Separatists But Not Others. *American Journal of Political Science* 50 (2): 313–30.

Weiner, M. (1967). *Party Building in a New Nation: The India National Congress*. Chicago: University of Chicago Press.

Widmalm, S. (1998). The Rise and Fall of Democracy in Jammu and Kashmir, 1975–1989. In *Community Conflicts and the State in India*, edited by Amrita Basu and Atul Kohli, 149–82. New Delhi, India: Oxford University Press.

Wightman, G. (1995). The Development of the Party System and the Breakup of Czechoslovakia. In *Party Formation in East-Central Europe: Post-communist Politics in Czechoslovakia, Hungary, Poland, and Bulgaria*, edited by Gordon Wightman, 59–78. Brookfield, VT: Edward Elgar Publishing Ltd.

Wildavsky, A. B. (1967). Party Discipline under Federalism: Implications of the Australian Experience. In *American Federalism in Perspective*, edited by Aaron B. Wildavsky, 162–81. Boston: Little, Brown and Company.

Wilkinson, S. I. (2004) *Votes and Violence: Electoral Competition and Ethnic Riots in India*. Cambridge: Cambridge University Press.

Wolchik, S. L. (1995). The Politics of Transition and the Breakup of Czechoslovakia. In *The End of Czechoslovakia*, edited by Jiří Musil, 225–44. New York: Central European University Press.

References

——(2000). The Impact of Institutional Factors on the Breakup of the Czechoslovak Federation. In *Irreconcilable Differences? Explaining Czechoslovakia's Dissolution*, edited and translated by Michael Kraus and Allison Stanger, 87–106. Lanham, MD: Rowman and Littlefield Publishers, Inc.

Wood, E. J. (2006). Variation in Sexual Violence during War. *Politics and Society* 34 (3): 307–42.

Wooldridge, J. M. (2002). *Econometric Analysis of Cross Section and Panel Data*. Cambridge, MA: Massachusetts Institute of Technology.

World Bank. (2002). *World Development Indicators Online*. Washington, DC: World Bank.

World Bank. (2005). *Fiscal Decentralization Indicators (WBFDI Country Database January 2005)*. Washington, DC: World Bank.

Young, C. (1994). *The African Colonial State in Comparative Perspective*. New Haven, CT: Yale University Press.

Zaidi, A. M. and Zaidi, S. C. (1980). *The Encyclopedia of the Indian National Congress Volume Eleven: 1936–1938: An Unwanted Constitution*. New Delhi, India: S. Chand and Company Limited.

Žák, V. (1995). The Velvet Divorce – Institutional Foundations. In *the End of Czechoslovakia*, edited by Jiří Musil, 245–68. New York: Central European University Press.

Zaller, J. R. (1992). *The Nature and Origins of Mass Opinion*. Cambridge: Cambridge University Press.

Ziblatt, D. (2004). Rethinking the Origins of Federalism: Puzzle, Theory and Evidence from Nineteenth-Century Europe. *World Politics* 57 (1): 70–98.

Endnotes

1. Sambanis (2001) defines ethnic war as "war among communities (eth-nicities) that are in conflict over the power relationship that exists between these communities and the state" (261). Sambanis further argues that not all wars involving ethnic groups as combatants are eth-nic wars, but only those in which the issues at the core of the conflict are integral to the concept of ethnicity. The term ethnic conflict, as it is used here, is more comprehensive, including ethnic war, as Sambanis defines it, as well as all forms of ethnic violence short of ethnic war. Secessionism is defined as the desire for an independent state (Hechter 1992), whereas secession is the act of declaring an independent state.
2. "A Conversation on Iraq with Senator Joseph R. Biden, Jr," *Council of Foreign Relations – Speeches and Debates*, February 15, 2007.
3. David Kaiza, "Federalism will Ensure Freedom and Equitable Sharing of Power," *Financial Times – Global News Wire – Asia Africa Intelligence Wire*, August 16, 2004.
4. Edison Stewart, "Clinton Weighs in with Plea to Quebec," *Toronto Star*, October 9, 1999.
5. The *Daily Telegraph*, November 13, 1997.
6. "Federalism is a Beguiling Serpent – H. L. de Silva," *Tamilnet*, July 28, 2003.
7. See Falleti (2005) for a discussion of other forms of decentralization, including administrative and fiscal decentralization, and their rela-tionship to political decentralization.
8. Although many scholars who work on issues of ethnic conflict and secessionism reserve the word "nation" for an ethno-linguistic or religious group, I follow the convention in this book of using the word nation to refer to the state.
9. See Freedom House (2007).

10. See Hug (2003) and Treisman (2007) for a discussion of the prob-
    lems associated with analyses that do not correct for selection bias
    in these and other data.

11. These different mechanisms are well illustrated by the Northern
    League in Italy. In order to make people living in Northern Italy think
    of themselves as Northern Italians, the Northern League produced
    and distributed special identification cards for the "Free Republic of
    Padania." It has also invented a flag to represent Padania, printed its
    own money, and built its own militia force. The Northern League
    has also held numerous rallies and demonstrations, one in which it
    formed a human chain along the river Po to symbolically separate
    Padania from the rest of Italy. The Northern League did not invent
    the term Padania. The term describes the plain area surrounding the
    river Po and is derived from the name of the river. The Northern
    League did, however, appropriate the word to describe the people
    of Northern Italy as a nation. The Savoy League has employed simi-
    lar tactics in France distributing "Sovereign Savoy" identity cards,
    adopting a flag for the Savoy region of a white cross on a red back-
    ground, and mass-producing car license plates for Savoy.

12. See Giuliano (2006) for a discussion on the importance of issue reso-
    nance in the formation of identities.

13. In 1960, the mineral-rich province of Katanga tried to secede from
    the Independent Republic of the Congo for this reason. Secession-
    ist tensions are still strong in Katanga today and driven by feelings
    that foreign companies and political groups outside Katanga benefit
    more from the mines than the Katangan people. Similarly, in Papua
    New Guinea in the late 1980s, a secessionist movement in Bougain-
    ville turned violent over concerns that people in Bougainville were
    not benefiting from profit-sharing agreements for the copper mine
    in this region.

14. Regional legislatures may exist in centralized systems of government
    to administer decisions made at the national level. They are usually
    not elected, however, and always lack the decision-making powers
    necessary to entice politicians to form regional parties since polit-
    icians would not be able affect decisions in these legislatures as part
    of regional parties or otherwise.

15. See note 10.

16. In a few countries, a prominent national figure, such as a president
    or monarch, may partially or fully appoint representatives to upper

houses based on their social position or technological expertise (e.g. Canada, India, Malaysia, Trinidad and Tobago, and the United Kingdom).

17. One exception to this rule may be the case of Brazil, where David Samuels finds that governors have more influence on national legislative elections than presidents (2000).

18. The Spanish Socialist Workers' Party of Andalusia (PSOE-A), a regional party, has worked together with the Spanish Socialist Workers' Party (PSOE) to coordinate the 2008 regional elections in Andalusia with Spain's national elections for this reason.

19. These figures are based on those who declared their ethnicity on the 1991 census (Federal Statistical Office 1991). The figures for Moravia include those who declared themselves as Moravian or Silesian. The remaining 5 percent of Bohemia identified themselves as Slovak, Moravian, Silesian, Hungarian, Romany, Polish, German, Ruthenian, Ukrainian, Russian, Greek, Bulgarian, Other, or did not state their identity. The remaining 5 percent of Moravia identified themselves as Czech, Slovak, Hungarian, Romany, Polish, German, Ruthenian, Ukrainian, Russian, Greek, Bulgaria, Romanian, Other, or did not state their identity.

20. The remaining 3 percent identified themselves as either Czech, Moravian, Silesian, Romany, Polish, German, Ukrainian, Ruthenian, Russian, Greek, Bulgarian, Romanian, Other, or did not state their identity (Federal Statistical Office 1991).

21. There were incidents of conflict between Czechs and Slovaks and the Roma population in the transition period. These incidents are not the subject of this study, however, since the Roma were widely dispersed throughout the country so that decentralization could not help reduce conflict among these groups. Parties that supported attacks against the Roma did not have much support in Czechoslovakia at the time among the electorate (e.g. Association for the Republic–Republican Party of Czechoslovakia (SPR-RSC) and Slovak National Party (SNS)).

22. Of the remaining respondents, 19 percent thought Slovaks and Moravians were "indifferent" to each other, while 8 percent thought that relations between them were "rather unfriendly" or "unfriendly".

23. The remaining 41 percent thought that relations between Bohemians and Moravians were "unfriendly".

24. Of the remaining respondents, 14 percent thought Bohemians and Moravians were "indifferent" to each other, while 5 percent thought that relations between Bohemians and Moravians were "rather unfriendly" or "unfriendly".

25. A referendum on national unity was never held in Czechoslovakia. The opposition made several attempts to hold a referendum but never had enough support to pass legislation to this effect. A referendum, according to some, may have prevented the division of Czechoslovakia into two separate states by allowing people to voice their opposition to the division (Pithart 1995: 332–4). Most scholars agree, however, that a referendum would not have prevented the dissolution of Czechoslovakia, pointing out that while people may have voiced their opposition to the division in a referendum, they would not have been able to demonstrate the particular type of system they were willing to accept in order to keep the country together (Rychlík 1995; Valko et al. 1992: 19–20; Pehe 1993).

26. "Pithart Criticizes 'Agitated' Moravia," *FBIS Daily Report – Eastern Europe*, February 6, 1991.

27. "KDH Issues Declaration on Independent Slovakia," *FBIS Daily Report – Eastern Europe*, December 24, 1992.

28. "Mečiar, Klaus Debate Causes of Split," *FBIS Daily Report – Eastern Europe*, December 30, 1992.

29. Workers in both the Czech Republic and Slovakia tended to vote for left-wing parties and extremist parties like SPR-RSC and SNS. Entrepreneurs and students, on the other hand, tended to vote for right-wing parties, like ODS in the Czech Republic.

30. Petr Tatar, Personal Interview, Bratislava, July 2, 2000.

31. Ibid.

32. "Mečiar Views End of ČSFR, Slovak Problems," *FBIS Daily Report – Eastern Europe*, December 21, 1992.

33. In the Civic Forum's own proposal for a constitution, it advocated a decentralized system of government where the national government had either exclusive or joint control over a considerable number of issues. These issues included the following: constitutional amendments, foreign affairs, international treaties, representation in international institutions, war and peace, defense, federal reserve materials, currency, normalization, weights and measures, copyrights, customs and duties, protection

of the federal constitution, federal legislation, and the operation of federal organs. The proposal also gave the federal government joint control over the following issue areas: legal arrangements of economic activity and enterprise, foreign economic relations, prices, transportation, post and telecommunication, planning, finance, work, wages and social politics, social economic information, taxes and duties, environmental protection, internal order and state security, and the advancement of science and technology (Občanské Fórum 1990).

34. One of Havel's more prominent bills gave the Czech and Slovak National Councils veto power over the constitution. This bill represented a compromise between the positions of the Czechs and Slovaks because it did not consider the constitution to be a treaty between two independent states, as the Slovaks wanted, but gave the two regions veto power over the constitution. The other bills of Havel allowed the parliament to be dissolved by the president in case of a constitutional deadlock, and also called for an electoral system based on a modified majority principle, a unicameral system of government, and voter-initiated referendums.

35. For a detailed discussion of the negotiations between Czechs and Slovaks throughout the transition period, see Stein (2000).

36. Miloslav Ransdorf, Personal Interview, Prague, July 24, 2000.

37. Ibid.

38. The Slovak branch of the party wanted to associate itself more closely with the former Soviet Union, while the Czech branch wanted to operate more independently of the Soviet Union (Ransdorf, see note 38). The Czech branch of the party also favored less government intervention in the economy and a more rapid transition to the market economy than the Slovak branch of the party (Vachudová 1993; Gryzmala-Busse, 2002).

39. "Pithart on Territorial Questions, Moravia," *FBIS Daily Report – Eastern Europe*, February 28, 1990.

40. "Čalfa Cited on Moravia, Silesia 'Problem'," *FBIS Daily Report – Eastern Europe*, February 4, 1991.

41. "Pithart on Territorial Questions, Moravia," *FBIS Daily Report – Eastern Europe*, February 28, 1990.

42. Rudolf Opatřil, "Nová Velkomoravská Šance," *Práce*, June 27, 1990.

43. David Olson does not try to explain the origins of regional parties in Czechoslovakia and argues elsewhere that nationalism, not decentralization, is responsible for the creation of regional parties in Czechoslovakia, at least in the case of OF in the Czech Lands and VPN in Slovakia (1994: 43).

44. On two occasions, however, in 1993 and 1996, statewide parties relied on the outside support of regional parties to control the national government.

45. There have been incidences of conflict in Spain involving Roma and Muslims. These groups are not the subject of this study, however, since they are widely dispersed throughout the country. Decentralization is not theorized to reduce conflict involving these kinds of groups.

46. In Catalonia, there was the Terra Lligue, which dissolved in 1990 claiming that violence was an outmoded means of achieving independence. In Galicia, there was the Armed Revolutionary Action and the Guerilla Army of the Free Galician People, and in the Canary Islands, a region that is not ethnically or linguistically distinct from the rest of Spain, there was the Movement for the Self-Determination and Independence of the Canarian Archipelago.

47. Specifically, 53 percent of Basques said that they are "greatly concerned" while 40 percent indicated that they are "somewhat concerned" by ETA's actions. Only 5 percent of Basques said that they are only "a little concerned" by ETA's actions and 2 percent said that they are "indifferent" to them.

48. An additional 20 percent of Basques polled said that they supported these movements "a little" while 18 percent of Basques said they did not support these movements at all.

49. In 1998, HB and EA together won 27 percent of the vote in the Basque parliament while in 1980, HB won 17 percent and in 1986, EA won 16 percent.

50. Independence-seeking parties in Galicia have in the past included: the Union of Galician People (UPG), the Party of Galician Workers (POG), the Galician Popular Front (FPG), and the National Block-Galician Populars (BNPG).

51. Other independence-seeking parties in Catalonia have included the National Liberation Leftist Bloc (BEAN) and the Party for the Independence of Catalonia (PIC).

52. These matters pertain to international issues such as defense, national security, nationality and immigration; domestic political issues such as justice and referendums; as well as economic issues such as banking, insurance, the national budget, transportation, communication, and international economic relations. Educational and scientific matters are also under the purview of the national government, including issues such as academic qualifications, national statistics, and arms and explosives.

53. *Constitución Española de 1978*. See http://www.constitucion.es/ Accessed December 3, 2007.

54. The financial system for the rest of Spain was established in 1980 by the Organic Law on the Financing of the Autonomous Communities (LOFCA). See *LO 8/1980, de Financiación de las Comunidades Autónomas, de 22 de Septiembre*, BOE del 1 de Octubre.

55. PNV is already included in Figure 4.4 for the years in which it competed in only the Basque Country. Recall that regional parties are defined as parties that compete in only one autonomous community (i.e. region) of Spain. Although PNV competed in more than one region of Spain for most of this period, policymakers and scholars consider PNV to be a regional party. Substantively, PNV is like other regional parties in this study because it advocates political autonomy. Its presence, moreover, in Navarra is very minor (averaging about 2 percent of the vote in Navarra over the 1977–2000 period).

56. The average vote for regional parties in the Basque Country is stronger (38 percent) if I include the vote for PNV in the 1984, 1986, and 1990 regional elections held in this region in the calculation of regional party vote. In these years, PNV was not considered a regional party because it competed in regional elections held in Navarra in 1983, 1987, and 1991.

57. The growth in regional parties in Melilla was even greater than in the Canary Islands in this period. However, the vote for regional parties in 2000 was significantly higher than in other proximate elections.

58. Adolfo Suárez, quoted in Gunther et al. (1986). Felipe González, Suárez' successor, has expressed similar sentiments – see "La Solución de las Autonomías Pasa por la Existencia de Partido Nacionales Fuertes, según Felipe González", *El País*, 8 de Octubre 1980, 16.

59. *Constitución Española de 1978.* See http://www.constitucion.es/ Accessed December 3, 2007.
60. See Ministerio para las Administraciones Públicas (1992).
61. The Organic Law on the Financing of the Autonomous Communities (LOFCA) specified the exact formula for the distribution of national taxes among the autonomous communities (see note 56).
62. Sebastián García, "La Comisión Constitucional Aprueba el Proyecto de Estatuto de Cataluña," *El País*, 14 de Agosto 1979, 11.
63. Other conflicts concerned Castilla-La Mancha's desire for its own autonomous community and its desire not to have Madrid included in this autonomous community because Madrid was much richer than Castilla-La Mancha and would dominate the community.
64. Alfons Quinta," 'La Generalitat Viene a Pediros el Sí', dijo Tarradellas a los Alcaldes Catalanes," *El País* 24 de Septiembre 1979, 11.
65. Carlos Garaikoetxea, "El Estatuto de Guernica," *El País*, 24 de Octubre 1979, 9.
66. "AP, Andalucistas y Extrema Derecha Negaron el 'Sí' al Estatuto Catalán," *El País*, 30 de Noviembre 1979, 15.
67. The connection between socialism and regional autonomy is apparent in PSOE's *Twenty-Seventh Congress.* In this Congress, the PSOE stated that "[t]he oppression that the nationalities and the regions suffer is more a facet and instrument of the oppression that the dominant class exercises over the people and workers of the Spanish state and is vindicated by the process of the class struggle.... In this line, the Socialist Party proposes the free exercise of the right to self-determination for all of the nationalities and regions, which they compose, in equal footing in a federal state." (quoted in Erkizia et al. 1988: 25–6). Similarly, Joan Reventós, the leader of PSOE in Catalonia, once remarked that "[w]e believe in the right of autonomy of all the nationalities and regions in Spain for without solidarity it would be impossible to construct a just society that we propose...Saying 'yes' to the Statute [in Catalonia] is saying yes to liberty and socialism is liberty" (1979: 13).
68. AP, quoted in Lagares Díez (1999).
69. "La VCD de Andalucía se Toma un Tiempo de Reflexión," *El País*, 18 de Enero 1980, 11.

70. The general elections in 1996 and 2000 occurred in March. The 1996 CIS survey was administered in November 1996 and the 2003 CIS survey was administered in September 2002.

71. "Acuerdo de Investidura y Gobernabilidad," *El País*, 29 de Abril 1996, 18–9. PP also promised CiU to reform the state administration, convoke a sectorial conference for European affairs, and consider ending the country's mandatory military service. PP further expanded Catalonia's powers to include traffic, the National Institute of Unemployment (INEM), and port management. In 1996, the party also made concessions to the Basque Country. In exchange for PNV's support, the party agreed to allow the Basque Country to rationalize its rules and regulations and increase its normative control over income taxes. It also agreed to coordinate the collection of taxes from non-residents of the Basque Country and special taxes on manufacturing, and to improve communication with the Basque Country.

72. Juan G. Ibáñez, "Aznar Logra el Apoyo de Coalición Canaria para su Investidura y para Gobernar los Próximas Cuatro Años," *El País*, 12 de Abril 1996, 15.

73. Manuel Silva i Sánchez, Personal Interview, October 23, 2001.

74. Ibid.

75. Iñaki Txueka Isasti, Personal Interview, October 23, 2001.

76. In 2007, for the first time, the regions also chose one-third of the magistrates to the Constitutional Court.

77. This figure is based on the 2001 national census (Office of the Registrar General, 2001).

78. Ibid.

79. It is difficult to determine how much support these conflicts have had within the larger population because support for terrorist organizations and regional parties may not necessarily be interpreted as sympathy for their goals. Unfortunately, comprehensive survey data on this issue does not exist in India the way it does in Spain and Czechoslovakia.

80. The analysis, thus, does not focus on Muslims outside Jammu and Kashmir or on scheduled castes and tribes. Scheduled castes and tribes are dispersed throughout India, although Punjab is the state with the largest proportion of scheduled castes while Mizoram has the largest proportion of schedule tribes. See Office of the Registrar General (2001).

81. *Indiastat.com: Revealing India Statistically*. New Delhi: Datanet India Pvt. Ltd.

82. Ibid.

83. A number of terrorist organizations were dismantled in this period including: United Akali Dal (UAD), All-India Sikh Student Federation (AISSF), Dumdami Taksal (DT), Panthic Committee, Khalistan Commando Force (KCF), Bhindranwale Tiger Force (BTF), Khalistan Liberation Force (KLF), and Bubbar Khalasa International (BKI).

84. These elections were not the first elections that were rigged in Jammu and Kashmir. Almost every election prior to this election since 1951 was rigged with the exception of the election in 1983. The 1987 election, though, was different from previously rigged elections because people expected these elections to be genuine.

85. The issues over which state legislatures have either exclusive or joint authority relate to the following areas: agriculture, public order, police and prisons, justice, health and sanitation, alcohol, pilgrimages within India, education, unemployment and disability, intrastate trade, natural resources, state institutions and monuments, weights and measures, markets and fairs, and gambling.

86. The issues over which the national government has exclusive control relate to the following issue areas: (international issues) defense, foreign relations, extradition, pilgrimages outside of India, piracy and crimes committed on the high seas, international trade and commerce; (internal issues) citizenship, education standards, transportation, post and telecommunications, currency, banking and stock exchange, property rights, lotteries, natural resources, institutions and monuments of national interests, standards for weights and measures, and statistics.

87. The Sarkaria Commission issued a report in 1988 recommending 247 revisions to India's political system that would increase the level of decentralization in the country, several of which have actually been implemented.

88. These powers relate to the following issue areas: crime, marriage, divorce and adoption, the transfer of nonagricultural property, food and drugs, and economic and social planning.

89. Ministry of Law and Justice. *Constitution of India*. New Delhi, India: Ministry of Law and Justice (Legislative Department). http://india-code.nic.in Accessed December 1, 2007.

90. Ibid.

91. Ibid.

92. The Planning Commission uses a different criterion to distribute grants. Since 1969, the Planning Commission uses the Gadgil Formula. Eighty-five percent of the Gadgil Formula is based on the population and per capita income of the states. The remaining 15 percent is based on the performance of the states in terms of their ability to meet national objectives and address special problems. Prior to 1969, the Planning Commission did not have an objective criterion for distributing grants.

93. The figures for each region presented in this table are based on different election years between 1952 and 1999 because some states and union territories did not exist for this entire period.

94. With the Congress Party unable to form a government on its own, the Janata Dal formed a coalition government, which included a number of regional parties, such as the Telugu Desam Party (TDP) of Andhra Pradesh, the DMK of Tamil Nadu, and the AGP party of Assam.

95. The Congress Party split into Congress (O) and Congress (R), led by Indira Gandhi, in this year because Indira Gandhi refused to accept the selection of Siddavanahalli Nijalingappa as party president. The O in Congress (O) signifies the word organization, while the R in Congress (R) represents the word ruling. In the 1970s, Congress (R) split again and became Congress (I) as a result of the displacement of Congress (R) from Youth Congress committees. Congress (I) was also led by Indira Gandhi from whom the initial I is derived.

96. These conclusions are based on a comparison on lower and upper house elections between 1952 and 1999. The regions identified here are regions for which the percentage of seats earned by regional parties in these two levels differs by more than 15 percent.

97. These conclusions are based on a comparison of national and regional elections, restricted to the 1977–1999 period. The regions identified here are regions for which the vote for regional parties at the national (lower house elections) and regional elections differ by more than 10 percent.

98. See Zaidi and Zaidi (1980).
99. The redrawing of India's borders helped to minimize the secessionist claims of the Nagas and Tamils in the country, although it may have increased the demands of other groups in India (e.g. the Mizos and the Punjabis) for their own linguistic states.
100. "National Vision as a Casualty" *Financial Express*, November 23, 2007.
101. The difference between these two means is significant at the $p \leq 0.01$ level.
102. This difference, while large, is not statistically significant, which may be due to small sample size.
103. In 1962, national elections were not held concurrently with regional elections in Kerala and Orissa, and in 1967 they were not held concurrently with regional elections in Nagaland and Pondicherry.
104. These countries are: Argentina, Australia, Belgium, Bermuda, Bosnia-Herzegovina, Bolivia, Botswana, Canada, Colombia, Costa Rica, Cyprus, Czech Republic, Czechoslovakia, Estonia, Finland, Germany, Greece, Hungary, Iceland, India, Indonesia, Ireland, Israel, Italy, Latvia, Lithuania, Luxembourg, Malaysia, Mauritius, Mexico, Moldova, Netherlands, New Zealand, Niger, Norway, Poland, Portugal, Romania, Slovakia, Slovenia, South Africa, Spain, Sweden, Switzerland, Trinidad and Tobago, Turkey, the United Kingdom, the United States, Venezuela, and Yugoslavia.
105. See the Caramani (2000) dataset on West European elections and the Scott Morgenstern dataset. http://www.pitt.edu/~smorgens/componentsdata.html. Accessed November 13, 2007.
106. Countries, such as Malaysia, in which all elections are not democratic in this period, are not excluded from the dataset for the years in which elections are not democratic. Countries are not included in the dataset until they experience a single democratic election and are not included at all unless they experience at least two democratic elections in this period.
107. A group is considered "at risk" if it meets one of the four following criteria: (a) the group is subject to discrimination, (b) the group is disadvantaged from past discrimination, (c) the group is advantaged but is challenged by another group, or (d) the group is supportive of political organizations that advocate greater group rights.

108. I used scholarly articles, newspapers, NGO reports, and so forth, to examine each instance of rebellion in the dataset to determine if rebellious groups demanded independence.

109. I determined how concentrated groups are in a country based on the group concentration index of the *Minorities at Risk Project*. The index places ethnolinguistic groups into four different categories: (a) widely dispersed, (b) minority in one region or primarily urban, (c) majority in one region and dispersed in others, and (d) concentrated in one region. Using supplementary data, I divided the second category of this index into two different categories – one representing groups that are primarily urban, and the second representing groups that are a minority in one region. This distinguishes groups like the Irish, who form a minority in Northern Ireland, from Asians and Afro-Caribbeans in the United Kingdom, who live primarily in urban areas of the country. I also determined the territorial concentration of groups excluded from the MAR dataset. After correcting either errors or discrepancies in the MAR data, I eliminated all groups from this study that are widely dispersed or primarily urban. These groups include: Jews (Argentina); indigenous people and non-Quebecois French (Canada); Roma (Greece, Spain, and Turkey); non-Kashmiri Muslims, Santals, and Scheduled Tribes (India); Chinese (Indonesia); Russians (Lithuania); Chinese and East Indians (Malaysia); other indigenous groups and Zapotecs (Mexico); Germans and Roma (Romania); Asians, Black Africans, and Europeans (South Africa); foreign workers (Switzerland); Afro-Caribbeans and Asians (United Kingdom); and African-Americans and Native Americans (United States).

110. It is necessary to aggregate the group-level data on anti-regime rebellion and intercommunal conflict to the national level because none of the variables in this analysis vary at the group level, and because groups and regions do not coincide perfectly in countries.

111. See note 112.

112. Decentralization can take place at the local level – either in conjunction with or in place of decentralization at the regional level of government. I do not incorporate this fact into my measure of decentralization since this study focuses on regional-level dynamics, although the logic of my argument may extend to local legislatures

and local parties as well. Local-level decentralization may be less effective, however, in reducing conflict since local legislatures tend to have control over significantly fewer important issues than regional legislatures.

113. The United Kingdom was centralized from 1985 to 1997 and decentralized from 1998 to 2000.

114. This is admittedly a crude way of measuring decentralization because constitutions are not the only documents that define how power is divided in a country, and may not be adhered to very closely in practice (although in democracies, which are the focus of this study, this is less of a concern than in dictatorships). Unfortunately, at this time, there are no better existing alternatives. I do not code countries based on whether or not regional legislatures have control over residual powers, i.e. powers not assigned to the national or regional level of government, as others have suggested (Treisman 2002). This is because the extent of regional authority depends on the number and types of powers that are not assigned to the national level of government.

115. These data reflect the most up-to-date data available from the World Bank and are different than those used in Brancati (2006). The most current data do not include figures on regional revenue (as a percentage of total revenue).

116. For the purposes of comparability, I have based these figures on lower house elections. Many countries do not have upper houses, and some are indirectly elected by regional legislatures. The analysis is based on only national elections because I would need information on all regional elections in centralized and decentralized systems of government to compare countries based on the overall electoral strength of regional parties, which is beyond the capacity of this study.

117. FIPS stands for Federal Information Process Standards. For more information, see http://www.census.gov/geo/www/fips/fips.html. These administrative divisions exist in both centralized and decentralized systems of government, although in centralized systems of government they do not have decision-making authority but may have administrative authority.

118. In alternative models, I have also defined regions as geographic regions (e.g. the North East and South in the United States), and

identified parties that compete in more than one region of a country but not every region of a country. In these models, regional parties generally increase ethnic conflict and secessionism, but their effects are smaller in size and significance. I expected this result because regional parties are much more broadly based and encompassing if they are defined this way.

119. Regardless of the potential effect of economic development on conflict and secessionism, I acknowledge the potential endogeneity between economic development (and even perceptions of economic development) and intrastate conflict (Miguel et al. 2004). Economic development is a control variable in this analysis and should not affect the results of decentralization and regional parties on intrastate conflict.

120. Previous studies of civil war have not found a robust relationship between overall heterogeneity and conflict (Fearon and Laitin 2003; Cederman and Girardin 2007; Fearon et al. 2007).

121. Applying the 1985 data to the entire 1985–2000 period is reasonable since country-level heterogeneity changes very little over time. The best possible data we could hope for would only vary about every ten years since this is the cycle national censuses typically follow.

122. I have not coded Niger, Spain, and Venezuela as mixed in this study, although they have a few single-member districts that allocate seats by majority/plurality rule, because the preponderance of districts in these countries are multimember districts that allocate seats by PR.

123. All countries are not represented every year of this ten-year period because some countries did not exist for the entire period (e.g. Bosnia-Herzegovina), and because some countries did not democratize until the 1990s (e.g. Estonia, Indonesia, Niger, Romania, and South Africa). Czechoslovakia is excluded from the analysis due to missing data regarding economic development and fiscal decentralization.

124. Countries in which the constituency level of government is greater than the regional level of government include countries that have electoral systems based on a single national constituency, such as Israel, the Netherlands, Moldova, Slovakia, etc. They also include countries that have multiple constituencies in which at least one constituency traverses several regions of a country, like New Zealand, which has an ethnic constituency representing the Maori who are dispersed throughout the country. I do not expect the omission of

these countries from the analysis to bias the results because these aspects of their electoral systems are not closely correlated with ethnic conflict and secessionism.

125. See Christin and Hug (2006) for a discussion of the importance of taking into account the geographic location of groups when analyzing the effect of decentralization on civil war. See note 111 for a list of groups excluded from the analysis because they are widely dispersed. Alternatively, I could have included a variable measuring the extent to which groups are territorially concentrated, and interact it with decentralization and regional parties. However, since I am more interested in this analysis in the interaction between decentralization and regional parties, I have kept the analysis simple and chosen to exclude these groups from the analysis.

126. The analysis does not include country fixed-effects since unit-specific effects are not consistent in nonlinear models (Wooldrige 2002), and because a number of variables of interest do not vary over time. If I cluster the standard errors (although clustering does not generally work well with fewer than 50 clusters (Bertrand et al. 2004), I find that my main variables of interest – political decentralization and the electoral strength of regional parties – are significant at the 0.10 level or better in nearly all models of anti-regime rebellion, and in many models of intercommunal conflict.

127. While including a lagged dependent variable may help correct for autocorrelation, I do not use a lag in this analysis following Achen (2000) and Keele and Kelly (2005). Achen (2000) shows that in OLS including a lag can lead to biased coefficients. Keele and Kelly (2005) refine Achen (2000) and demonstrate the conditions under which this bias is likely to be most severe.

128. If I drop the ELF index from all models in this section of anti-regime rebellion, decentralization continues to significantly reduce conflict while regional parties continue to increase it, although the size of the effect is modestly smaller.

129. In alternative models, I replace regional party vote with the percentage of parties that are regional parties in an election and the percentage of seats that they win. In both models, the variables for regional parties are positive and significant. I also replace regional party vote with denationalization. The main effect for decentralization is significant in this model, but the effect of denationalization is

not, suggesting that regional parties are more of a problem for secessionism than are parties competing in multiple regions of a country with an uneven distribution of votes throughout.

130. The following countries lack data for one or more of the three fiscal decentralization measures used in this chapter: Bosnia-Herzegovina, Botswana, Czechoslovakia, Finland, Greece, Indonesia, Niger, Turkey, and Venezuela. Some of these countries, like Bosnia-Herzegovina and Czechoslovakia, are highly decentralized fiscally while others are not.

131. In an alternative model, I measure fiscal decentralization in terms of subnational expenditure (percentage of GDP). This model does not converge unless I drop the ELF index from the model. Upon doing so, the effect of fiscal decentralization is negative and significant. Of the three measures of fiscal decentralization used in this chapter, this measure of decentralization has the least data.

132. There is one exception to this statement: subnational revenue (as a percentage of GDP) is negative and significant at the $p \leq 0.05$ level if I drop political decentralization and restrict the model to the same population as subnational expenditure (as a percentage of total expenditure). Additionally, if I restrict all previous analyses to the same population as Models 4 and 5, I find that decentralization and regional party vote continue to have the same effects on anti-regime rebellion, suggesting that the effects are not due to different samples.

133. Fiscal decentralization reduces conflict if I measure it in terms of subnational expenditure (percentage of GDP), but the number of observations in this model is even smaller than in Models 16 and 17.

134. In order to implement this procedure, I aggregate the group-level data to the national level of government according to the mean level of intercommunal conflict and anti-regime rebellion in a country so that I can use linear specifications of my models. Although transforming the data by its mean does not preserve differences in the categories of my dependent variables, models where the dependent variable is not continuous pose a challenge to researchers. In particular, the orthogonality conditions of IV regression do not necessarily extend to nonlinear transformations. Scholars have developed a number of techniques (Achen 1986; Foster 1997) to address this

issue where the dependent variable is binary, but this remains an issue for data where the dependent variable is a multicategory discrete variable, as in this analysis.

135. The null hypothesis of the Anderson cannon correlations likelihood ratio test is that the model is not identified.

136. I define regions here, as I do throughout this book, as the administrative divisions in a country (i.e. the level of government directly below the national level). In alternative models, I also define regions and measure regional parties in terms of the geographic regions of a country, which often traverse multiple administrative divisions in a country. While decentralization also increases the electoral strength of regional parties defined in these terms, the effect is smaller and generally not significant. The weaker effect is expected since geographic regions typically span more than one administrative division of a country, and regional legislatures, which I argue are the driving forces behind regional parties, generally coincide with the administrative divisions of a country.

137. For regional elections, I operationalize regional parties as parties that compete in one region of a country per regional election cycle. I define a regional election cycle as all regional elections that occur between two national elections. I also explore alternative operationalizations, the results of which are substantively and statistically the same as those presented in this chapter.

138. I was not able to collect data on upper house elections for which regional legislatures are the electing body, except for those already included in the case studies. These two elections are not included in the statistical analysis as a result.

139. I consider elections concurrent if they occur on the same day and year. If information on the day of the election is not available, I code elections as concurrent if they occur in the same year.

140. Unfortunately, there is no alternative source of cross-national data over time for fiscal decentralization that separates out both grants and transfers from all other sources of funding.

141. The data used in this analysis reflect the most up-to-date IMF data on fiscal decentralization available from the World Bank and, therefore, is different than the data in Brancati (2008a).

142. These controls focus only on social cleavages that are ethnic or linguistic in nature. Unfortunately, sufficient data is not available for this study to measure cleavages that are economic in nature.

143. This is reasonable since overall heterogeneity changes very little over time and censuses are generally taken every ten years. The Roeder dataset does not provide the ELF index for Bermuda. In order not to lose this data, I calculated the ELF index based on data in the *CIA World Factbook*. https://www.cia.gov/library/publications/the-world-factbook/. Accessed February 12, 2008.

144. Groups that are not included in the Fearon (2003) database because they constitute less than 1 percent of the overall population may have a regional base. Thus, the regional base variable used in this analysis specifically refers to the proportion of the population over 1 percent of the population that has a regional base.

145. All majority/plurality systems do not have single-member districts, including the following countries in the dataset: Bermuda (lower house), Mauritius (lower house), and Poland (Senate) and Spain (Senate).

146. The assembly in Northern Ireland has been suspended multiple times throughout its history.

147. I do not use country fixed-effects since most of the variables in this analysis vary very little over time. In separate analyses, however, I include fixed-effects for regions of the world. These fixed-effects are not significant and do not change the size or significance of the coefficient for decentralization. I also cluster the standard errors by country and by region, although clustering, in the case of the former, does not work well when the number of clusters is small (i.e. less than fifty) as they are in this study (Bertrand et al. 2004). Clustering does not change the results for decentralization either. Finally, I also analyze the relationship between decentralization and regional party vote using only the mean value of every variable in the dataset per country so that all countries are represented equally by a single observation. In this analysis, decentralization has a positive effect on regional parties, but with only as many observations as countries in this analysis, the results are not surprisingly, not significant at the 0.05 level or better, although they are significant in some models at the 0.10 level.

148. Interacting average district magnitude with the regional base variable, I find that the main effects for average district magnitude and the regional base variable, as well as the interaction term between the two, are jointly significant at the $p \leq 0.10$ level.

149. The correlation between political decentralization and subnational expenditure (as a percentage of total expenditure) and between subnational revenue (as a percentage of total expenditure) are 0.45 and 0.43, respectively. The correlation between political decentralization and subnational expenditure (as a percentage of GDP) is 0.22. They are significant at the $p \leq 0.01$ level.

150. Chhibber and Kollman's (1998) statistical analysis is based on forty-six elections in one country, the United States, and does not include any control variables. Their case study analysis (2004), though, controls for a number of factors since all four of their case studies have plurality systems and decentralized systems of government (although the United Kingdom did vary in this respect over time), and three of the four case studies (the United States being the exception) have parliamentary systems of government.

151. The following are examples of countries in which only certain regions have decision-making authority. The regions that have independent decision-making authority within each of these countries are identified in parentheses. These countries and regions are as follows: Denmark (Faeroe Islands and Greenland), Finland (Åland Islands), Portugal (Azores), Mauritius (Island of Rodrigues), Moldova (Gaugazia and Transdniestria), the Philippines (Mindanao and Cordilleras), Trinidad and Tobago (Tobago), and the United Kingdom (Northern Ireland – 1921–72 and Northern Ireland – 1998, Scotland and Wales – 1999–present).

152. Colombia is excluded from the analyses presented in Table 7.3 because I do not have seat data for elections held in this country. As a result, I cannot calculate the proportion of seats that each region in Colombia holds in the national legislature. Excluding this variable from the models so that Colombia is included in the analysis, yields the same substantive and statistical results for my main variable on autonomy.

153. In alternative models, I cluster the standard errors by country and by region, recognizing that clustering is not effective unless the numbers of clusters is approximately fifty or more (unlike in the case of countries) (Bertrand et al. 2004), the results of which are discussed in the text.

154. I do not explore the effect of fiscal decentralization in this analysis since the IMF data on fiscal decentralization is not disaggregated by region.

155. For regional elections, regional parties are operationalized as parties that compete in only one region of a country within a regional election cycle. A regional election cycle includes all regional elections that occur in a country between two national elections.

156. Although clustering is not effective unless the number of clusters is fifty or greater (Bertrand et al. 2004), I explore the effect of clustering by country in alternative models. The results are statistically and substantively the same as those in Table 7.5, with one exception. In models where I distinguish between nonconcurrent presidential and parliamentary elections, the individual coefficients on these variables are not significant if I cluster the standard errors by country, but they are jointly significant. In other models, I cluster the standard errors by region – the results of which yield the same substantive and statistical conclusions as those in Table 7. 5.

157. There are no mixed systems in this analysis.

158. I did not use population as an instrument for decentralization in the previous chapter even though more populous countries tend to be decentralized, because studies have shown a relationship between population and civil wars (Fearon and Laitin 2003; Collier and Hoeffler 2004). I use it, however, as an instrument for decentralization in this chapter because there is no theoretical and empirical relationship between population and regional party strength. The data on population are drawn from the *World Development Indicators Online* (2002). I filled in missing population data for Czechoslovakia based on the country's national census (Federal Statistical Office, 1991).

159. The absolute value of the correlation coefficients examining the relationship between each of these instruments and the percentage of seats regional parties win in an election, as well as denationalization, is less than 0.20 in all cases. The correlation coefficients for the relationship between each of these instruments and the percentage of parties that are regional parties in an election are notably higher, but still less than 0.45 in all cases.

Index

Figures and tables are indexed in bold.

Abadie, A. 1
Achen, C. H. 172, 176
Afghanistan 2, 171
Agarwal, U. C. 132
AGP, *see* Asom Gana Parishad
Agranoff, R. 97
AIDS 2
Aizpún, J. 112
Aja Fernández, E. 99
Alberti Rovira, E. 119
Alcántara Sáez, M. 104
Alesina, A. 52, 55
All-Parties Huriyat Conference (APHC) 141
Andalusia (Spain) 98, 102, 107, 109, 111–12, 114, 116
anti-regime rebellion 160–1, 162–3, 167, 171–2, 172–4, 174**t**, 175, 175**t**, 176–7, 177**f**, 178, 178**f**, 179–80, 182, 184–5, 186, 187, 188, 189–90, 192, 207, 208
anticommunism 71
AP, *see* Popular Alliance
APHC, *see* All-Parties Huriyat Conference
Aragon (Spain) 102, 105
Argelaguet, J. 18
Armet, L. 119
Arora, B. 138
Asom Gana Parishad (AGP) 142
Assam 144
    languages 125–6, 141
    separatist organizations 142
    violence 126, 142
Assam Accord 144
Association for the Republic-Republican Party of Czechoslovakia (SPR-RSC) 75–6
autonomous communities (Spain) 92, 94, 100, 106–7, 108, 109–10, 112, 119

FCI transfers to 99**f**
regional legislatures 95
taxes 97
votes 102–3, 103**f**
autonomy 10, 35, 56–7, 66, 80, 91, 100, 128, 132, 143, 144, 194, 195, 213, 214, 216
    demands for 53
    and minority groups 11
    and regional parties 13, 15, 52
    see also under individual countries
Aznar Grasa, A. 98

BAC, *see* Bodoland Autonomous Council
Baker, R. M. 186
Bakke, K. M. 12
Balearic Islands 92, 105, 107, 113, 117
Ballentine, K. 4, 11
Banerjee, K. 18, 138
Bangladeshi Muslims 125–6
Bañón i Martínez, R. 97
Barrera, H. 110, 111
Bartels, L. M. 186
Basque Country (Spain) 3, 18, 20–1, 40, 92, 96, 102, 105, 106, 109, 110, 112–13, 114, 115
    and autonomy 56–7
    elections 203
    extremist organizations 91, 93
    flag 112
    independence 93, 94, 115
    languages 113
    taxes 97–8, 109
    and violence 22
Basque National Party (PNV) 102, 110, 111, 115, 117
Basque Solidarity (EA) 93

Index

Bates, R. H. 167
Belgium 220
Beltrán, M. 94, 95
Bengalis 141
Beramendi, J. G. 99, 100
Beramendi, P. 99
Bermeo, N. 2, 8, 9
Bertrand, M. 172, 202, 213
Bharatiya Janata Party (BJP) 135, 143–4, 145
Bhargava, P. K. 129
Bhatnagar, S. 18, 138
bicameralism 7
Biden, US Senator J. 4
BiH, see Bosnia-Herzegovina
Birnir, J. K. 193
Biswas, G. 138
BJP, see Bharatiya Janata Party
Blumi, I. 18
Bodo Accord (1993) 144
Bodoland Autonomous Council (BAC) 144
Bodos 126
Bohemia (Czech Lands) 66, 67, 88
    federation 85
    independence 68
    and Moravia 68, 80, 85
    and Slovaks 68
Bolton, P. 33, 52, 55, 167
Bombwal, K. R. 143
Bookman, M. Z. 33, 167
borders 2, 31, 35, 51, 84, 93, 124, 125, 126,
        139, 143–4, 148
Bosnia-Herzegovina (BiH) 164, 171, 172,
        196, 198, 201, 210, 217
Bossi, U. 18
Bound, J. 186
boundaries 13, 31, 42, 51, 214, 224, 229,
        214, 229
Bowman, A. O'M. 53, 200
Brady, H. E. 18
Brambor, T. 176
Braña, F. J. 98
Brancati, D. 12, 22, 37, 150, 158, 160,
        270**n**, 274**n**
Brass, P. R. 14, 143, 169
Brassloff, A. 99
Braumoeller, B. F. 176
Brazil 48
Brubaker, R. 4, 10, 18
Brzinski, J. B. 48
Buchanan, J. M. 33, 167
Budge, I. 33
Bunce, V. 4, 10, 11, 14, 18, 39, 71, 194
Burgess, M. 10
Buse, M. 104

Byman, D. 228

Caha, L. 81
Čalfa, M., Prime Minister,
        Czechoslovakia 86
Campbell, T. 55
Campenni, M. 169
Canada 3, 54
Canary Coalition (CC) 114
Canary Islands 96, 102, 105, 107, 117
Candland, C. 142
Caramani, D. 158
Carey, J. 47, 204
Čarnogurský, J. 77
caste system 48, 122, 135
Castilla-La Mancha 98
Catalonia (Spain) 18, 20–1, 92, 96, 102,
        105, 106–7, 109–11, 112–13
    and autonomy 56–7, 110, 115
    elections 203
    independence 93, 94
    languages 113
    taxes 109, 115
Convergence and Union (CiU) 110, 114, 117
Catholicism 92
causality 19
CC, see Canary Coalition
Cederman, L.-E. 166
centralized parties 46–7
centralized systems 49, 51, 52, 55, 197
CHA, see United Aragon
Chandler, W. M. 35, 47
Chandra, K. 14, 42, 146
chief executives 171, 204, 219, 229
Chhibber, P. K. 48, 49, 50, 129, 138, 142,
        149, 167, 196, 200, 212, 213
Chong, D. 32
Christian Democratic Movement (KDH)
        67, 77
Christian Democratic Movement-
        Czechoslovak People's Party
        (KDH-CSL) 72
Christian Democratic Party (KDS) 75
Christiansen, T. 18
Christin, T. 172
Chueca Rodríguez, R. L. 104
city-states (Africa) 92
CiU, see Convergence and Union
Civic Democratic Party (ODS) 75, 86
Civic Forum (OF) 74, 75, 83, 85–6
civil rights 3–4, 41–2, 43, 152, 168–9, 179, 227
civil wars 3–4, 23, 54, 160, 162, 188–9
Clark, W. R. 176
Clavero, M. 112

CLE, *see Constituency-Level Elections dataset*
cleavages 15, 26, 30, 32, 34, 48, 89,
    138–9, 225
Clinton, B., former US President 4
CMP, *see* Common Minimum Programme
coalitions 36–7, 43, 50, 74–5, 171, 204
    two-party 76
    see also India, coalitions
coat tails effect 17, 58., 59
collective identities, *see* identities, collective
Collier, D. 18
Collier, P. 23, 167, 188, 217
Colombia 163
Colomer, J. M. 104
colonialism (UK) 55
Common Minimum Programme (CMP) 144
communism 24, 69, 79–80, 170
Communist Party of Czechoslovakia
    (KSC) 74, 85–6
concurrent elections 59, 120, 151, 189
Congress of Deputies (Congreso de los
    Diputados) 95
Congress Party (India) 123, 132, 134, 135,
    137, 141, 142–3, 144, 145, 147, 148,
    149, 227
Conservative Party (UK) 53
consociationalism 43, 168, 228–9
Constituency-Level Elections (CLE) dataset
    22–3, 158–9, 160, 172, 205, 217
constitutions 53, 164–5, 198, 227
    see also Czechoslovakia; India; Spain
corruption 134
Cotarelo, R. G. 104
countervailing 37
Coursen, K. 8, 9, 18
Cox, G. W. 59, 201, 203, 204
Cox, R. H. 81, 82
Croatia 35
cross-regional voting laws 21, 189, 190,
    192, 201, 202, 209, 213, 220, 224,
    227, 230
Czech Lands 21, 35, 65, 67
    and autonomy 66
    and centralized state 69
    coalitions 74
    and communism 80
    and independence 83
    and market economy 77
    regional legislatures 73, 88
    regional parties 81, 83–4, 88
    revenue 70
    and secessionism 68
    unemployment 78
    unity 89

Czech Republic 73–4
    independence 85
    and Moravia 86
Czechoslovakia 3, 20, 78
    anticommunism 71
    constitution 24, 65, 70, 72, 73, 82, 83,
        84–5, 88, 227
    democracy 24, 65, 74–5, 226
    dissolution of 21, 35, 65–6, 68, 71, 77, 78,
        81, 82–3, 85, 86, 88, 89
    ethnic groups 66–7, 71, 79, 80
    fiscal authority 70–1
    interwar 24, 66, 78, 79, 79f, 89, 80, 89
    languages 65, 67, 71, 79
    leaders 71, 82
    legislation 70, 72, 83, 84, 87, 88
    minority groups 78, 79–80
    and mobilization 38–9
    national elections 76, 78
    national governments 69, 70, 71, 79, 83,
        84, 85, 88
    and national legislatures 65, 87
    and party systems 66, 77, 81, 82–6, 87, 88
    and peaceful secession 3, 21
    political parties 65, 67, 68t, 73, 81, 85
    and political systems 65, 68t, 72, 73,
        83, 86
    postcommunist 19, 35, 43, 65, 66, 71,
        72, 80
    regional identities 71
    regional legislatures 65, 69, 73, 83, 86,
        87, 88, 89
    and regional parties 20, 66,74, 81,
        87–8, 227
        electoral strength of 75, 75f, 76, 76f,
            78, 79f, 81; topdown policies 81
    statewide parties 75, 77, 84
    upper houses 20
    veto 65, 72, 87, 88, 89
Czechs and Slovaks 82, 82, 84, 89
    differences between 77, 78, 79–80
    independence 69
    political powers 72
    relations between 3, 65, 66–7, 72–4
    regional identities 71

de Burgos, J. 119
de Esteban, J. 103, 104
de Silva, H. L. 5
de Winter, L. 14, 33, 34, 52, 158, 193
decentralization:
    definition 6–7
    methodology 17–23
    and opposition to 4–5

Index

decision-making 13, 72, 119
  authority 26, 49, 56, 60, 87, 89, 95, 127–8,
    150, 153, 160, 164, 198, 217, 228
  independent 6, 8
  and legislatures 7, 60
  rules 43
Dědek, O. 78
democracies 2, 3, 8, 157, 160, 171–2,
    188, 220
  age of 170, 173, 180–1, 204, 209, 213, 220
  and centralized systems 55
  and Czechoslovakia 24
  and division of power 7
  elections 170, 204
  post-World War II 21
democratic transitions 21, 24, 40–1, 67,
    77, 90, 91, 95, 106, 119, 170, 204,
    220, 226
Democratic Party (DS) 76
democratization 55
denationalization 167, 173–4, 182, 196,
    208–9, 212, 213, 221, 223
Denmark 56
Desposato, S. W. 47
Diamond, L. 55
Dikshit, R. D. 4, 9, 10
district magnitude 42, 169, 173, 202, 209
DMK, see Dravida Munnetra Kazhagam
Dorff, R. H. 73
Dravida Munnetra Kazhagam (DMK)
    141–2, 145
Druckman, J. N. 32
DS, see Democratic Party
Dua, B. D. 147
Duchacek, I. D. 8, 7, 10
Duflo, E. 172, 202, 213
Dutta, A. 138
Dutta, N. 138
Duverger, M. 201
Dvořaková, V. 81

East Asian Christians 125
Eastern Europe 18, 21, 170
Eaton, K. 53
economic development 168
  underdevelopment 167
economic wealth 20, 21, 33, 54–5
effective number of electoral parties
    (ENEP) 167
Eidelson, R. J. 8, 9
Elazar, D. J. 9, 10
elections 169–70, 201, 210, 212
  concurrency 189, 190, 204, 230

democracies 158
  first 203–4, 209
  legislative, concurrency of 192–3
  proportionality 201–2
  and regional parties, strength of 5, 13–14,
    29, 192–3, 206
  rigging (Jammu and Kashmir) 127
  sequencing/timing 189, 229
  and voters 15
  see also under individual countries;
    legislative elections; national elections;
    presidential elections; regional
    elections; upper houses, elections
Electoral College (USA) 204
electoral competition 42, 45, 46, 119
electoral laws 45
electoral systems 42, 44, 169, 179, 204, 209,
    224, 230
  and age of democracy 180
  competitiveness 60
  and incentives 45
electoral outbidding, see outbidding
Elkins, Z. 31
Elster, J. 77
endogeneity 61, 190, 221
ENEP, see effective number of electoral parties
English (India) 125
ERC, see Republican Left of Catalonia
Escobar-Lemmon, M. 53
ETA, see Euskadi Ta Azkatasuna
ethnic conflict, failure of decentralization to
    reduce 9–12
ethnic groups 2, 8,13, 20, 25, 39, 44, 45, 161,
    162, 168, 171–2, 201, 202, 210, 213
  India 152
  Spain 95
  territorially concentrated 30, 60
  see also Czechoslovakia, ethnic groups
ethnicity 10, 31, 44, 48
Ethno-Linguistic Fractionalization (ELF)
    Indices 168, 200, 205–6
ethnolinguistics 4, 19, 20, 25, 34, 37, 77,
    90, 91, 167, 202
  heterogeneity 168, 179, 205–6
  see also India, ethnolinguistics; Spain,
    ethnolinguistics
European Union 83, 114
Euskadi Ta Azkatasuna (ETA) 15, 93, 115
exogeneity 221
executive systems 47, 59, 204, 219
  national elections 204–5
extremist organizations 39–40, 91, 141,
    152, 225

Faith, R. L. 33, 167
Falleti, T. G. 49
FCI, *see* Interterritorial Compensation Fund
Fearon, J. D. 1, 23, 33, 161, 166, 167, 188, 200, 201, 217
federalism 4, 6
federation 67, 83, 85, 86
Filippov, M. 12, 18, 46
financial powers 49–50
financial subsidies 13
Finland 56
first-past-the-post elections 146
fiscal authority (India) 129
fiscal autonomy 42, 109, 113–14
fiscal decentralization 49–50, 175–6, 179, 182, 194, 224
former Yugoslavia 1, 21, 39
  and civil war 3
  and Serbs 35
Forst, V. 68, 69
Fossas, E. 95, 99, 119
Foster, E. M. 176, 182
fractionalization 42, 160
Fraile, M. 104
France 55, 187
Frankland, E. G. 81, 82
Franklin, M. N. 230
Fusi Aizpurua, J. P. 99, 100

Gagnon, V. P. 14, 37, 39
Galicia 92, 93, 96, 102, 105, 107, 109
Gandhi, I., Prime Minister, India 148, 149, 227
Ganguly, S. 131
Garaikoetxea, C. 110
García Ferrando, M. 94, 95
García-Retamero, R. 33
Gardeazabal, J. 1
Garmendia Martínez, J. A. 104
Gassah, L. S. 18
Gavela, D. 119
GDP 168, 173, 176, 179, 200
Geddes, B. 20
Germany 53, 57, 196, 198
Ghobarah, H. A. 1
Gibson, J. L. 33
Girardin, L. 166
Giuliano, E. 14, 23, 30, 42, 146, 167
Gleason, G. 4, 10, 52, 194
globalization 55
Goa 128, 136
Golder, M. 176
Gouws, A. 33

governance 34
  decentralized 9–10, 29
Government Finance Statistics 165
governments:
  expenditure (Spain) 97
  hierarchical division of power 6
  influence of citizens on 8
  systems 230
Grau Creus, M. 104, 119
Great Britain, *see* UK
Gregor, M. 81
groups, *see* ethnic groups; minority groups
Grzymala-Busse, A. M. 75
Guerrero Salom, E. 102
Gunther, R. 104
Gurr, T. R. 1, 8, 9

Habyarimana, J. 33
Hale, H. E. 12
Hamann, K. 104
Hamilton, A. 55
Hampl, S. 68, 69, 80
Hardgrave, J. L. 4, 10, 131
Hardin, R. 39
Hartzell, C. 2
Hasan, Z. 138, 139
Havel, M. 70
Havel, V., President, Czech Republic 77–8, 82, 84
Hearl, D. J. 33
Heath, A. 142
Hechter, M. 2, 10, 33, 52, 194
Henderson, K. 72, 77, 82
Herbst, J. 55, 187
Herrera, Y. M. 14, 30, 167
Herri Batasuna (Basque Country) 40, 93, 115
heterogeneity 15, 40, 152, 168, 173, 179, 200–1, 205–6, 221, 224, 226
Hewitt, J. J. 1
Hindi 125
Hindus (India) 124, 131–2, 140
  nationalism 127
Hirczy, W. P. 230
Hlinka's Slovak People's Party (HSLS) 78–9
Hoddie, M. 2
Hoeffler, A. 23, 167, 188, 217
Holzer, A. 18
Honajzer, J. 75
Horowitz, D. L. 4, 8, 11, 18, 42, 45, 146, 167, 168
House of Nations (Sněmovna Národů) 69, 87–8

House of People (Sněmovna Lidu) 69, 87–8,
133**f**, 134**f**
HSD-SMS, *see* Movement for Self-Governing
Democracy-Association for Moravia
and Silesia
HSLS, *see* Hlinka's Slovak People's Party
Hubbard, C. 32
Hug, S. 19, 33, 167, 172
Humphreys, M. 33
Hungarian Coalition (MKDH-ESWS)
75–6
Hungarians 67
Hungary 202
Huth, P. 1
HZDS, *see* Movement for a Democratic
Slovakia

Ibáñez, J. G. 113
Iceland 210
identities:
and beliefs 32–3
collective 32, 33
formation of 10, 14, 29, 42
national 60
and regional parties 30–4
religious 20, 32
and statewide parties 31
see also regional identities
ideology 10, 120
Illegal Migrants Act 1983 144
IMF, *see* International Monetary Fund
immigration 113, 115
independence 3, 9, 10, 11–12, 33, 55, 94,
164, 187, 194, 226
demands for 34, 36, 52
fighting for 39
and legislation 38
see also under individual countries
Independent Republic of the Congo 33
India 18, 19, 20, 123, 126–7, 214
autonomy 132
boundaries 229
coalitions 135, 141, 144–5, 150
constitution 128, 129
decentralization 122, 127–31, 131–2, 139,
143, 146–7, 152–3
decision-making authority 56, 128, 150
democracy, weakness of 147, 152
and economic wealth 21
elections 134–5, 146
sequencing/timing 151–2, 153
and electoral competition 45
ethnic groups 152

ethnolinguistic 122–3, 124, 131, 138,
139, 143, 146
and extremist organizations 40, 152
fiscal authority 129
independence 132, 141
and intrastate violence 22, 122, 124–5,
131–2, 141
languages 125–6, 138, 140–2, 144
legislation 122, 140, 148, 151, 152
lower house 133, 136, 139, 149–50
national elections 127, 132–3, 151
and national governments 20, 123,
127–9, 131, 133–4, 138, 147–8, 150
expenditure 129
national legislatures 136
party systems 122, 123, 132–3, 139–49,
149–52
and pivotalness 122, 132, 146–7, 149, 152
political parties 123, 126, 135, 138, 140
political systems 143, 145–6
President's Rule 128–9, 147, 148, 149
regional elections 123, 149, 151–3
regional identities 132
and regional legislatures (Vidhan
Sabhas) 20, 25–6, 56, 123, 127, 129,
136, 138, 143, 148, 150–2
regional minority groups 140, 141, 146,
152, 226
and regional parties 20, 25–6, 51, 122,
123, 134, 135, 136, 136**f**, 137–8,
138–43, 145, 149, 152, 226
electoral strength 133**f**, 152; votes
132–3, 136–7, 137**f**
religion 122–3, 124, 138, 139, 143, 146
and statewide parties 25, 122–3, 132, 134,
140, 141, 143–6, 147–8, 149, 152
subnational government:
expenditure 130**f(a)**; revenue 129,
130**f(b)**, 131
union territories 124, 127, 128, 139,
143–4, 150, 153
upper houses 20, 25, 123, 136, 139,
150–1, 198
election procedures 152–3
veto 151
see also Congress Party; House of Nations;
House of People; individual regions
India Act (1935) 143
Indigenous People's Front of Tripura
(IPFT) 142
Indo-Pak War 1971 138
Indonesia 4, 45, 57, 203, 220
infectious diseases 2

information, dissemination of 31–2
Innes, A. 82
institutions 10, 14, 46–7, 55–6
 and regional differences 34
intercommunal conflict 162, 163, 171–2,
 179, 180, 180t, 181t, 181–3, 183t, 184,
 185, 185f, 186–7, 188, 189–90, 192,
 193, 207, 208
International Monetary Fund (IMF) 165, 200
Interterritorial Compensation Fund
 (FCI) 98, 99f, 110
intracommunal conflict 160–1
intrastate conflict 2, 5, 15, 22, 225
IPFT, see Indigenous People's Front of Tripura
IRA, see Irish Republican Army
Iraq 2, 33
 and Kurds 4
 reconstruction 231
Ireland 210
Irish Republican Army 15, 54
irredentism 51
Italy 53
Iyengar, S. 32
Iyer, V. R. K. 147

Jaeger, D. A. 186
Jammu and Kashmir 124, 125, 140, 141
 autonomy 128, 143, 144, 146
 decision-making authority 128
 elections, rigging 127, 147
 violence 126–7
 votes 136–7, 139
Janda, K. 46
Jay, J. 55
Jensen, N. M. 1
Jozífková, B. 77

Kahneman, D. 32
Kaiza, D. 4
Kalyvas, S. N. 30
Kasara, K. 166
Kashmir, see Jammu and Kashmir
Kaufmann, C. 8, 9
KDH, see Christian Democratic Movement
KDH-CSL, see Christian Democratic
 Movement-Czechoslovak People's
 Party
KDS, see Christian Democratic Party
Keating, M. 15
Keele, L. 172
Kelly, N. J. 172
Kenya 170
Keohane, R. O. 18

Khalistan 126
Khanna, H. R. 147
King, G. 18
Klaus, V., President, Czech Republic 77
Kohli, A. 145
Kollman, K. 48, 49, 167, 196, 200, 212, 213
Kopecký, P. 77, 82
Kostelecký, T. 71, 81
Kothari, R. 148
Kovář, J. 82
Krause, G. A. 53, 200
Krejčí, O. 81
Kroupa, A. 71, 72, 80
KSC, see Communist Party of
 Czechoslovakia
Kučera, M. 80
Kumar, P. 18, 138
Kunc, J. 81
Kurds, in Iraq 4
Kusý, M. 67
Kymlicka, W. 4, 10, 11, 18, 39, 52, 194

Labour Party (UK) 53
Lagares Díez, N. 111
Laitin, D. D. 1, 14, 23, 30, 33, 39, 166, 167,
 188, 217
languages 3, 9, 10, 31, 32, 33, 38, 65, 159, 187
 Basque 113
 Catalonia 113
 Czechs and Slovaks 67
 English (India) 125
 Kok-Barak 126
 Slovakia 79
 Spain 92
 Tamil 144
 Tibetan 141
 see also under Assam; Czechoslovakia; India
Latin America 180
leaders 4, 7, 15, 41, 42, 46, 71, 82–3,
 108, 146
 party 4, 14, 18, 19, 32, 46, 82, 148, 226
 political 4, 10, 14, 30–1, 54, 71, 123, 152
 regional 11, 14, 32, 71, 73
leadership style 15, 42–3, 46–7, 60, 123,
 146, 148–9, 227
Leff, C. S. 4, 11, 18, 39, 72, 73, 77, 194
legislation 10, 19, 29, 34–8, 50, 164,
 226, 227
 harmful to other regions 5, 15, 24, 25, 30,
 35, 37–8, 41, 43–4, 60, 91, 108, 140,
 152, 169, 225
 national 24
 subnational 11

legislation (*continued*)
  vetoes 72
  see also Czechoslovakia, legislation; India,
    legislation; Spain, legislation
legislatures:
  control of 43
  decision-making authority 60, 165
legislative elections 23, 189, 192, 195, 199,
    202, 204, 210, 219
  concurrency 199, 204–5, 209–10, 219, 230
  national 51, 59, 167, 213–14, 215**t**,
    216–17, 219
  nonconcurrency 209, 210, 219
  regional 199, 217, 218**t**, 219–20
  sequencing/timing 219
Levi, M. 33
Lieberman, E. S. 18
Lijphart, A. 2, 8, 9, 10, 11, 43, 131, 168, 228
Linz, J. J. 48, 102, 104, 171, 220
Lipset, S. M. 33, 167, 169
Llera Ramo, F. J. 18, 104
López Aranguren, E. M. 94, 95
López Guerra, L. M. 103, 104
López Laborda, J. 98
lower house 158
  see also India, lower house; Spain, lower
    house
Lukyamuzi, J. K. 4
Lundell, K. 46
Lustik, I. S. 8, 9

Macek, M. 73, 74
McGarry, J. 12, 34
McGraw, K. M. 32
Madagascar 54
Madison, J. 55
Máiz, R. 99
Major, J., former UK Prime Minister 4–5
majority, *see* prohibition of the majority
    (Czechoslovakia)
majority/plurality 135, 146, 169, 172–3,
    201–2, 206–7, 209, 219–20
Malcolm, N. 14, 18, 39
Manor, J. 8, 131, 143, 149
Mansfield, E. D. 170
Marcet, J. 18
market economy 76, 77
market-oriented reforms 55
Martínez Rodríguez, A 104
Mates, P. 86
Meadwell, H. 11
media 11, 15, 39, 41, 73
Meguid, B. M. 34, 52

Mexico 203
Miguel, E. 166
militia 11, 15, 39
Milošević, S. 18
Milovy Draft Treaty 84
Minorities at Risk (MAR) *Project* 23, 160–2,
    163, 188, 201
minority groups 2, 3, 4, 8, 37, 78, 139, 146,
    162, 163
  and autonomy 11
  geographically-located 9
  regional 140, 141, 145, 146, 152
  and subnational governents 9, 11
  territorially concentrated 9, 124
Miodownik, D. 8, 9
Mišović, J. 68
mixed electoral systems 169, 173, 202,
    206–7, 209
Mizo Accord 125, 142
Mizo conflict 125
Mizo National Front (MNF) 142
Mizoram 125, 139
MKDH-ESWS, *see* Hungarian Coalition
MNF, *see* Mizo National Front
mobilization 29–30, 38, 39–40
  of groups 60, 225
Montero Gibert, J. R. 48, 102, 104
Moravia (Czech Lands) 24, 66, 67, 80, 86,
    88, 89
  autonomy 80
    regional 85
  federation 85
  independence 68
  regional parties 89
  self-government 85–6
Moreno, L. 99, 100
Movement for Self-Governing Democracy-
    Association for Moravia and Silesia
    (HSD-SMS) 85, 86
Mueller, J. 14, 39
MUF, *see* Muslim United Force
Mughan, A. 16, 50, 57, 199
Mullainathan, S. 172, 202, 213
multimember districts 202
Murdoch, J. C. 1
Musil, J. 67
Muslim United Force (MUF) 127
Muslims (India) 124, 131–2, 141, 146–7

Nagaland 136
  independence 124–5
Narang, A. S. 8, 9, 10
Narula, R. S. 131

National Councils (Czechoslovakia) 69–70, 76f, 85, 87, 88
National Democratic Alliance (NDA) [India] 135
National Development Council (NDC) [India] 144
national elections 52, 195, 198, 203, 205, 207t, 208t, 211t, 215t, 219, 220, 221
  concurrency 199 51,
  Czechoslovakia 76, 78
  nonconcurrency 223–4
  regional parties 13, 16, 17, 52, 58–9, 165–6, 193, 196, 213, 217
  sequencing/timing of 16, 17, 56, 58, 195, 220, 223–4, 229
  see also elections; individual countries; legislative elections; regional elections
National Front government (India) 134
national governments 3, 13, 35, 38, 41, 43, 49, 59, 69, 165, 169, 170,188, 200, 212
  and autonomy 53
  decentralization 53
  funding 200
  and legislative authority 6
  and subnational governments 7, 20
  see also under individual countries
national legislatures:
  control of agenda 50
  and Czechoslovakia 65, 87
  number of 56
  proportion of regional seats 24, 25, 29, 44–5, 50–1, 56, 199, 213
  and regional legislatures 58–9
  share of 50–1
National Liberation Front of Tripura (NLFT) 142
nationalism 100, 127
Navarra (Spain) 56–7, 96, 102, 105, 109, 110, 112–13
  independence 94
  taxes 97–8, 109
Nayar, V. K. S. 134
NDC, see National Development Council
NDA, see National Democratic Alliance
Nehru, J., Prime Minister, India 124, 148
Netherlands 55
Newell, J. L. 18
Nigeria 33
  and decentralization 55
  and democracy 3
  and presidential candidates 59
  and Shari'ah 11

NLFT, see National Liberation Front of Tripura
noncontiguous territories 188–9, 221
nonconcurrent elections 17, 58, 116, 151, 195, 199–200
nondemocracies 7
Nordlinger, E. A. 4, 10, 11, 18, 52, 194
Norris, P. 229
North Atlantic Treaty Organization 83
North Eastern Areas (Reorganization) Act 1971 143
Northern Ireland 43, 52–3, 53, 54, 203, 204, 214, 216
Northern League 18
Núñez, X.-M. 100

Obrman, J. 86
ODS, see Civic Democratic Party
O'Leary, B. 11, 34
Olson, D. 86, 87
Olson, M. 39
Oñate Rubalcaba, P. 48, 104
O'Neill, K. 53
Opatřil, R. 86
Ordeshook, P. C. 12, 18, 46
Ornstein, N. 8, 9, 18
outbidding 42
overidentifying restrictions 223

Padró-Solanet, A. 104
Pai, S. 138
Pakistan 126–7, 138
Pal, C. 131, 132
Pallarés Posta, F. 48, 104
Panizza, U. 55
Papua New Guinea 33
parliamentary systems 21, 53, 59, 189, 204, 224, 229
  concurrent elections 199–200
Parraluna, F. 104
partition 228
party discipline 47
party systems 44, 48–9, 196, 207–8, 224, 225, 230, 231
  see also under individual countries
patronage 149
Patterson, S. C. 16, 50, 57, 199
Pavlík, Z. 80
PCE, see Spanish Communist Party
Pearson, B. 33
Pehe, J. 82
Penn, E. M. 10, 30
Pérez Vilariño, J. 104

Index

Pérez-Agote, A. 104
Pérez-Nievas, S. 18, 104
Perulles Romero, J. M. 97, 98
Petrocik, J. 138, 142
Pithart, P., former Prime Minister, Czech Republic 74, 84, 85, 86
pivotalness 15, 37, 45, 120, 226–7
 see also India, pivotalness
Planning Commission (India) 129
plurality, *see* majority/plurality
PNV, *see* Basque National Party
political decentralization, *see* decentralization
political leaders, *see* leaders, political
political parties 12, 35, 41, 47, 48–50, 158, 159–60
 see also under individual countries
political rights 169, 173
political systems 8, 13, 14, 30, 33, 41, 46, 47, 54, 158, 160, 168, 213, 225–6, 228
 see also under individual countries
politics 8, 9, 77, 82, 111, 131, 132, 138, 212, 230–1
 and statewide parties 45–6
Popkin, S. L. 32
Popular Alliance (AP) 111
Popular Party (PP) 109, 111, 114, 117
population 188, 201, 204, 206, 213, 221, 228
Portugal 56
Posner, D. N. 30, 33
PP, *see* Popular Party
presidency 59, 204, 210
President's Rule, *see* India, President's Rule
presidential candidates 47
 and Nigeria 59
 and USA 59
presidential elections 59, 204–5, 210
 concurrent 192–3, 199–200, 205
 and Kenya 170
 nonconcurrent 209, 224
presidential systems 47, 48, 59, 189, 199–200, 204, 210
presidentialism 171, 179–80, 201
Příhoda, P. 67
prime ministerial elections 204
privatization 76
prohibition of the majority (Czechoslovakia) 72, 73, 88
proportional representation (PR) 42, 45, 169, 201–2, 206, 220
Průcha, V. 80
PSLA, *see* Social and Liberal Party of Andalusia

PSOE, *see* Spanish Socialist Workers Party
Public Against Violence (VPR, Slovakia) 74, 75
public goods 53
Punjab (India) 125, 126, 139, 144

Quebec 3

Rabushka, A. 42
Rajiv-Longowal Accord 126, 144
Ramos Gallarín, J. A. 97
Ransdorf, M. 84
Rao, M. G. 129
Reangs 125
rebellion, *see* anti-regime rebellion
referendums 82, 110, 112, 161
regional elections 23, 52, 76, 87, 158, 159, 193, 195, 195, 196, 198, 203–4, 217, 218**t**, 220, 227, 229
 concurrency 20, 199, 205, 219
 nonconcurrency 20, 224
 sequencing/timing of 5, 16, 17, 29, 56, 58–, 224, 195, 220, 223–4, 229
 see also elections; India, regional elections; Spain, regional elections
regional elites 10–11, 55, 81
regional identities 5, 10, 14–15, 25, 30, 31–3, 35, 39, 60, 71, 105, 106**f**, 107, 112, 113, 119, 120, 132, 225, 228–9
regional leaders, *see* leaders, regional
regional legislatures 5, 7, 16–17, 20, 25, 29, 39, 50, 52, 56–9, 160, 164, 165, 166, 198, 227, 229
 elections 217
 and national legislatures 58–9
 and regional parties 50
 regional minorities 15
  and discrimination 11
 see also under individual countries
regional parties 12, 14–16, 17–19, 20–1, 23–6, 29, 30–1, 33–8, 40–2, 48, 157–8, 159, 160, 165, 174, 176–8, 178**f**, 179, 181–5, 185**f**, 189, 190, 192–3, 193–4, 195–224, 225–7, 229–30
 and autonomy 13
 and electoral strength 5, 16, 20, 29, 33–4, 48, 55–9, 158, 165–71, 184–5, 185**f**, 196, 196–7, 197**f**, 207, 210, 213, 217, 223–4, 227, 230
 and ethnic conflict 14–15
 and increase in conflict 18–19
 and leaders 14
 mobilization 38–40

and regional legislatures 16–17
and statewide parties 12, 23–4
    strength 165–71
    votes 174, 177–8, 178**f**, 192, 210, 214,
        219–20
    see also individual countries
regional primaries 47
regression analysis 185–90, 191**t**, 92–3
    instrumental variable 185–193, 221–223,
        222t
Řeháková, B. 81
religion 3, 31, 32, 33, 38, 65, 80, 128, 140, 142
    Czechs and Slovaks 67
    see also India, religion
religious identity, *see* identities, religious
Republican Left of Catalonia (ERC) 93,
        110–11, 115
Requejo, F. 95, 99
Riker, W. H. 6, 11, 12, 18, 46
Rocca, F. X. 18
Rodden, J. 49
Roeder, P. G. 4, 10, 18, 39, 168, 194, 201
Rogowski, R. 2, 11
Rokkan, S. 33, 34, 52, 158, 169, 193
Roland, G. 33, 52, 55, 167
Romanians (Transnistria), and Russia 11
Ross, M. L. 33
Rothschild, J. 78
Rousseau, D. L. 33
rump states 228
Russett, B. 1
Russia, and Romanians (Transnistria) 11
Rwanda 1
Rychlík, J. 71

Saideman, S. M. 169
Sambanis, N. 2, 228
Samuels, D. 52, 219
Sandler, T. 1
Sani, G. 104
Sargenti, E. 166
Sartori, G. 201
Satyanath, S. 166
Schwegler, B. 18
Scotland 52–3, 203
Scottish National Party 18
secessionism 1, 3
    as expression of public will 3
    peaceful 3, 21
    within countries 3
self-determination 115
self-government (Moravia) 85–6
Sen, S. R. 147

Senate (Senado) 95, 117–18, 118**f**, 119
Sengupta, A. 138
separatism 30
separatist organizations 36, 90, 107, 142
separatist regions 3
Serbia 35
Serna de los Mozos, V. M. 98
Seshia, S. 138, 143
Shabad, G. 99, 100, 104
Shepsle, K. A. 42
Shugart, M. S. 47, 204
Shvetsova, O. 12, 18, 46
Sikhs 126
Silesia 67, 80, 86
Silva i Sánchez, M. 114
Singh, G. 132, 143
Singh, S. D. 134, 138
single-member district systems 45
Slavíková, J. 77
Slides, J. 31
Slovak Lands 21
Slovak National Party (SNS) 67
Slovakia 21, 24, 67
    and autonomy 35, 66
    and communism 80
    and Czech Republic 73–4
    federation 85
    and independence 67, 68, 83
    and languages 79
    and national legislatures 65, 87
    regional legislatures 67, 73, 88
    regional parties 81, 83–4, 88
    and revenue 70
    and secessionism 68
    state subsidies 77
    unemployment 78
    upper houses 67
Slovaks, *see* Czechs and Slovaks
Slovaks and Moravians 67–8
SNS, *see* Slovak National Party
Snyder, J. L. 4, 11, 14, 18, 39, 170, 194
Social and Liberal Party of Andalusia
        (PSLA) 111, 112
Socialist Party of Serbia 18
South Africa 55
Soviet Union 18
Spain 19, 22, 187
    and autonomy 56–7, 91, 100, 108–9, 113,
        120, 216–18
    constitution 91, 96, 108, 109, 110,
        111–12, 119
    and decentralization 54, 90–1, 95,
        99–101, 104–6, 110–11, 116–17, 120

Spain (*continued*)
  democracy 90, 91, 94, 95, 99, 106, 107,
    111, 226
  elections 120
    national 220; sequencing 203
  ethnic groups 95
  ethnolinguistics 91, 92, 104, 107, 117, 120
  fiscal authority 95
  and independence from 24–5, 90, 94,
    94f, 95
  legislation 91, 107, 108, 118, 119–20
  lower house 91, 118, 119–20
  national elections 116–17, 120
  national governments 90, 95–6, 97, 98,
    102, 108, 109, 114, 115, 116, 119, 120
    expenditure 97, 97f
  national legislatures 116
  nationalism 100
  party systems 92, 101, 116–17, 118–20
  and pivotalness 120
  political parties 93, 104, 107
  political systems 107–8, 110, 112, 119
  regional elections 93, 102, 111, 116–17, 120
  regional identities 105, 106f, 107, 119
  regional issues 90
  and regional legislatures 90, 91, 95, 97,
    102, 108, 117, 119
  and regional parties 20, 24–5, 91–2,
    102–4, 107–8, 112–13, 116, 119–21,
    226
    electoral strength 105–6, 107, 117–18,
      210; votes 101, 101f, 102, 116
  regions 95–6, 108–9
    decision-making powers 96
  and secessionism 24–5, 93
  and separatist organizations 90, 91, 93,
    95, 107
  statewide parties 90–1, 102, 103, 104–5,
    107, 108, 109, 110–11, 112–14, 115,
    117, 120–1
  upper houses 20, 25, 58, 117–18, 119–20,
    198
    Senate 95, 117–18, 118f, 119
  veto 91, 119
  see also autonomous communities
Spanish Communist Party (PCE) 111
Spanish Socialist Workers Party (PSOE) 109,
  111, 114, 115
Spolare, E. 52, 55
SPR-RSC, *see* Association for the Republic-
  Republican Party of Czechoslovakia
Sri Lanka 54
Sridharan, E. 138

Stanger, A. 73
Stanton, S. 169
state subsidies 77
state unity 3
statewide parties 12, 13, 15–16, 19, 23, 24,
    25, 29, 31, 166–7, 199–200, 204–5,
    212, 226
  and decentralization 48, 225, 227, 230–1
  and leadership 227
  and legislation 38
  and national elections 17
  and party unity 36
  and regional interests 13, 14, 34, 35–6,
    45, 47, 60, 229
  and regional parties 12, 15–16, 23–4,
    37, 40, 44, 46, 52, 53, 58–9, 166–7,
    204–5, 226
  see also under individual countries
Stein, E. 77, 83
Stepan, A. C. 8, 9, 50, 199, 220
Stewart, E. 4
Stock, J. H. 186
Suárez, A. 108
Suberu, R. T. 4, 11
Subirats i Humet, J. 119
subnational elections, sequencing 16
subnational governments 6, 7, 9, 11, 20,
    49, 53
  see also governments; national
    governments
subnational legislatures 6–7, 16, 20, 24, 49,
    228
  and regional leaders 11–12
  and regional parties 44, 60
subnational revenue 200
Suresh, K. 138
Svejjnar, J. 80
Svitek, I. 70
Switzerland 161
symbols 31

Tajfel, H. 33
Tamayo, M. 97
Tamil Nadu 125, 135, 139, 141–2, 145
Tarchi, M. 18
Tartar, P. 82
taxes 32, 35
  autonomous communities (Spain) 97
territorial contiguity 188
terrorism 93, 144–5
terrorist organizations 15, 142
Thandavan, R. 138
Tibet-Burma 126

TNV, *see* Tripura National Volunteers
Tomek, I. 68, 69
Tornos Más, J. 96
Treisman, D. 19, 55, 188
Tremblay, R. C. 131
Tripura (India) 125
  elections 142
  extremist organizations 141
  violence 126
Tripura National Volunteers (TNV) 142
Tripura Tribal Autonomous District Council
  (TTADC) 142
Trudeau, P. 4
Truman, D. B. 47
Tsalik, S. 55
Tsebelis, G. 8
TTADC, *see* Tripura Tribal Autonomous
  District Council
Türsan, H. 14, 33, 34, 52, 158, 193
Tummala, K. K. 147
Turkey 45, 190, 203
Turner, J. C. 33
Txueka, I. 117
Tversky, A. 32

UCD, *see* Union of the Democratic Center
Uganda:
  and decentralization 54
  and federalism 4
ULFA, *see* United Liberation Front of Assam
unemployment 78
union territories, *see* India, union territories
United Front (India) 135
UK:
  colonies 55, 187, 190, 221
  and decentralization 54
  elections 169
    national 220; sequencing 203
  India, independence from 26, 123
  and regional parties 52–3
Union of the Democratic Center (UCD)
  [Spain] 108, 109–110, 111–12
Union of the Navarran People (UPN)
  [Spain] 112
union territories, *see* India, union territories
United Aragon (CHA) 116–17
United Liberation Front of Assam
  (ULFA) 142
United People, *see* Herri Batasuna
United Progressive Alliance (UPA) 135
unity, sense of 9–10
UPA, *see* United Progressive Alliance
UPN, *see* Union of the Navarran People

upper houses 7, 20, 50, 198
  elections 29, 52, 158
    direct 229; procedures 55, 57–8
  method of elections 16, 17
  Slovakia 67
  see also under individual countries
Ugarte, B. A. 18
Urwin, D. W. 34, 52, 158, 193
USA 40
  and decentralization 54, 231
  and economic wealth 54–5
  and presidential candidates 59
  and regional primaries 46, 48

Vachudová, M. A. 261**n**
Vadas, M. 73
Valencia 92, 102, 105, 116
Valentino, N. A. 32
Valenzuela, A. 171
Valko, E. 82
van Houten, P. 33, 42
Varshney, A. 143
Verba, S. 18
veto:
  India 151
  minority 43, 228
  powers 24, 44, 164, 165, 198, 227, 228
  Spain 91, 119
  see also Czechoslovakia, veto
violence 1, 13–14, 162
  and Basque Country 22
  and elections 169–70
  and regional parties 42
Vodička, K. 77
vote splitting 116
voters 32
  intimidation of (India) 40
  regional 51–2
  and regional parties 48, 51, 214,
    216, 220
voting laws, *see* cross-regional
    voting laws
VPR, *see* Public Against Violence

Wales 52–3, 203
Walter, B. F. 3, 38, 52, 54
water 2, 35
Weaver, R. K. 2, 11
Weiner, M. 132, 149
Weinstein, J. M. 33
Western Europe 158
Wibbels, E. 12
Widmalm, S. 131, 138

Index

Wightman, G. 81
Wildavsky, A. B. 47
Wilkenfeld, J. 1
Wilkinson, S. I. 37, 45, 141, 145, 146, 169, 229
Wolchik, S. L. 72, 82
Wood, E. J. 2
Wooldridge, J. M. 172
World Bank 231
World Development Indicators Online (World Bank) 168, 188, 217

Yadav, Y. 142
Young, C. 55, 187
Young, D. J. 1
Yugoslavia, *see* former Yugoslavia

Zaidi, A. M. 139
Zaidi, S. C. 139
Žák, V. 81, 82
Zaller, J. R. 32
Zelenay, R. 82
Ziblatt, D. 53